Ecclesiastical Law, Clergy and Laity

Discipline in an ecclesiastical context can be defined as the power of a church to maintain order among its members on issues of morals or doctrine. This book presents a scholarly engagement with the way in which legal discipline has evolved within the Church of England since 1688. It explores how the Church of England, unusually among Christian churches, has come to be without means of effective legal discipline in matters of controversy, whether liturgical, doctrinal, or moral. The author excludes matters of blatant scandal to focus on issues where discipline has been attempted in controversial matters, focussing on particular cases. The book makes connections between law, the state of the Church, and the underlying theology of justice and freedom. At a time when doctrinal controversy is widespread across all Christian traditions, it is argued that the Church of England has an inheritance here in need of cherishing and sharing with the universal Church.

The book will be a valuable resource for academics and researchers in the areas of law and religion, and ecclesiastical history.

Revd Neil Patterson (MA BD) is Director of Vocations and Ordinands (Hereford), Rural Dean of Hereford, and a Member of the General Synod and the Ecclesiastical Law Society. He has published on ecclesiastical issues in books and periodicals.

Law and Region

The practice of religion by individuals and groups, the rise of religious diversity, and the fear of religious extremism, raise profound questions for the interaction between law and religion in society. The regulatory systems involved, the religion laws of secular government (national and international) and the religious laws of faith communities, are valuable tools for our understanding of the dynamics of mutual accommodation and the analysis and resolution of issues in such areas as: religious freedom; discrimination; the autonomy of religious organisations; doctrine, worship and religious symbols; the property and finances of religion; religion, education and public institutions; and religion, marriage and children. In this series, scholars at the forefront of law and religion contribute to the debates in this area. The books in the series are analytical with a key target audience of scholars and practitioners, including lawyers, religious leaders, and others with an interest in this rapidly developing discipline.

Titles in this series include:

State and Religion
The Australian Story
Renae Barker

Ecclesiastical Law, Clergy and Laity
A History of Legal Discipline and the Anglican Church
Revd Neil Patterson

For more information about this series, please visit: www.routledge.com/Law-and-Religion/book-series/LAWRELIG

Ecclesiastical Law, Clergy and Laity

A History of Legal Discipline and the Anglican Church

Revd Neil Patterson

Routledge
Taylor & Francis Group
LONDON AND NEW YORK

First published 2019
by Routledge
2 Park Square, Milton Park, Abingdon, Oxon OX14 4RN

and by Routledge
52 Vanderbilt Avenue, New York, NY 10017, USA

First issued in paperback 2020

Routledge is an imprint of the Taylor & Francis Group, an informa business

British Library Cataloguing in Publication Data
A catalogue record for this book is available from the British Library

Library of Congress Cataloging in Publication Data
A catalog record for this book has been requested

ISBN 13: 978-0-367-58625-6 (pbk)
ISBN 13: 978-0-8153-5264-8 (hbk)

Typeset in Galliard
by Taylor & Francis Books

Contents

Foreword

The study of Ecclesiastical Law in the Church of England has undergone a renaissance during the past 30 years, partly through the dynamic influence of Professor Norman Doe and others, with many books and articles being published. It is thus surprising that the rich ground relating to clergy discipline has thus far been untilled in any substantial way. Neil Patterson's present volume is therefore most welcome, addressing, as it does, the topic of clergy discipline from both an historical and a theological perspective. The author's approach, not undertaken in any previous work, is to begin from the problematical outworking of law as discipline before drawing ecclesiological conclusions from its history in the Church of England. The result is a book which will be of genuine interest not only to lawyers but also to a much wider readership. The historical narrative, rather than being a dry recital of the key dates and big names of the day, is peppered with many accounts of hapless individuals who have found themselves having to account for their behaviour or, more importantly, their beliefs, before one of the numerous institutions that have, from time to time, purported to exercise discipline over the clergy. It is both interesting and useful to have the history of the development of this jurisdiction set out in one flowing account and there is a bonus in that Neil Patterson's writing style, despite the density of some of the material, remains light and highly readable throughout. At all stages the historical narrative is teased out and challenged against relevant doctrinal concepts, so that the reader may see any movement of the theological tectonic plates which must underpin any process of clergy discipline.

I am writing this Foreword less than a week after The Archbishop of Canterbury, when giving evidence to the Independent Inquiry into Child Sexual Abuse, stated that the Clergy Discipline Measure 2003 is 'not fit for purpose' with respect to safeguarding cases and, more generally, involves a process which may cause extraordinary damage both to survivors and those against whom a complaint has been made. A review of the CDM is to take place. In addition, the revealing account that Neil Patterson gives, using previously unpublished material, of the church's handling of the issue of gay marriage within the context of the CDM underlines the need for a such review. The publication of this book is therefore timely and it should, I would suggest, be essential reading for all those who may now have to consider the shape of the clergy discipline process in the Church of England as we move on to the second quarter of the twenty-first century.

The Rt. Hon. Sir Andrew McFarlane
President of Tribunals and Chair of the Clergy Discipline Commission
Maundy Thursday 2018

Preface

I cannot now trace for certain when I first thought I might have something to say about the relationship between the ecclesiastical law and canon of the Church of England and her discipline. Perhaps it was inevitable that an ordained graduate of PPE and Theology should be led in that direction, although it might not be expected that the final result be essentially a work of legal history. Certainly though, the idea that the weakness of her discipline is a distinctive and valuable mark of the Church of England, among all churches, had long been in my mind. What I did not expect was to uncover such a fascinating seam of research, in part through general reading but also the widening awareness that came with membership of the Ecclesiastical Law Society from 2013.

Decisive shape came, however, with the thought that this presented an opportunity to fulfil my dormant permission to supplicate for the now-discontinued Oxford degree of Bachelor of Divinity, and I therefore sought advice from Professor Mark Chapman at Ripon College Cuddesdon. With his support, confirmation was obtained from the Theology Faculty that they would accept a thesis, and he was appointed my official Advisor. The BD demands no fees of students nor offers them to tutors, and so Mark's advice was offered informally amid a certain amount of Cuddesdon reminiscence and current gossip, in return for occasional pub lunches. Though select, this advice was crucial: the guidance to structure the work as a clear historical narrative; invaluable snippets of comment and direction along the way; and the patient reading-through of the draft text before offering necessary feedback over a pint on the terrace of York University during July 2016 General Synod. I like to think that some of the characters referred to herein had similar research discussions in the coffee-house margins of Convocation in the 1710s.

I am most grateful to my parishioners in the six parishes of the Ariconium benefice where I was Rector until late 2015 for allowing me the capacity to study at this depth, and to both them and the Diocese of Hereford for a short sabbatical break in summer 2015 when I was able to begin writing up. Whilst in my sermons then and now I intend to show signs of some learning, I hope I have not bored anyone with abstruse details such as are found here. The thesis was duly examined by Professor Brian Young and Dr Judith Maltby later in 2016 and accepted. Some of their helpful comments have been reflected in the subsequent revision, although

I here apologise to Professor Young that I chose not to pursue his interesting suggestion of examining parallels between controversies in the Church and the University. It was with appropriate gratitude and rejoicing on my part that Mark Chapman should be able to act as substitute for the Regius Professor and present me to be admitted BD in 2017. Although I understand there are others still able to and possibly intending to supplicate, as one of the last and youngest to be accepted I have the peculiar expectation of being in time the last living holder of a degree with its origins in the Middle Ages.

Early in the development of the thesis I had conversations with a number of informed people whom I will try to remember to thank below, but among them Professor Norman Doe stands out for his enthusiasm and encouragement. Although relatively few are cited below, I was able to read a number of relevant theses written by his past LLM students, including some lent by him personally, and they led me to vital cases and themes pursued. I was therefore pleased when I returned to Norman with a completed thesis that he gave his full endorsement to its publication under his supervision in this Routledge series, and also provided his editorial comments, not least to improve the standard of conformity to the expectations of the legally trained, which I am not. I shall never put an 'e' in the middle of judgment again.

As a clergyman attempting amateur study alongside parish and then diocesan work, my chief research resources have been my own expensively growing library and periodic excursions to use my reader's membership of the Bodleian, for which I have been very grateful. I also extend my thanks to Gladstone's Library, the libraries of Blackfriars, Oxford; Hereford Cathedral; Lambeth Palace; Middle Temple; Ripon College Cuddesdon; the Church of England Records Centre; and particularly the National Library of Wales, who retain copies of those Cardiff LLM theses deemed Outstanding. Indirect thanks to Anthony Priddis, who on his retirement as Bishop of Hereford left various useful books free to covetous homes, including a run of several years of the Ecclesiastical Law Journal. With the help of John Rees and Darren Oliver I was then able to secure, and therefore read, the remaining portion. Particular thanks are also due to the staff of General Synod, especially Nick Hills, who gave me access to their records room and were unfailingly polite and helpful.

It is inevitable that as a member of the ELS and General Synod, I have benefited from relevant conversations with more people than I can remember, but amongst those in and out of those bodies, I note the following in particular: Robert Ombres OP, who at an early stage of study gave valuable challenge to some of my assumptions; Thomas Culver, who lent me his personal copy of his LLM thesis when it became apparent that no other was still extant; Anthony Freeman and Andrew Foreshew-Cain, who generously shared papers from their own cases; Canon Clay Knowles and Dr Andrew Foster (Literary Executors to Bishop Eric Kemp), Bishops Hewlett Thompson, Michael Langrish and Peter Wheatley for permission to quote their letters from those correspondences, and for relevant conversations I do recall: Will Adam, Simon Butler, John Clark, Alex McGregor, Jeremy Pemberton and Geoffrey Thompson; Sion Hughes Carew and

Sir Andrew MacFarlane, who shared their different perspectives on the workings of the current CDM system, Andrew also giving permission to quote one of his own official letters, and then providing the gracious and charming Foreword.

As noted above, Mark Chapman and Norman Doe read the text at different stages and did their best to redeem my faults there; thanks are also due to Alison Kirk both for commissioning the book and advising on presentation and pitch, and Alex Buckley for patiently advising on the details of production in which I am wholly inexperienced. Finally, to my partner David Wyatt, who has retained implausible enthusiasm for me and my book beyond the bounds of logic; I hope he is not too disappointed when he reads it in full, and that it offers some wisdom for the ministry for which he is now also training.

Introduction

This study is a longitudinal examination of a particular type of religious conflict, in a particular Christian denomination, the Church of England, but it has relevance beyond that specific context. The idea that faith is a source of conflict is anything but new, as Jesus himself said, "*I have come to bring fire on the earth*" (Luke 12.49) and the history of Christianity alone is replete with conflicts between nations and factions, competing in their understanding of religious truth, to the point of violence and warfare. In this early twenty-first century, violence appears to be largely the preserve of other faiths, most obviously militant Islamism, and it is rare for Christian groups to possess either the effective means (through state support) or the inclination to resort to force. However, cultural and legal conflict around all religions remains as vigorous as ever.

It could be argued that these conflicts, so persistent in spite of the growth of liberal democracy with its acceptance of diversity and freedom, say something important about the nature of religious belief, especially in the Abrahamic religions which are most influential in conflicts in the Western world. Christianity, Judaism and Islam all recognise different varieties of expression, and all make some use of apophatic language about God, denying that he can be fully known or described. Yet it remains the case that to proclaim some understanding about God, as traditionally understood, is philosophically to make a claim to absolute truth. And so from the believer's viewpoint, those who deny or threaten that truth are therefore not merely promoting a different way of human flourishing, but are wrong about the nature of the world. The desire to prevail in religious truth, and, crucially for this study, to control dissent from that truth, is as it were the shadow side of monotheism.

In practice in developed liberal democracies today, these conflicts now frequently take the form of human rights cases contested in national and (in Europe) supra-national courts. Frequently where the state in question is a signatory of the European Convention on Human Rights, this takes the form of a claim under Article 9 (freedom of religion), often having to be judged in tension with Article 14 (freedom from discrimination). In the United States, as explored for English readers recently by Frank Cranmer,[1] the key text to be interpreted is the First Amendment to the Constitution, forbidding the establishment of religion and permitting its free exercise.

In a recent conference address,[2] the (then) Deputy President of the UK Supreme Court, Baroness Hale of Richmond, judged that cases involving freedom of and freedom from religion were becoming more complex, and in particular that European courts were coming to recognise, against Article 8 of the European Convention, that sometimes the potential harm arising from religious belief (for example, the decision of a Muslim family to move to an area governed by militant Islamism) could outweigh the right to family life and justify state intervention. She concluded by observing that this seemed to contradict the existing tradition of neutrality, and that it raised hard questions.

However, whilst the nature of conflicts between religions and wider human rights are complex, they are still, ironically, not presented as complex enough, not least perhaps because of the lack of knowledge on the part of civil servants and lawmakers about the intricacies of particular faiths. And in broad analyses of conflict around religion the point is often lost that the most vital conflicts are often not between the holders of a religious view and those who oppose them, but between members of the same religious group struggling to determine who has authority among them to declare what counts as truth.

To remain for the moment with an Islamic example: imagine a Muslim student who causes controversy in her university by only attending fully veiled, and never leaves home except veiled and accompanied by a male relative. It is possible to present this as a conflict between her rights to observe her faith in distinctive dress as against the rights of her tutors and fellow students, for whom it may be argued that their education is impeded by the difficulty of communication and the presence of a non-member in their classes. However, the conflict is quite different if the student explains that she would happily lose the chaperone and face veil (but not, let us say, the headscarf), but her faith does not give her the freedom to defy the wishes of her father, who insists that she not go out unveiled in public. The difficult question, into which the courts are reluctant to stray, is whether paternal authority of this sort is a necessary part of Muslim observance.

Or to take a Christian example, as this will be from here on a study of conflict in Christianity. Roman Catholic schools expect, as a genuine occupational requirement, that their head teachers be faithful Catholics. It is easy to imagine an RC school where the head, a faithful attender at Mass and always ready to promote the faith throughout the school life and curriculum, nonetheless enters a same-sex relationship. This would be likely to cause controversy, and the desire of the school's governors to dismiss him for this apparent breach of Catholic morality. But if the head protests that he remains a faithful Catholic by observance and belief, any attempt to dismiss him turns on an internal question; who has the power to determine what constitutes faithfulness to the Catholic Church?

This tension has a long history in Christianity, and in the era of Christendom had a particular salience, because when all Christian practice was united in one overarching structure, any dissent might be expressed, or felt, as a challenge to the authority of that structure. And the whole evolution of canon law from the Middle Ages onwards can be seen as an attempt to respond to such challenges by both defending the origins of religious authority and defining its limits. Since the coming of religious pluralism from the seventeenth century onwards, the predominant response of those unhappy with the opinions of their own church or group has been to exercise their freedom to leave, and that continues to be the case today.

Within the breadth of Christian churches, the Church of England occupies an unusual place which is only in part due to lying somewhere in the middle of the conventional spectrum from Catholic to Protestant. In terms of questions of authority, that spectrum can be seen, if such a generalisation is helpful, to begin with the overarching and hierarchical structure descending from the Magisterium providing great clarity on the Catholic side. Although this study does not embark on a comparison, it may be noted that this structure is resourced by a dedicated framework of law and has recourse to internal courts answering to the Roman Rota.[3] At the other end, whilst the locus of authority is typically local in Protestant churches, including down to the individual congregation or even member, there is a clearer sense of defined membership, with powers to exclude, resourced often by specific creedal statements. Whilst this would in the past have been historic documents like the Westminster Confession, it is most often in my experience today the ecumenical Declaration of Faith adopted by the Evangelical Alliance and other bodies, which defines a clear but not extreme evangelicalism.

The distinctiveness of the Church of England lies not only in claiming to be both Catholic and Reformed, enjoying or suffering aspects of both, which is the common inheritance of the wider Anglican Communion. In England, however, that inheritance has always been worked out, as this study shows in one particular aspect, in the particular context of abiding Establishment. This has meant that even down to the present day, the Church of England retains a belief in its own universal mission within a particular geographical area.[4] The result is that "because of the continuing integration of the national church in the national life, historical tensions felt elsewhere as tensions between the church and something else have been felt in England as tensions within the church."[5]

The objective of this work, therefore, is to explore a particular aspect of the English Anglican experience, the negotiation of conflicts which can be described as disciplinary, in the belief that these have relevance for any church proclaiming that it represents the fullness of Christian truth, and which finds itself wrestling with internal dissent. It will be argued that the worked-out ineffectiveness of discipline within the Church of England, although historically a happy accident, is worthy of wider understanding and appreciation. A subsidiary motive, of one engaged in the inner conflicts of the Church through General Synod among other places, is to bring to mind the past history of the Church as a coercive institution, and to resist those who would re-impose narrowing legal strictures against those of whom they disapprove.

The concept of discipline

It is no accident that the words discipline, discipleship and discipling are closely related, for all are about the exertions of Christians, individually and corporately, to live the life to which God calls them. But whereas discussion of and exhortation to better discipleship, and for some, discipling, is widespread and even popular, *discipline* is a word used rarely and with reluctance. It is necessary therefore to begin by setting out what is meant by ecclesiastical discipline in general, before noting its particular meanings within different contexts such as the discipline of clergy in a particular church.[6]

Discipleship in the broadest sense is the striving of Christians to follow Christ faithfully, and the caring ways in which Christians (particularly ministers or leaders) guide and direct in the way.[7] For the purposes of this work, discipline is identified as a subset of the discipling of one Christian (or group of Christians) by another, and in a way which involves some sort of coercion or punishment if the person fails or refuses to meet the standard expected. It is, therefore, always an exercise of authority, usually but not absolutely always of the Church corporate or its senior officers over individuals. It needs to be distinguished from *self-discipline*, a normal and indeed necessary part of Christian living. The proposition is that one of the most distinctive characteristics of the Church of England among churches is the extreme ineffectiveness of her forms of discipline, and what follows is an exploration of why that may have come to be so. It will be apparent that the scope of this study could be vast; before explaining the parameters which narrow down the field to a manageable scale, it is worth highlighting some aspects which may help to clarify potential issues.

Perhaps the most obvious form of discipline in Christian history is the active criminal persecution of Christian minorities and their subjection to physical penalties, including burning at the stake. Although such punishment had ceased in England by the time under consideration, the memory of centuries in which extreme punishments could be exacted of fellow-Christians for holding views identified as deviant plays a large part in shaping perceptions of the place of discipline in church life. There is also an important sense in which the Church has never really repented corporately for these persecutions – down to the extent that as recently as 1995 the Chancellor of Durham diocese refused a faculty for a memorial at St Edmund's Chapel, Gateshead, describing John Ingram, d.1594 as a martyr. His grounds were that Ingram, a Roman Catholic priest, had in fact been hung, drawn and quartered as a traitor and it would be inappropriate for Her Majesty's Ecclesiastical Court to authorise a memorial to a condemned traitor for whom no pardon had been issued.[8] Throughout modern history members of the Church of England have also made comparison, not always well-informed, with the apparently more rigorous disciplinary provisions of other churches.

Stepping away from the extremity of burning heretics, it is now largely forgotten that the same Chancellors and consistory courts who now supervise the Faculty jurisdiction over church buildings in England are only the remnant of a great network of church courts, originating in a famous ordinance of William the Conqueror, whose main function was to correct the morals of the nation *pro salute animae*, keeping spiritual discipline by the very real means of ordering public penance. The decay of these courts and the discipline they maintained, traced in Chapters 1 and 2, owed far more to neglect and ineffectiveness than anyone's plan to liberate the people of England from the oppressive power of the Church. Their final demise in the old form at the hands of rational Victorian law reformers came just before church controversy burst back into the courts from the 1850s onwards.

A third meaning of discipline is specific to the Reformed, broadly Calvinist tradition, referring to the belief that discipline, in the sense of the active correction of moral and spiritual sin, is a mark of a true church. The characteristic form of this, seen in Geneva and Scotland for example, is the church led by a body of Elders who make it their business to enquire into the lives of all in a small community, and hold power to punish sin by physical or spiritual penalty and by shame. On the whole such communities are now seen (often in memory) with horror or suspicion, but it should not be forgotten that in the disorder of the seventeenth century and for some since, they hold great appeal. As MacCulloch comments of the Scottish Kirk "Reformed discipline provided structures for controlling a frighteningly violent and arbitrary world, and involved the whole community in doing so."[9] Underlying the commentary of many critics of the undisciplined Church of England is a desire for something like a Calvinist structure to reliably identify and punish sin, or if necessary, expel the sinner from the pure Church. It will be seen that in our present travails over homosexuality, this Puritan conception remains a real motivation for some present-day campaigners.

Finally, in the modern context, discipline in the Church of England means clergy discipline, still administered internally by a legal structure, but of tribunals rather than courts, with power to hear cases and determine penalties all the same. The scope of the present tribunals, however, is almost entirely limited to matters that are considered breaches of professional good conduct, rather than substantive spiritual error in ministers of the Church (although many of the breaches of course also suggest such error). In many ways this study will trace the path of how we came to be where we are, with such limited legal means for responding to the notoriously myriad matters over which the Anglican clergy (never mind the laity) are often felt to be in scandalous error.

The meaning of discipline in the Anglican context has been limited to the act of seeking to control or punish individuals in relation to a particular station (whether baptised and communicant member, cleric, office-holder or bishop) they occupy within the Church, and exclude most of those occasional controversies which were mainly about whether a person should or should not be ordained, or consecrated a bishop. Certainly, these often revolved around the same issues as were also a question of discipline. But whilst some of the same issues of justice arise, discipline *per se* is the attempt to control or reform the behaviour of a Christian in their station, and different (and more difficult) than simply preventing them from occupying that station in the first place.

Scope and context

Three main parameters limit the scope of this book: subject, context and date. Within the wider subject of ecclesiastical discipline, it is immediately apparent (particularly looking at the work of the present-day Clergy Discipline tribunals) that much of the potential subject matter concerns what is called, for the sake of a defining word, 'scandal'. That is to say, matters on which clergy (or others in posts of responsibility) have either committed criminal acts, or engaged in behaviour obviously and indisputably inappropriate to their position, generally either sexual or financial irregularity, or disastrous drunkenness.[10] Such matters have been generally excluded, not simply because they will tend to trivialise the subject, but because the nub of this study is how the Church has used law to deal with controversy, and these subjects, though sometimes interesting, are not controversial. Those excluded are those where the accused accepted the jurisdiction of the court, and that the offence would be an offence, but whose defence was broadly 'I didn't do it'.

By contrast, in most of the cases and subjects under consideration, there is at least an element of 'I did do it, but it isn't wrong' or 'I did do it, and it's no business of yours to punish me for it.' This means that the boundary moves around through history. The eighteenth-century adulterers and bastard-begetters are included, because although they were not often able to contest the courts' jurisdiction, there was growing doubt as to whether penance in a white sheet was in any way a useful social response to the accidents of lust. Or later, a clergyman discovered in an indecent situation with another man in 1911 would certainly have resigned instantly on being confronted by his bishop, and be of no interest to us, whereas in 2011 he may be found living with the other man in a civil partnership, and protesting his right to do so, and very much a subject for discussion. In many cases the interest lies in the fixing of the boundary – those prosecuting (particularly those not necessarily in authority but pushing from outside for the case to be brought) are usually sure that the wicked thing done is plainly outside acceptable bounds; whereas the defendant believes it is not; time and again it will be found that judges preferred the side of greater liberty.

Context means that within broader ecclesiastical discipline this is basically a study of how that discipline has been exercised through the courts. This is partly because of the simple fact that cases are recorded and commented upon, and so it is the place where records can be found as they usually cannot when informal pressure has been brought upon individuals to quietly conform or leave. But it is also because fortunately for the historian the structures of the Church of England are such that it is often only through the courts that action can be taken. The 'parson's freehold,' or more accurately, the fact that parish clergy are usually legal personalities in their own right (still true under common tenure), and the general freedom under the law of all in England, means that moral persuasion is only effective with consent. The history of the Church of England is filled with characters who would not be told what to do, and the willingness of others to take them to law provides a rich resource for study.

Finally, time settled upon 1688, the most important neglected date in the history of the Church of England, as the start date. Certain key decisions in the Reformation period (notably the refusal to adopt any version of the Calvinist eldership system) are a vital backdrop to the subject. It is the appearance of Toleration, in the form of the Toleration Act 1689, and the freedom of all people disgruntled with the impositions of the Church simply to stay away or go elsewhere, that sets the frame for the slow death of ecclesiastical discipline in England. Many Anglicans are still ready to celebrate the theology of the seventeenth century; we have forgotten that it flourished by being imposed with force upon the English population, both before and after the Civil War.

There is also a good deal of wider context which has to be borne in mind as the study proceeds. Church culture in England has always nested very closely into the culture of society at large, and so standards of clergy conduct, for example, have often owed as much to changing understandings of the acceptable behaviour of gentlemen as any specifically religious, never mind canonical, expectations. Respect for spiritual authority, which waned in the eighteenth century, returned for a brief (and perhaps in retrospect anomalous) period in the mid-nineteenth, before diminishing in the face of real pluralism. In the last hundred years, the Church of England has struggled to define itself apart from ever-changing society, and this whole study can only be understood in the context of that immensely complex process. The law, too, has undergone great change, and the abolition of most of the jurisdiction of the ecclesiastical courts in the 1850s was to contemporaries part of a wider process of rationalisation and modernisation.

A further complexity of context is the unavoidable use of the classification of thinkers or positions as liberal. 'Liberal' is what my bishop likes to call a 'greedy word,' assimilating to itself multiple meanings until it loses clarity of purpose. The problem is that, for many, liberal means a particular church tradition (also sometimes called 'modernism'), favourable to biblical criticism, predominantly left-wing and committed to overthrowing the heterosexist patriarchy, and in politics can mean allied views. However, liberal also, in the more austere and Victorian way of John Stuart Mill, means the principled acceptance and promotion of toleration of difference, and the legal provision of space for competing models of human flourishing to exist. Depending on the time and the circumstances, the latter may well favour the former, but it can also be distinctly conservative in effect, what has been called 'neo-liberalism' since the 1980s. Within this work, it is probably fair to say that liberal has more to do with John Stuart Mill than the Liberal Democrats. But to say any more would be to brush over great subtleties which need to be understood in the context to follow.

Also only appearing as background is the ecumenical context. In the earlier periods, Anglican writers were very willing to compare the life of the Church of England with 'Popery' and 'Dissent' with implied criticism and little analysis – it will be necessary sometimes to follow these lines of argument for what they tell us about how the Church of England saw itself without intending to endorse their lack of charity. In the last century, the ecumenical movement has transformed ecclesiology, and relativized all the structures of authority within the churches. This study concentrates solely the particular undisciplined nature of the established Church of England, understood as an example for all churches to consider.

Apparent at every period is that the study of discipline within the Church is tied up, both in practice and in ideology, with the established status of the

Church of England. Legal establishment on the whole has been a key factor in preserving the freedom of individuals within the Church from the authority of clergy or bishops. A theme of Anglican history since 1689 has been the striving of the Church of England for her own autonomy from the state, and those who have written on the subject have often used the rhetoric of freedom for the Church. But this freedom from the State in practice usually means less freedom for individual Christians within the Church, something which only a few campaigners for a freer Church have had the honesty or insight to recognise, but more have quietly intended. An underlying objective is to show that the liberalising effects of establishment have been a gift to the Church of England worth treasuring even as the ties that bind to the nation may be on the verge of rusting away at last.

Structure

The work falls into three parts. The first two chapters concern the old system of ecclesiastical courts overseeing the morals of England. Chapter 1 observes how in the first generation after 1688, the fear of the effects of Toleration motivated the Tory High Church movement, anticipating rightly many of the later effects of removing compulsory religion. Chapter 2 charts how the courts declined to become what seemed an irrelevance to church life, using the case of the extraordinary Bedfordshire parson Dr Free to illustrate the moribund state of the courts in the 1820s. This phase closes by noting the survival of white sheet penance in a few cases until 1850, and how the consequent scandal reflects their anachronistic feel.

Chapters 3 to 5 cover the nineteenth century in a thematic way. The first two look at contrasting aspects of clergy discipline, in relation to heresy and ritual. In Chapter 3 we find that the hierarchy were disinclined to pursue heresy closely. The complexity of process and the difficulty of legally defining error meant that successive judgments widened the breadth of acceptable Anglican opinion. In Chapter 4 it can be seen that ritual, by contrast, attracted specific persecuting legal provision, but the law was defeated in practice by civil disobedience, revealing the voluntary nature of liturgical discipline. Chapter 5 looks at the current of thought among some clergy in favour of the discipline of the laity by restricting communion, which when tested in court proved toothless, notably the responses to the 1908 *Bannister v Thompson* case.

From that era of fierce legal controversy, the twentieth century, as surveyed in Chapter 6, displays no less controversy, but a systematic reluctance by bishops to engage legally, which might be thought to reflect a settled wisdom, then worked out in the Ecclesiastical Jurisdiction Measure 1963. This wisdom can be seen tested in the muddle of canon, discipline and personality that was the 1972 case of *Bland v Archdeacon of Cheltenham*. In Chapter 7 it is seen that the yearning to pursue errant opinion or conduct by judicial means is by no means dead in the Church of England. The narrowly failed attempts of 1996 and 2004 to revive an effective tribunal system for doctrinal error are discussed, and the story brought up to date by applying some of the principles of the whole study to the current controversy about same-sex marriage.

It should be noted that from an academic viewpoint, the chapters described above deal with widely varying levels of previous scholarly interest, and it is necessary to explain that this study, to avoid distortion, engages with them with similar inequality. The Tory crises either side of 1700 (Chapter 1) have been widely studied, but mainly for their interest in the history of Britain as a whole. The doctrinal and ritual debates of the nineteenth century (Chapters 3 and 4) have also attracted extensive and more theological scholarship. In these the engagement has been more limited, in the latter concentrating on returning to the sources in the relevant court judgments, whilst aiming to remain aware of the surrounding scholarship. By contrast the decline of the courts (Chapter 2) and the failure of repulsion (Chapter 5) have been of interest mainly to specialists in ecclesiastical law and not linked into a wider narrative. The twentieth century (Chapters 6 and 7) does not really seem to have been brought together under this theme at all, and the originality of this work is to bring the whole thread together with its relevance for current controversies, including research directly from some key participants. So this is to say that there has been a necessary minimisation of engagement with the late seventeenth and mid-nineteenth century scholarship, not because it is not good but to prevent those periods dominating the whole.

Themes

It is important in all periods to recognise the gap, particularly deep in the Church of England, between law and reality. There have been many studies of the law books of the Church of England over time, most recently the great works of Norman Doe. It would be possible to read these and believe that one had understood how the Church's laws functioned. In most periods, this belief would be completely unjustified (a naivety of which scholars such as Doe are of course aware). The reality is that at any time large parts of the canons and law extant on paper have been either quietly ignored or actively defied. This state of indiscipline appears to be endemic in the Church of England; as will become apparent, part of the objective is to ask what that tells us about the Church and about the utility and theology of its laws in its life. What it may mean is that the ultimate purposes of Christian law in the Church of England are different from those suggested by the internationally agreed *Statement of Principles of Christian Law* recently approved by a range of distinguished experts,[11] a question returned to in the Conclusion.

This is because running through the whole study is the deeper question of what *law* is within the Christian Church. It will become apparent that there is a slender yet continuous thread of scholarship, through Gibson, Wood, Kemp and Moore, willing to adopt a slimmed-down but still fundamentally Catholic understanding of church law as a part of revelation, a gift from God for the right ordering of his Church and her protection from error. This tradition appeals to the medieval concept of the *jus commune*, the idea that a commonality of ecclesiastical law can be distilled by judges to arrive at a declaration of the *sensus fidelium* of Christendom. This is sometimes referred to as the 'canonical' tradition. At least some of those who approved the *Statement of Principles* mentioned above may feel themselves in that tradition, although it is probably fairer to regard Doe's comparative work on which they are based as an act of more neutral observational scholarship. On the Protestant side, instead, is a clear emphasis on ecclesiastical law as the means by which the Church and her potentially overbearing clergy can be kept in subjection to the needs of the nation as expressed through Parliament, often referred to conveniently if simplistically as 'Erastianism.'

The study of actual cases over a little more than 300 years shows that the action of law in discipline must always theologically be considered a *failure* of the Church to be what Christ wills her to be. Like just war, church discipline is a necessary evil. But in a church which accepts its own corporate fallibility as the Church of England does, it can be argued that the disciplining of its own members who hold dissenting positions in good conscience will never be a Christian act. And, so, this leads to an understanding of law as not the expression of the Church's gathered will, but something more limited and yet higher, the means to enable the freedom of all. This is, of course, the conclusion of the legal liberalism that grew out of Anglicanism reflected back into the Church herself. And understood well and believed in, it may be the most precious gift the Church of England has to offer to a world full of religions still in hock to the allure of coercion.

Notes

1 Frank Cranmer, "How relevant to the United Kingdom are the 'Religious' cases of the US Supreme Court" 18 EccLJ 300–15.
2 A version is published at 19 EccLJ 3–13, but the author was also present for the address itself and subsequent questions.
3 Doe, Norman, *The Legal Framework of the Church of England* (Clarendon 1996) 150–1
4 This remains the abiding outlook of, for example, the Church Commissioners, whose recent (2016–17) project support to Hereford diocese was guided directly by the relationship between church attendance and population distribution, as if possible adherence to any other faith or denomination was irrelevant.
5 Robert E. Rodes Jr., *Law and Modernisation in the Church of England* (Notre Dame 1991) 363.
6 As compared in e.g. Mark Hill (ed.) *Faithful Discipleship. Clergy Discipline in Anglican and Roman Catholic Canon Law* (Centre for Law and Religion, Cardiff University 2001).
7 Stephen Pattison, *A Critique of Pastoral Care* 3rd ed. (SCM 2000) 56–9.
8 Timothy Briden and Nigel Mason (eds) *Recent Court Cases,* 3 EccLJ 426–7.
9 Diarmaid MacCulloch, *A History of Christianity* (Allen Lane, 2009) 638.
10 I am grateful to Sir Andrew MacFarlane, President of the Tribunals, for confirming from his own experience my impression of the main subject matter of modern tribunal cases.
11 At 19 EccLJ 138–55.

1. Toleration and its effects

The church court system as inherited from the Middle Ages

This chapter stands as a preliminary, tracing the last and for our purposes critical phase of formation of the Anglican polity by the Glorious Revolution of 1688 and its effects, and perceptions of those effects then and since. Subsequent chapters will narrow in on the operation of the church courts, with a focus on particularly revealing cases in each chapter. This is more of a general account offered as background, and to make clear how a concern for ecclesiastical discipline played a part in key developments in the formation of the Church of England.

Many histories of Anglicanism, after retelling the long and bloody story of the Reformation through until the Civil War, seem to reach 1662 with something of a sigh of relief, and move on to the Tractarians in the following paragraph. It is indeed true that the Act of Uniformity 1662 is still in a sense in force, and the Book of Common Prayer annexed thereto was used by the Church from then on and remains the default legal liturgy of the Church of England alongside newer services authorised since the Worship and Doctrine Measure 1974. But collective amnesia reigns over the huge contextual difference to 1662 made by the Toleration Act 1689, which fundamentally altered the ecclesiastical polity of England. This amnesia is of long standing, perhaps even since Walpole let the sleeping dogs lie, but it was preceded by the generation of the Convocation Crises between 1688 and 1718, when the Tory High Churchmen were very aware of the danger to the Church in the loss of universality. Their anger and fear were paralleled by a decline in the effective disciplinary work of the church courts. This process reveals for the first time some of the main trends of this study; the accidental loss of authority coupled with angst about the consequences.

Those clergy who still use the service of Holy Communion from the Book of Common Prayer, and read the long intercessory text sometimes called the Prayer for the Church Militant, will find themselves praying that those set in authority under the Crown will engage in *the punishment of wickedness and vice, and the maintenance of thy true religion and virtue.* Today this can be interpreted as a pious hope that the Government will promote social wellbeing. Within the Church of England there has been a tendency to forget that immediately after 1662 among those set in authority under the Crown were the judges of the ecclesiastical courts, whose daily business was indeed the punishment of wickedness and vice. The presence and activity of this jurisdiction had a major impact on contemporary views of the Church, and the desire for toleration which grew in the late seventeenth century.

These courts and their work were ancient indeed, their origins in England being conventionally dated to the ordinance of William the Conqueror in 1072, ordering the bishops and archdeacons to withdraw from local witan-moots, and set up their own courts to try ecclesiastical matters.[1] This was within a Europe-wide context of church reform, and it was clear that the proper concerns of the Church included not only judgment over its own personnel, but all matters of sexual propriety and what would now be called family law (notably probate and marriage), whereas almost all matters of property, even church property, tended to be assigned to secular jurisdiction. The boundaries between these made fertile work for medieval canonists.[2] What is remarkable is that the oft commented-upon obsession of the Church with sex and family life, as opposed to how Christians used and abused their material goods, was so deep seated as to pass unquestioned into a legal distinction which endured for centuries. It was not a complete separation, most importantly crossed by the writs of prohibition, some, like *Middleton v Crofts* (1736) of great importance, but the principle of two spheres of legal jurisdiction underlies the whole study. An exception by our period, ironically in the light of its current prominence in Anglican divisions, was the traditional sin of sodomy, which was criminalised under a 1534 statute of Henry VIII and so removed from ecclesiastical jurisdiction.[3]

Like the Church of England's beloved cathedral foundations, and many other particularities, the ecclesiastical courts survived the Reformation, with both an unbroken tradition of jurisprudence and a bewildering complexity of local jurisdictions. The basic unit of the Church, the diocese, was equipped with its proper court, the Consistory Court, sitting under the bishop's Official Principal (also called the Chancellor for some purposes). As dioceses were divided into archdeaconries, so archdeacon's courts with their own Principals sat more locally, and above the consistory courts sat the provincial Court of Arches (for Canterbury, although always based in London) and the Chancery Court of York. The simple three-tier pattern was confounded by a vast range of peculiar jurisdictions, derived from monastic territories or local arrangements, so that courts existed for areas ranging from single parishes to large parts of dioceses, in some cases subject to the logical higher court, in some cases not.[4]

Whatever their jurisdiction, these courts administered a body of law which drew on relevant statute, the 1604 Canons, and medieval canon and precedent inasmuch as these were not abrogated by statute, as provided by the Submission of the Clergy Act 1533. Statute provided, for example, for the penalties for non-attendance at church and the 1604 Canons provisions for clergy conduct. In relation to their disciplinary jurisdiction over personal morality, there is a core of what is sometimes called 'general ecclesiastical law' which recognised sins such as adultery, fornication and defamation in a similar way to how the common law recognised offences such as murder and theft, and these occupied a large part of the courts' work. Of 416 presentments from the deanery of Doncaster in 1619, for example, only 93 were for non-attendance at church, whereas 206 were for some sort of sexual sin.[5]

It is vital to recognise, however, that the church courts were defined very much as *not* being under the common law except by writ of prohibition from Chancery. They had their own differences of procedure as well as their own body of law, among the most important being that all evidence was submitted in the form of the written depositions. These are now helpful sources for historians eager to show that Shakespeare's uncle was, or was not, sued for defamation by Marlowe's cousin, to imagine an example. The church courts also employed a specialist profession of lawyers, known as the civilians, as their proctors and advocates, with Doctors' Commons as their inn of court, a profession whose dwindling plays a part in the long decline explored in the next chapter.

The significance of the church courts for ecclesiastical discipline lies not so much in their law or procedure, but in their method of punishment, which immediately manifests the deep but problematic theological roots of the system. Those found guilty of the recognised sins, adultery, fornication and the like, were required to perform public penance. The normal form of this, prescribed in a schedule issued by the court (many survive) orders the guilty party to appear, usually in their parish church at service time, dressed in a white sheet. They were often required to stand by the door as parishioners arrived, in this penitential attitude and seeking forgiveness from all who passed, and then at a specified time to stand up and read aloud a prepared confession of guilt and plea for forgiveness. The minister was then to absolve them and their penance was done. A typical schedule from Gloucestershire as late as 1785 runs as follows (my italics):

> A schedule of penance to be performed by William Stephens in the parish church of South Cerney on Sunday the sixteenth day of January, 1785: "Whereas the said William Stephens stands judicially convicted by his own confession that he has been guilty of *the foul sin of fornication*. It is therefore ordered by the Archdeacon of Gloucester that he shall come to the said Church at the tolling of the bell for Morning or Evening Service … and shall stand in the porch … until the first lesson is ended *bareheaded and barefooted and having a white sheet over his wearing apparel* and a white rod in his hand and shall ask forgiveness of all that have passed by him, and after the first lesson is past he shall come into the said Church and stand in some eminent place by the reading desk … and shall make an humble confession of his fault saying … I William Stephens do in the presence of God and this congregation confess and acknowledge with shame and confusion of face that not having the fear of God before mine eyes and being seduced *by the temptation of the Devil and mine own filthy lusts* have been guilty of the foul sin of fornication.[6]

It will be apparent that this represents a formalisation of the very Christian conception that those who have offended by sin should have the opportunity to repent, and do so publicly in order that their fellow Christians may forgive them and welcome them back into fellowship. It could even be argued that the courts were an admirable institution of Christendom, taking unavoidable and sensitive matters of offence arising from personal relationships under the wing of Mother Church, able to gently reform the sinner and guide him or her back into the path of righteousness, as suggested by e.g. Matthew 18.15–17. It is equally apparent that public penance can be viewed as an appalling opportunity to heap public shame upon people for private sin, affording gratification to the righteous, particularly the offended, and to behold the humiliation of the sinner.

The forms of punishment are complicated by the employment of excommunication. In principle those ordered to do penance would not communicate until their penance was performed, but in the context of infrequent communion (both before and after the Reformation) this does not seem to have been a major concern. Of more importance was that right back in the 1070s, the church courts, with the agreement of the Conqueror, had adopted summary excommunication as the punishment for contempt of court, including non-appearance. In medieval Christendom this represented exclusion from church life altogether, besides other social and legal disadvantages (e.g. the inability to prove a will). However, Outhwaite notes that even in the seventeenth century before Toleration, there were very few prosecutions for "consorting with excommunicates"[7] and that although it was possible to obtain the writ *de excommunicato capiendo* and require the sheriff to imprison the excommunicate until they submitted to the penance or other penalty, this was slow and expensive, and not often done.[8] After Toleration it led to the perverse result that a dissenter, refusing to attend his parish church (and so not wishing to receive Anglican communion) would be then excommunicated if he refused to submit to the penance ordered by the church court. The further consequences of this as the courts became more distant from English life will be seen in the next chapter. To the frustration of churchmen, the defiant excommunicate might simply defy the church courts, and there was little more that could be done.

In the context of the Reformation period, there is a particular sharpness to this. All the churches of the sixteenth and seventeenth century were concerned to move away from the perceived laxness of the late Middle Ages and improve moral standards. For Counter-Reformation Rome, this meant a hard-working pastoral priesthood, hearing the sins of the faithful in the secrecy of frequent confession, and directing the sinners confidentially into reformed lives on condition of exclusion from the sacraments, with the Inquisition offering a judicial last resort to be feared. This was of course impossible for a Church of England so clearly built upon the repudiation of priestly power and where regular confession had ceased to be required. On the other hand, if one turned to Calvinism,

> accompanying the Genevan polity was always the Genevan "godly discipline" whereby the moral lapses of the laity were ruthlessly brought to light and rigorously reformed. This program was no more attractive to the ordinary Englishman than the fires of Smithfield had been.... To be sure, the traditional mechanism of parochial visitation was supposed to serve the same ends as the godly discipline, but it had its inefficiency to recommend it.[9]

So, parochial visitation it was, particularly as Parliament had planned for, but never fully implemented, the Calvinist system under the Commonwealth.[10] This meant that a major responsibility of churchwardens (incredible as this will seem to their successors today) was to bring before the relevant court (usually the local archdeacon's court) either at the annual visitation or as need arose, any recognised sinners for due trial. The judgment of historians of the church courts is that, owing to the demise of the confessional and the desire for greater holiness, the courts' business grew after the Reformation. In his monumental three-volume study, Rodes concludes of the Elizabethan period:

> it seems to me that a good deal of work was done to try to catch sinners who would not have been caught before. Perhaps the bishops were stung by their Calvinist brethren; perhaps their own nostalgia for Geneva moved them. In any event, the dominant impression I get from medieval material is that people were turned in only when their neighbours were annoyed at them, whereas the Elizabethan materials show the neighbours being systematically prodded to turn people in.[11]

Similarly, from Outhwaite,

> The corrective work of the church courts increased after the Reformation, partly to impose new religious orthodoxies and partly to fill the regulatory vacuum that was created by both the ending of auricular confession and the decline in levels of activity in manorial, hundred and borough courts.[12]

Queen Elizabeth may not, proverbially, have wished to open windows into men's hearts, but her Church was very willing to open windows into their bedrooms now and again, as well as regulate their public prayers.

It was this system of ecclesiastical courts which was resurrected, along with the rest of the traditional Anglican hierarchy (and the accompanying critical resentment of the Puritan movement) in 1660 when the king came into his own. The system had been trimmed of a few of its most oppressive elements by the Long Parliament, and these were not revived. The Court of High Commission and the Court of Star Chamber, renowned as mechanisms of arbitrary royal justice, had been abolished. The former in particular had regularly been used to try religious cases. Also abolished, in the 1670s, was the notorious 'oath of compurgation' whereby the accused was tried by being given the opportunity to find a body of witnesses who knew him and would swear to his innocence.[13] As with the concept of public penance itself, this makes some sense in the context of a Christian community aspiring to pure lives, but fell an obvious victim to the insistence of Coke and the common lawyers that no-one should be tried on the strength of their reputation, rather than on the basis of evidence. Helmholz also draws attention to the fact that compurgation shared many characteristics with wager of law at common law, which fell into disuse with the rise of trial by jury, discrediting compurgation as an obsolescence.[14] Although their zeal was diminished by the growth of Arminianism, it can be noted that for some Puritans like Baxter, the Restoration was still nonetheless a let-down in not setting up the longed-for godly discipline.[15]

How Toleration happened

Within the vast historiography of the events of 1688–89 two main points are relevant here. The first is that the Anglican dominance of 1660–88 was not merely the assured possession of the only legal liturgy for public worship and the churches, parsonages and endowments wherewith to perform it, but the operation of the church courts actively engaged in enforcing Anglican conformity in every parish of the land. John Coffey summarises:

> the Restoration settlement proved that support for religious uniformity was very strong among the nation's elites, and during the quarter-century after 1660 England witnessed a persecution of Protestants by Protestants without parallel in seventeenth-century Europe. Dissenters were fined and imprisoned in their thousands for defying the penal laws [e.g. the Five Mile Act and Conventicle Act] against non-conformity and holding illegal conventicles.[16]

The splendours of a strong Restoration Church celebrated in subsequent eras depended on a system of enforcement which today must rank with other police states of history.

Coffey's assertion of unparalleled persecution is supported by impressive figures in an earlier study, showing that, for example, over 3,800 dissenters were arrested in London in 1681–86,[17] but with recognition that the vigour of persecution varied from place to place and year to year. G. V. Bennett, in his study of the life of Atterbury, joins Coffey in noting Archbishop Sancroft's zeal for discipline through strengthening the courts, noting how much of his correspondence is taken up by the matter. Examples from 1676 suggest Sancroft had been able to maintain regular communicant numbers at 80–90% of the population.[18] Sancroft was no doubt very worried about the 10–20%, but in comparison with every period from 1688 on, it goes to demonstrate that, "when virtually the whole population of a village from the squire down to the labourers and their wives knelt at the altar rails, the power of the Church, at least in the countryside, was still strong."[19]

The second point, to be explored in more depth, is that the vast majority of those, Anglican and dissenter, who contended against and for the freedom to worship outside the Church, believed in the existence of some system of authority to restrain sin, and worried that the end of uniformity would mean the breakdown of morality. Yet the accident of history meant that against all their intentions, the power of the church courts to respond to dissenters from agreed morality was fatally weakened, and the seeds sown of the undisciplined Church of the future.

It is perhaps bold to describe the Toleration Act as an accident of history but, seen in the context of the contending ideologies and proposals of the preceding period, it is difficult to come to any other conclusion. The historical situation is fairly clear: until 1689 the Church of England was the only legal church, with power to enforce its rule on the nation. However, those who could not accept the formulae of the Church of England, either those who would not worship according to her liturgy or those who believed she lacked the discipline of a true church (these were often, but importantly not always, the same people), were proving ultimately impossible to coerce by the power of the courts alone. The memory of the Civil War and the European context made the political class ill-disposed towards the greater use of force. The Declaration of Indulgence issued by James II in 1687 in effect conceded the point by suspending the penalties for dissent whilst not yet proving permanent legal means for its implementation.

It was in this context that the idea of toleration was mooted before 1689. However, those who proposed it were seldom proposing the 'freedom of religion' guaranteed by modern human rights, traced back to Locke's *Letter concerning Toleration*. Crucially, Locke's letter was only published in England *after* the Toleration Act had been passed, and so far from being the ideological justification for it, represents the wellspring of the thought which has been inspired to identify Toleration with the freedom of Englishmen, and subsequent liberal democracy down to the present day. But the Toleration Act was in fact passed by a Parliament formed of Anglicans with no understanding of liberal democracy, never mind enthusiasm for it. What then did they think they were doing?

The key to the historical accident of the Toleration Act is that the Toleration Bill was introduced to Parliament by the Earl of Nottingham in February 1689 together with a Comprehension Bill, to modify the formularies, particularly the liturgy, of the Church of England by removing those parts which were most offensive to dissenters, with a view to their being 'comprehended' into the Anglican fold. The liturgical offer made various texts and ceremonies optional, and is of interest to historians of the Prayer Book.[20] Seen from today, and particularly from a Church of England where liturgical variety has been accepted for generations, this looks like "*Common Worship* three centuries early." The reality is, of course, far less cosy.

In his recent study of the build-up to 1689, Scott Sowerby notes a sustained degree of discretion amongst Anglicans in response to calls for toleration, as they did not wish to be thought of as persecutors in an age when that called to mind the Inquisition. Nonetheless:

> The ministers of the Church of England had been fighting dissent in their parishes for their entire careers. Many of them believed that if a man or woman left the Church of England to attend a conventicle – whether it was a Quaker, a Baptist, or a Presbyterian one – that soul was in danger of the fires of hell.[21]

The difficulty is that there is a subtlety, not always clearly expressed by individual writers, as to whether a willingness to bend from this narrow status quo is a willingness to accept difference within or without the Church of England – a theme which can be traced right down to the present day – and this means the motives of those such as who proposed schemes of comprehension were mixed, to a degree now difficult to untangle.

One attempt to classify is offered by Coffey, who suggests a fourfold scheme: toleration combined with comprehension, sought by Locke and many dissenters; the opposite, neither tolerance nor comprehension (i.e. the 1660 status quo), held to by High Church Tories; toleration without comprehension (what actually happened), sought by sectaries only concerned to establish their pure holy huddles; comprehension without toleration, sought by bishops like Stillingfleet, some subsequently called Latitudinarians.[22] It is the last which is most interesting, as it represents, in variations, the viewpoint of most of the leading figures who were striving to find a way forward.

Bennett attempts a division of concept with respect to comprehension:

> It is possible to misunderstand these schemes of comprehension, and I think we cannot put them in context unless we see that there were two types of comprehension scheme. There was one type which was actually favoured by High Churchmen like Sancroft, Fell, Turner, Hickes and others; they desired Christian reunion because they wanted a united church in which they could exercise discipline: reform church attendance, control morals, and ensure that children were catechised and confirmed. They feared a divided religious situation for fear that this might lead to toleration and the making of religion a purely voluntary activity … Tillotson and his allies had a somewhat different view … a subtle attempt to reduce the dogmatic character of the church.[23]

An alternative would be that Sancroft and Tillotson were in fact not so much proposing different schemes as seeing the same scheme different ways.

Historical debate has been complicated by the use of the blanket term 'Latitudinarian' without clarifying which thinkers and bishops should be contained under it. Bennett, at any rate, stands in a school of thought presenting the Latitudinarians as the direct ancestors of today's Anglican liberals, anxious to reduce mystery and present a soft-option Christianity acceptable to the greatest number. There is a good deal of this in Tillotson, and more so later in Hoadly. But theological liberalism does not necessarily go with acceptance of dissent – there is a consistent sense that those seeking comprehension did so in order to get the greatest number on side to apply solid pressure excluding the remaining minority. In Ashcraft's trenchant words, "Latitudinarianism is not a moderate middle ground between contending extremes; it is, rather, *part* of one of the extremes. It is the acceptable face of the persecution of religious dissent" (italics original).[24]

In the event, it was recognised that the High Church party, dominant in Convocation (which was meeting at the same time) was opposed to any changes to the Prayer Book, and would prevent approval there, and also that, for the Dissenters, the probability of Toleration rapidly removed the attractions of comprehension. Bennett attributes the failure of the Comprehension Bill to King William III's ill-prepared introduction to Parliament of a proposal to abolish the Test and

Corporation Acts[25] arousing Tory ire. Ashcraft prefers to say "details relating to this event are still shrouded in mystery"[26] (not least because there was no Hansard and recording parliamentary debate was illegal), but the Comprehension Bill fell and the Toleration Bill passed into law, as a grudging but necessary recognition that if dissenters were going to persistently refuse to conform to the Church of England, they could be relieved of the penalties that would otherwise fall on them for so doing. Reassurance was also given by the oath required of dissenters to abjure popery, and the stipulation that their worship could not be behind closed doors (where sedition might be plotted).[27]

The effects of Toleration

Any attempt to assess the effects of the Toleration Act on the functioning of the church courts is hazardous owing to the ungathered nature of the data from the vast range of courts. Even as he attempted his overall summary, Brian Outhwaite noted "most of the church courts of Restoration England remain unstudied, and consequently all generalisations about them remain fragile."[28] Nonetheless, it is possible to find some numbers which suggest a fairly rapid decline in the work of the courts, and non-attendance presentations being the first casualty. In the deanery of Holderness, non-attendance cases, numbering 165 in 1665 and 121 in 1674, had fallen to 29 in 1691. In the deanery of Buckrose there were 317 in 1670 against 12 in 1691.[29] Another local study, again acknowledging the difficulties of poor recording, notes a drop in presentations for non-attendance in Hereford archdeaconry from 370 in 1687 to 92 in 1695. A long decline is noted by the same study in Oxford, where the average number of presentations across 14 annual sittings fell from 34.4 in 1662/63, to 13.7 in 1691/92, to 8.87 in 1701, and to negligible numbers by the 1740s.[30]

A famous 1692 remark of Archdeacon Humphrey Prideaux of Suffolk is often cited in support of the contention that the Toleration Act had introduced religious freedom:

> now such liberty is given to others, it cannot be avoyded but everyone takes to doe what he pleases in matters of religion, it being too difficult a matter to distinguish between those absentees from church that goe to conventicles, and those that doe not, that everyone is now free to do what he pleaseth.[31]

In practice, however, my predominant impression is of a slower and subtler process over two generations. In the first generation, presentations for non-attendance did indeed drop off, and amongst the Tory High Church, as will be noted, within the wider rhetoric of 'the Church in danger' was a theme of lament for the lack of enforcing authority to compel all except the officially-tolerated licensed Dissenters to adhere to the Church.

However, it is not until the 1720s that a breadth of sources lament the ineffectiveness of the discipline exercised by the church courts, and still later before they reach the peculiar condition of neglect which introduces the next chapter. A recent study has noted significant regional variations in the decline of cases, with certain unexplained rural jurisdictions (Nottingham and Carlisle, but not Hereford or Derby) hearing many fornication cases well into the mid-eighteenth century.[32] Troy Harris argues from a number of studies that the church courts remained busy throughout the first half of the eighteenth century[33] but his detailed figures for the consistory courts of Lichfield and Durham show a significant overall decline in cases across his three chosen periods 1725–31; 1732–38; 1739–45, with fluctuating figures for defamation and discipline.[34]

Toryism and the hope of restored discipline

The period from 1688–1720 saw a transformation of the public life of the country in which religion played only a part along with a wider context of political uncertainty, international tribulations and the prolonged uncertainty of the royal succession leading to the uneasy acceptance of the Hanoverians. The Tory movement was in its essence a backward yearning for what seemed to have been a clearer age of Anglican-Stuart hegemony, but as times changed showed itself in alarmist ways. As one writer commented of the wave of support for Sacheverell in 1709, "The old England struck out blindly in the dark, struggling against its transformation into the home province of a Greater Britain."[35]

Yet the High Church Tories came to be remembered by the Tractarians, and still are by some Anglo-Catholics with good historical sense, as heroic forebears, the defenders of the true Church in the face of the worldly Whiggery that Toleration made possible and the Hanoverians made dominant. Without denying that possible train of thought, it is useful to make a gentle reminder that integral to the Tory vision of the period was the revival of a coercive discipline upon the nation. Whilst that yearning for discipline can be found in a minority thread of Anglo-Catholic thought, it was in fact the refusal of Anglo-Catholics to accept the actual if ineffective discipline of the Church of England which gives a major theme to this study of an undisciplined church. But not all Whigs wished to abandon ecclesiastical discipline either.

The particular locus of Toryism in the context of the Church was the Convocation of Canterbury, the ancient assembly of bishops and leading clergy of the province (chosen by a complex electoral system giving a heavy weighting to cathedral dignitaries). Discussion of Convocation is complicated by the historiographical divergence over its true long-term role. Whig historians from the eighteenth century on emphasised that its major function in the Middle Ages had been to vote taxation on the clergy, and argued that once this role had been abandoned at the Restoration (on the basis of mere verbal agreement between Archbishop Sheldon and Lord Chancellor Clarendon[36]) it had no real purpose and was reasonably suppressed. Tories, including nineteenth century Anglo-Catholics such as Wood, below, preferred to see it as the legitimate provincial governing body of the Church of England (or at least the Province of Canterbury; the generally uncontroversial Convocation of York tends to get ignored) without which the Church was emasculated for the long eighteenth century. The most significant modern account, in Eric Kemp's Bampton Lectures of 1961, articulates an account of a body with medieval roles with relation to both taxation and the expression of church opinion, but even from his Anglo-Catholic perspective he has to concede that Convocation played little role in the English Reformation, and that the Tory period of the early 1700s is anomalous.

The key to this anomaly was Francis Atterbury, who campaigned consistently for "a uniquely English vision of the union of a national Church and a regime of absolute monarchy, deriving from Archbishop Laud and developed under Sheldon and Sancroft in the era after 1660"[37] but for which he was fated to campaign in an era when it was not wanted. Atterbury's particular conception, articulated in the anonymously published *Letter to a Convocation Man*[38] and his later writings, was that Convocation had a political role akin to Parliament, and the Lower House parallel to that of the House of Commons. Atterbury's camp rose and fell with the fluctuating favour of Queen Anne and his own political successes, finding a voice to confront the bishops as Prolocutor of the Lower House of the Convocation of Canterbury before becoming Bishop of Rochester in 1713. Yet in spite of his "essential Tory refusal to accept the fact that Dissent had become a permanent feature of English life"[39] it is possible to find earlier in Atterbury's career an example of the two-sided nature of law as a vehicle for church controversy.

One of the major Tory objectives under Queen Anne was to obtain an Occasional Conformity Act, which would outlaw the practice of dissenters receiving communion in the Church of England purely for the purpose of satisfying the requirements of the Test Act, before accepting public office. The Tories regarded this as hypocrisy and an abuse of the sacrament, pointing for example to Lord Mayor of London in 1697 Sir Humphrey Edwin, who "took the sacrament in an Anglican church simply to qualify to hold the office of Mayor before walking to his usual place of worship, the Congregational Chapel at Pinner's Hall."[40] Atterbury brought to this campaign, among many other writings, a set of sermons published with Queen Anne's endorsement in 1708 and a preface stating that, "the discipline of the Church courts was to be revived, the rights and revenues of the clergy secured, and blasphemers and heterodox writers suppressed."[41] Atterbury was determined that the loophole of the Toleration Act should not prevent the affirmation of the Church's power. Yet at precisely the same time, in his then capacity as Dean of Carlisle, assisted *in situ* (since Atterbury was busy politicking in London) by Dr Todd, one of the canons, he was fiercely resisting the rights of his own bishop to carry out a Visitation of the cathedral, on slender legal grounds that the Queen was the only possible Visitor. Atterbury is thereby exposed in the pattern of many others very keen to assert the authority of the Church over those they perceived as ungodly, but ready to use any means to resist authority imposed upon themselves.

The attraction of the Tory programme can be seen in the popular reaction to the trial of Dr Sacheverell in 1709 for the preaching of an intemperate High Church sermon for the 5 November, identifying Dissenters as 'False Brethren,' where he was feted by the crowds and given a very mild penalty. The Tory-dominated Lower House of the Convocation of Canterbury in 1711 sent a

Representation of the State of Religion to Queen Anne (a text generally attributed to Atterbury) blaming the Great Rebellion for undermining the order of the Church, and yearning (rather optimistically) that, "some way might be found to restore the discipline of the Church, now so much relaxed and decayed, to its primitive life and vigour; and to strengthen the ordinary jurisdiction of the ecclesiastical courts."[42] In 1711 Parliament was finally prevailed upon to pass the short-lived Occasional Conformity Act, and for a few years before the death of Queen Anne there might have seemed to be a chance of a Tory polity prevailing, with the passage of the even more short-lived Schism Act 1714.

The failure of Convocational censure

As well as deploying Convocation to demand legal changes to benefit the Tory position, "Atterbury and the High Churchmen … sought to make the Convocation the instrument of censure and, by doing so, brought down the institution."[43] In fairness to them, this was a function of Convocation in the Middle Ages, as chronicled intermittently by Kemp,[44] but not exercised in a serious way since the Reformation. The first target of censure was the clerical mathematician William Whiston, who had discovered the early Christian text known as the *Apostolic Constitutions* and was drawing from it heterodox conclusions, arguing in his *Primitive Christianity Revived* that Arianism had been the creed of the early Church.[45] These cost him his chair in Cambridge in 1710 and brought public denunciation of his writings by Convocation in 1711.[46] Yet Whiston represents the first of many cases where the legal structures of the Church proved unable to respond effectively to a challenge to orthodoxy. Before the Civil War, he would have been tried by High Commission, but "the Act abolishing the Court of High Commission had forbidden the creation of a court with similar jurisdiction."[47] A suit for heresy was brought against Whiston by a Dr Pelling, but owing to his residence in the peculiar of the Dean and Chapter of St Paul's, the courts struggled to assign him to a jurisdiction competent to try him for heresy, and the case was dropped in 1714.[48] Nonetheless, Whiston's case, and that of Samuel Clark, denounced by the Lower House and protected by the Upper in 1714,[49] led to a perception of Convocation as the seat of persecuting opinion and hostility to the Whig principles of the Hanoverian Succession.

The strongest Whig leaders among the bishops, such as Burnet and Hoadly, did believe in liberty of thought, even within the Church. Yet within those sometimes classified as Whigs there was significant variety of opinion about the question of discipline. Every, writing in 1956, offers a division which is also demonstrative of how utterly slippery the terms 'Whig' and 'Latitudinarian' can prove:

> Whig High Churchmen, like Potter and Gibson, believed in civil liberties, and therefore in a certain measure of latitude in Church affairs, but not beyond the bounds of orthodoxy. Their Whiggery resided, not in their Churchmanship, but in their readiness to accept Dissenters as fellow-citizens. Latitude

> men, like Hoadly and Francis Hare, had put their trust in Whiggery, because the Whigs alone would protect them against a revival of Church authority.[50]

For Benjamin Hoadly, whose views we might call liberal even by today's standards, this protection was not hypothetical. In 1717, Hoadly's famous sermon to the Court on "The Nature of the Kingdom of Christ," taking the line that it is wholly 'not of this world' in a contemporary legal and political sense, and that the Church had no authority to impose doctrinal tests, provoked the pamphlet outburst known as the Bangorian Controversy (he was at the time Bishop of Bangor). With tracts circulating in their hundreds, the Lower House of Convocation on 3 May 1717 appointed a committee to investigate Hoadly's opinions, whose critical report a week later was received *nem con* by the Lower House.[51] The protection of the Whig government manifested itself impressively, proroguing Convocation within the month, and repeatedly until as an institution it was wholly silenced for over a century. Hoadly himself progressed through the episcopate to reach Winchester, and his writings had an enduring influence on the eighteenth century Church.

Although Tractarian historians have depicted this as a purely cynical and Erastian move, it was a reversion to the policy of William III[52] and the end of an in fact very short period in which the Convocations, or more accurately, one House of one Convocation, attempted to act as a voice for part of the views of the Church of England, with self-defeating effect.

> [T]he fractious meetings of Convocation were the last splutterings of a body that had not met between 1690 and 1703. Its silencing in 1717 was not occasioned by Hoadly or the House of Bishops, but by the insistence of the Tory High Churchmen between 1710 and 1717 to use it as an instrument of censorship and repression.[53]

From the point of view of the history of discipline, this was one of several abortive attempts by those of a High Church perspective to assert their will over chosen opponents, thwarted by the nature of the establishment of the Church of England.

Gibson and his Codex

A more substantive figure in legal history is Edmund Gibson, who occupied the middle ground of the Whig High Church. Like many in the middle ground down the centuries, Gibson is striking for the variety of ways in which he was perceived, which say a great deal about the confusion as to where the Church was going. Politically, Gibson was a Whig who was happy to accept office from George I, becoming in due course Bishop of London in 1723. Although of by no means the same political views, he was close to Walpole, and was the major source of advice on church patronage to the first Prime Minister, becoming known as 'Walpole's Pope.'[54]

Gibson's great contribution to legal thought is his mammoth *Codex Juris Ecclesiastici Anglicani*, first published in 1713, and a revised edition in 1761, and which gave him the earlier nickname 'Dr Codex.' The Codex is, as the name suggests, a thematic compilation of all the ecclesiastical statue law and canon extant at the time, together with a formidable range of Reformation and medieval material adduced as precedents. It is therefore largely a work of relatively impartial scholarship, and a valuable source for legal historians; more debatable is the extent to which simply by compiling and publishing it, Gibson was making a claim for the authority of the Church as some felt. He did feel able to include in it some modest suggestions towards the better functioning of the church courts. He recommended the removal of business like probate, which he felt not strictly spiritual in nature, from the church courts, and was one of many who sought to end the use of excommunication as the penalty for contempt, replacing it with imprisonment.[55] These feel like modest modernisation.

But when Gibson comes to consider the former oath of compurgation, his objectives are revealed (capitalisation and italics original):

> I shall not make any Observation upon the time, when this important Branch of Ecclesiastical Discipline [i.e. compurgation, the trial by seeking sworn witnesses of innocence] was abolished, nor take it upon me to say, how much the loss of it has contributed to that unusual *Boldness* and *Openness* with which Lewdness and other immoralities have since reigned, and do reign, in this Nation: But this I may venture to affirm, that it cannot but be a matter of Grief to all good Men, to all who are Lovers of Virtue and Religion, and have a concern for the Honour of God, to see the *Church* (to which the Suppression of Vice more especially belongs, and in whose Hands the Work is most likely to prosper) thus *restrain'd* and *fetter'd* in the Exercise of her Discipline.[56]

Gibson can, therefore, be seen as a natural heir to Stillingfleet, for example, in accepting the political realities of his time in the need to accommodate Dissent as an unavoidable part of English life, whilst still believing firmly in the purpose of the Church to be the moral agent in the nation.

Gibson also may have felt he had to reckon with competition. W. M. Jacob tracks the largely one-generation phenomenon (roughly 1690s–1710s) of the Societies for the Reformation of Manners.[57] These were voluntary organisations seeking to identify and shame sinners in the interests of public morality and drew moral support from several royal proclamations against profaneness and vice between 1697 and 1708. But they were suspect in the eyes of Churchmen as they often involved enthusiastic Dissenters keen to keep the Puritan spirit alive, and for their willingness to bring sinners before the secular courts if the church courts would not act. They represent that element of Christian thought which is always ready to spot "the general overflowing of vice"[58] and their concern with petty morals can be seen by their provision of blank warrants to make prosecution easier for constables and magistrates (by saving them stamp duty) for such offences as profane swearing and tippling on Sunday.[59]

Gibson's attempt to codify the laws of the Church, and aspire to a more efficient functioning of the church courts for moral reform, drew a strong reaction. Norman Sykes, in his 1926 biography, remarks:

> The cry of "Church Power" was raised against him and the *Codex* became the symbol of aspiration to ecclesiastical tyranny.... The temper and hostility aroused were so great that Gibson did not dare to publish to the world the conclusion he had reached, after a thorough consultation of all the extant episcopal registers of the various English and Welsh sees, that ecclesiastical canons were binding on the laity.[60]

Even omitting this controversial detail did not prevent the fury of Michael Foster, a London common lawyer. Foster was among those who denounced Gibson's Codex as a 'Scheme of Church Power,' seeing his fairly modest proposals for reform of courts, which were after all already in place at the time, as something like a wholesale imposition of popery. He follows Hoadly's argument about the unworldliness of the Kingdom, and recounts the classic English Protestant story of the Reformation as the delivery of the nation by good rulers and wise lawyers from bondage to obscurantist clergy. As far as he is concerned, the Civil War only goes to prove his point, for it was caused by "a general Alienation of Affections at Home, occasion'd in great measure by a rigorous Exercise of Ecclesiastical Discipline."[61]

Foster's solution, echoing in part what was beginning to happen in society, was for civil magistrates and courts to take responsibility for public morals, and that Gibson's contention that this was somehow the special responsibility of the Church was a nonsense, for far from being experts on morality, the clergy "may with no great impropriety by compared to *Quack Medicines*; which promise great Matters, *Speedy, Safe and infallible Cures*; but in the End, destroy rather than preserve the Constitution."[62] He concludes briskly, "The Temporalty in Parliament surely did not shake off one Sett of Spiritual Pædagogues, only to subject themselves and Posterity to the Discipline of another."[63] It is, of course, difficult to gauge the reception of Foster's work (which went through several editions), but it goes to demonstrate the ebbing of the popular tide of Toryism in favour of celebration of the liberty of Englishmen.

A different critical perspective is offered by the 1733 tract of W. Bohun, *A Brief View of Ecclesiastical Jurisdiction*, which is linked by Outhwaite with a 1734 Bill to abolish the penal jurisdiction of the church courts.[64] However, the content of Bohun's text scrupulously avoids suggesting there is anything wrong with the religious concept of spiritual courts, but simply denounces the cost to the nation of "an *over-numerous body of ecclesiastics* among us, and by the exactions, extortions and oppressions, of what are called *spiritual courts* and *jurisdictions*."[65] He counts up the costs of both bishops and courts, seeming to regard all alike as needless and luxurious expenses, and concludes by endorsing an opinion he claims to have had in person from Bishop Gilbert Burnet, that "*the Canon law and ecclesiastical jurisdiction were originally derived from Hell, and thither it ought to be sent again*."[66]

Local angles on the decline of discipline

As already noted, the almost accidental nature of Toleration, and the real vigour of Tory hopes for the restoration of a confessional state for as long as Queen Anne lived, meant that ecclesiastical discipline still held some force, certainly over moral matters (as opposed to non-attendance at church) for a generation after 1689. However, in the early Georgian period it becomes easy to find writers lamenting the weakness of the church courts in upholding morality. Johnson's *Clergyman's Vade Mecum* in 1731 notes that dissenters were still liable to penance for their sins, "for the Act of Toleration was never intended to Patronize Lewdness or Immorality,"[67] but seems accepting that they will not be easily caught. In a sermon to the Mayor and Corporation in Hereford in 1725, my distant predecessor as Rector of Weston-under-Penyard, Thomas Bisse, considers the dilemma of how to defend the true Church when alternatives exist side by side, recommending favouritism to better people, and laments the limitations of ecclesiastical discipline memorably (italics original):

> There was a time, when the Sword of the ecclesiastical Ruler was a terror to evil doers, and the amputations of it more dreaded than the temporal. But more dreaded, as that sword ought to be, exceeding, like *Goliath's*, the swords of men, yet, like *Goliath's* too, it is now, in effect, laid up as behind the Altar, without much use or regard: And no marvel, in these days of Latitude, when it cannot so much as smite the hand that writes against the Altar. But were it borne with its primitive authority, yet there are some kinds or degrees of wickedness, that are beyond the reach of spiritual censures, and almost below the cognisance and correction of the secular arm. There are some sinners, dregs of sinners, that lie about the streets like common nusances, bestial drunkards, outrageous swearers, *foaming out their own shame*, obscene wretches *glorying in it.* [68]

The high-minded Tory Bisse, brother of a previous bishop, a founder of the Three Choirs Festival, a member of the committee of Convocation which had censured Bishop Hoadly,[69] (but who had to endure Hoadly succeeding his brother in 1721) sounds to have been himself foaming in the pulpit as he denounced the low life of Hereford, without any practical means of amending them (Hoadly had moved on to Salisbury in 1724, possibly giving Bisse the freedom to preach thus).

A generation later, the vicar of Blecheley lamented to his diary that he had no choice but to agree to a baptism and churching in a domestic parlour, "as the discipline of our church, through the practice of dissenters, is now so relaxed as to come to nothing, there is no parleying with one's parishioners on any point of doctrine or discipline."[70] Although the church courts continued to function, and had cases brought to them when need arose, the Church of England had for all practical purposes become a voluntary organisation, albeit an immensely privileged one, unable to enforce either the liturgical practice or the public morality its own laws demanded.

The Manx exception

An important exception, remote from the experience of mainstream early eighteenth -century society, stands by its exceptionality to demonstrate the general decline in the Church's disciplinary control. The see of Sodor and Man was, and is, part of the Church of England, and began the period governed by the same inheritance of ecclesiastical law and canon. However, although under the Crown, the Isle of Man is not subject to Parliament, and therefore exempt from the provision of the Submission of the Clergy Act 1533 which forbids the making of new canons without royal licence, and which inhibited serious reform of the canons in England until the twentieth century. The Manx bishops, by contrast, were able through their own synod to enact new canons.

Thomas Wilson began his long episcopate in 1698, and is remembered for devoting himself wholly to the close care and direction of the spiritual life of Man. Before considering the discipline question, it is worth noting this diligence, his restoration of churches, and that he aided the economy and the needs of the people by pushing through land reform. However, his significance for our purposes is that he used the power to enact new canons in 1703 to increase the level of moral enforcement, and with little Dissent on the island, made full use of it. Punishments were more varied than the usual white sheet: the scold's bridle could be employed from 1714 on scolds or gossips.[71] The 1703 Canons also provided that 'common whores' were to be dragged in the sea behind a boat, a cruelty endured more than once by one Katherine Kinrade.[72] The most celebrated case resulted from Wilson's sentencing Mrs Horne, the wife of the Governor, to penance for slander, which led to the bishop and his vicar-general themselves being imprisoned for exceeding their jurisdiction in 1722.

The strong moral rule of Wilson over the Isle of Man is notable for the wider picture in two ways. The way in which it was noted at the time as an exception to the English norm highlights the extent to which the mainstream Church of England was felt to have lost its discipline. The judgment of Bishop Short in the 1840s that the diocese under Wilson had resembled "an English Diocese as it was before the days of Charles I"[73] was borne out by a horrified Attorney General Searle, who reported after visiting Man in 1761 that the church courts were "avowed enemies of liberty and peace. The Spiritual Court exults here in its fullness of power and despotism."[74] However, after Wilson the church courts of Man seem to have undergone a similar process of decline to the rest of England, and excommunication was never imposed after 1780.[75]

Yet the example of Wilson was not forgotten, and this is the second point of note. Wesley recorded with approval the state of religious discipline on Man, and attributed to it the success of Methodism there among a population eager for a more rigorous religion. More importantly for later Anglicans, Keble wrote Wilson's *Life* and republished his complete works, as the very first volumes of the celebrated Tractarian *Library of Anglo-Catholic Theology*. As we shall note later, the yearning for a lost England where the Church could rule and bring her corrective powers to bear on sin and heterodoxy, is a small but vital theme in the whole Anglo-Catholic movement.

On the path of decay.

The ending of church discipline over society in the early eighteenth century can be seen simply as a cultural phenomenon, that "no-one in that permissive age was interested in having his vices detected."[76] However, the vigour of the Tory High Church movement in the reign of Queen Anne and the exertions of the Societies for the Reformation of Manners suggest that there were still many in the first generation after the Glorious Revolution who were full of interest in detecting the vices of others, and wanted the means to deal with them when they were detected. But the unreformed church courts, slow of process and equipped only with the rusty sword of excommunication against those who ignored them, were unable to offer much help. The Church of England, not yet corporately distinct from the nation at large, entered the Georgian period in increasing enjoyment of freedom from religious discipline, and in many cases, believing this to be the happy fruit of the Glorious Revolution.

Notes

1 *The Ecclesiastical Courts. Principles of Reconstruction* (SPCK 1954) 1–4.
2 Robert E. Rodes, Jr., *Ecclesiastical Administration in Medieval England (*Notre Dame 1977) Ch. 2–4.
3 Robert E. Rodes, Jr, *Lay Authority and Reformation in the English Church. Edward I to the Civil War* (Notre Dame 1982) 237.
4 R. B. Outhwaite, *The Rise and Fall of the English Ecclesiastical Courts, 1500–1860* (CUP 2006) Ch 1.
5 Ibid., 58.
6 In William Gibson (ed.) *Religion and Society in England & Wales 1689–1800* (Leicester University Press 1998) 160–1.
7 Outhwaite, *Rise and Fall,* 12.
8 Ibid., 13.
9 Rodes, *Lay Authority* 105.
10 Rodes, *Modernisation* 86.
11 Ibid., 137.
12 Outhwaite, *Rise and Fall,* 57.
13 Robert E. Rodes, Jr., *Law and Modernisation in the Church of England* (Notre Dame 1991) 24–5.
14 R. H. Helmholz, *The* Jus Commune *in England* (OUP 2001) 82–8.
15 cf. George Every, *The High Church Party 1688–1718* (SPCK 1956) 21.
16 John Coffey, "The Toleration Controversy during the English Revolution" in C. Durston and J. Maltby, *Religion in Revolutionary England* (Manchester University Press 2006) 60.
17 John Coffey, *Persecution and Toleration in Protestant England 1558–1689* (Longmans 2000) 173.
18 G. V. Bennett, *The Tory Crisis in Church and State 1688–1730. The Career of Francis Atterbury, Bishop of Rochester* (Clarendon Press 1975) 6.
19 Ibid., 8.

20 For example, Francis Proctor and Walter Howard Frere, *A New History of the Book of Common Prayer* (Macmillan & Co. 1929) 206–22.
21 Scott Sowerby, *Making Toleration. The Repealers and the Glorious Revolution* (Harvard University Press 2013) 170.
22 Coffey, *Persecution*, 12.
23 Geoffrey Rowell (ed.), *Gareth Bennett: to the Church of England* (Churchman Publishing 1988) 82–3.
24 Richard Ashcraft, "Latitudinarianism and toleration; historical myth versus political history" in Kroll, Ashcraft and Zagovin (eds) *Philosophy, Science and Religion in England 1640–1700* (CUP 1992) 155.
25 G. V. Bennett, "Conflict in the Church" in Holmes, Geoffrey (ed.) *Britain after the Glorious Revolution 1689–1714* (Macmillan, St Martin's Press 1969) 161.
26 Ashcraft, "Latitudinarianism" 151.
27 The Toleration Act 1689, in Gibson, *Religion*, 31–2.
28 Outhwaite, *Rise and Fall*, 80, citing Spurr, *The Restoration Church of England 1646–1689* (New Haven 1991) 209.
29 Ibid., 81.
30 William Marshall, *Church Life in Hereford and Oxford, 1660–1760. A Study of Two Sees* (Carnegie Publishing 2009) 64.
31 Cited in Jacob, W. M., *Lay People and Religion in the Early Eighteenth Century* (CUP 1996) 52–3.
32 William Gibson and Joanna Begiato, *Sex and the Church in the Long Eighteenth Century* (I. B. Tauris 2017) 95.
33 Troy L. Harris, "The Work of the English Ecclesiastical Courts 1725–1745" in Troy L. Harris (ed.) *Studies in Canon Law and Common Law in Honor of R. H. Helmholz* (Robbins Collection 2015) 251–4
34 Ibid. , 275.
35 Every, *High Church*, 135.
36 Eric Kemp, *Counsel and Consent* (SPCK 1961) 166.
37 Bennett, *Crisis*, 295.
38 Kemp, *Counsel*, 165.
39 Bennett, *Crisis*, 179.
40 William Gibson, *Enlightenment Prelate: Benjamin Hoadly, 1676–1761* (James Clark & Co 2004) 61.
41 Bennett, *Crisis*, 93.
42 Cited in Bennett, *Crisis*, 137.
43 Gibson, *Hoadly*, 32.
44 Kemp, *Counsel*, 89–90, 116–17.
45 Gibson, *Hoadly*, 122.
46 Ibid., 122.
47 Every, *High Church*, 138.
48 *Pelling v Whiston* (1712) 1 Comyne 199.
49 Gibson, *Hoadly*, 123.
50 Rowell (ed.), *Bennett*, 82–3.
51 Gibson, *Hoadly*, 174.
52 Ibid., 179.
53 Ibid., 197.
54 Edward Pearce, *The Great Man. Sir Robert Walpole: Scoundrel, Genius and Britain's First Prime Minister* (Pimlico 2008) 265–70.
55 Edmund Gibson, *Codex Juris Ecclesiastici Anglicani* (2nd ed. London 1761) Introductory Discourse.
56 Ibid., 1042.
57 Jacob, *Lay People*, 125–35.
58 Woodward 1797 in Gibson (ed.) *Religion* 54.

59 Examples given in Gibson (ed.) *Religion* 57.
60 Norman Sykes, *Edmund Gibson, Bishop of London 1669–1748. A Study in Politics and Religion in the Eighteenth Century* (OUP 1926) 69–70.
61 Michael Foster, *An Examination of the Scheme of Church-Power, laid down in the Codex Juris Ecclesiastici Anglicani, &c*, (published anonymously, London 1735) 73.
62 Ibid., 105–6.
63 Ibid., 110.
64 Outhwaite, *Rise and Fall,* 116–17.
65 William Bohun, *A Brief View of Ecclesiastical Jurisdiction, as it is at this day practised in England* (London 1733, reprinted Boston, New England, 1765) 1.
66 Bohun, *Brief View*, 12.
67 John Johnson, *The Clergyman's Vade Mecum* (London 1731) 29.
68 Thomas Bisse, *The Ordinance and Office of the Magistrate* (sermon preached to the Mayor of Hereford 4th October 1725, published by Innys, London 1726) 32.
69 Gibson, *Hoadly*, 174.
70 Cited in Norman Sykes, *Church and State in England in the XVIIIth Century* (Birkbeck Lectures, CUP 1934) 249.
71 Peter Clamp, "Bishop Wilson's Discipline: Language, Schooling and Confrontation in the Isle of Man, 1698–1755" *Journal of Religious History 15.2* (1988) 191.
72 P. W. S. Farrant, *The History and Development of Ecclesiastical Law and the Bishop's Courts in the Diocese of Sodor and Man* (unpublished Cardiff LLM thesis 1998) 47.
73 Farrant, *Sodor and Man*, 51.
74 Ibid., 46.
75 Ibid., 48.
76 Rodes *Modernisation*, 7.

2. The old discipline lingers

The ineffectiveness of the courts

The ecclesiastical courts in the latter part of the eighteenth century were decayed, but they were not dead. Apart from the question of discipline, the profession of ecclesiastical law was sustained by the administration of the probate jurisdiction of the nation. But increasingly the church courts were regarded as one of the many quaint features of the English judicial system, serving a purpose in the area of 'relationship law' with only an accidental connection to their origins as a structure to maintain the rigour of Christian discipleship. This partly explains why when faced with a real disciplinary matter like the case of Dr Free, it was so difficult for the Church corporately to take effective action. In the early Victorian period, there was a recovery of understanding that the sentences of the church courts constituted religious judgments, but this only hastened the demise of their jurisdiction over lay morals in a pluralist age.

One of the criticisms of the courts was that cases could be brought which were never pursued, and that suits were delayed to a degree great even in an age not renowned for legal efficiency. A thorough example from Oxford is given by Rodes:[1] On 17 October 1761, 24 persons were introduced to the Consistory Court, all for sexual offences. The cases are traced through until the last records of them four years later. Only in one case were any costs recovered. The main proctor promoting the cases, Edward Bilstone, seems to have been inefficient and was often ill. A few individuals were excommunicated, but since it was necessary then to issue a 'schedule of excommunication' and then 'letters denunciatory' before the excommunication could be proclaimed in the relevant parish, each step requiring the court to sit, fees to be paid, etc., the excommunications were of little effect because they never got round to taking them. Following the introduction of stamp tax in 1694, each step of the procedure also cost more to carry out than in the secular courts hearing evidence *viva voce*.[2] The court did not sit for long periods in the summer, "perhaps it was a good summer for fishing."[3] In the end, not one of the 24 supposed offenders was tried, never mind sentenced.

There were, though, worldlier reasons for preserving the jurisdiction for certain purposes. Fornication might not have been regarded as a scandalous sin, but an illegitimate child was potentially a charge on the parish, and if bringing a presentment for fornication was the way to persuade the father to marry or at least support the mother, the churchwardens had an incentive to try it. The ecclesiastical charge of defamation remained the principal way to defend oneself against spoken reputational damage. In the many cases where a penance was commuted to a money payment, this could be usefully applied to local church repairs.[4] And at least until Hardwicke's Marriage Act in 1753, there was a certain amount of work for the courts clarifying marital questions. Jacob gives a less totally pessimistic picture than Rodes in suggesting "only about a half to a third"[5] of cases reached sentence.

Individual stories and references serve to show that even if less common, the practice of public penance continued. Penance for fornication and/or incontinence sometimes seems to have been recognised as wiping the reputational slate clean before marriage. In 1766, a gentleman in Worcestershire did penance for incontinence with his housekeeper on the morning of his marriage to a wealthy heiress.[6] Parson Woodforde refers a few times to carrying out a penance by order of the court, with a sense that it was a rather regrettable event. In 1794, a neighbouring parson seeks his advice on the administration of a penance for defamation, suggesting the rarity of the practice.[7] The picture is complicated by the fact that sentences of penance were often carried out more privately between the offender and those offended, in a locked church, the vestry, or even the hall of the parsonage. It was also possible particularly for the better-off sinner to commute them into a fine.[8] All this contributed to the remoteness of the system of penance from its origins in the correction of sin.

Several commentators note a sharper decline in presentments from the 1780s on, Gibson and Begiato noting that religious reformers seemed to be placing their faith in the new Sunday Schools to reform the morals of the nation in place of the old discipline.[9] Not all seem to be aware of an important change in the law which was a major cause of this. A Devon MP, who rejoiced in the surname of Bastard, campaigned steadily to introduce limitations on the possible prosecutions for ecclesiastical offences, introducing a succession of bills during the decade.[10] These were at first defeated or talked out – interestingly, the Bishop of Bangor offering the disingenuous argument to the Lords that the infrequency of cases rendered the changes unnecessary. However, Mr Bastard persisted, and in 1787 an act, sometimes called the Statute of Limitations, passed, limiting prosecution for defamation to six months after the alleged offence, for brawling and fornication eight months, and preventing prosecution for fornication if the parties had subsequently married. As the most reliable evidence of fornication is usually only visible after nine months, this rapidly reduced the number of presentments for that offence.

The final late rationalisation came in 1813 when, as proposed by Gibson over a century before, excommunication was finally abandoned as the means to deal with disregard for the courts' jurisdiction. It had always been possible as noted above for the church courts to issue a writ *de excommunicatione capiendo* to compel the sheriff to imprison any who refused to comply with the sentence, but ultimately a contemptuous sinner was not going to jib at being cut off from a Church he did not attend. The new procedure abandoned the excommunication process in favour of the writ *de contumace capiendo*, whereby the church courts could seek the gaoling of those guilty of contempt without either the bureaucracy or the controversy of first imposing a spiritual sentence upon them.[11] However as will be seen, this convergence with secular procedure may have served in time to increase the difficulty of the church courts exercising any penal role at all.

One should also note that at the same time as the ancient moral discipline of the Church ebbed away, England was living under the regime of penal legislation prescribing hanging for a vast range of offences known as the Bloody Code.[12] It is a historical commonplace that this represented the defensive action of the propertied classes but is less often noted that it was put in place in the early eighteenth century at the same time as the power of the church courts diminished. One might surmise that the rich and respectable had come to the conclusion that if they could not discipline the poor man for drinking or whoring, they could at least hang him for stealing their sheep. The many clergy serving as magistrates during the eighteenth century testified to the Church's ready acceptance of the ethic of the ruling class.

Lax discipline of the clergy

As the spiritual discipline of the laity by the church courts slowly but surely diminished, it is not surprising that that of the clergy no longer lived up to that of the rigorous and controversial seventeenth century. A clear theme in the history of the Church of England, noted from places as incidental as the novels of Jane Austen, is how thoroughly integrated by marriage and habits the Anglican clergy have been with society at large, and into the early nineteenth century, and with 'polite society' in particular. So, it should be no surprise that a more relaxed age, with better-off clergy, saw the ordinary standards of behaviour for a gentleman as good enough for the clergy. "The eighteenth century church … asked nothing of the clergy that ordinary working Christians were not willing to give."[13]

It is important, however, to be as specific as possible (given the vast and uncollected range of evidence) about what this means for the question of ecclesiastical discipline. In the early nineteenth century, the Evangelical movement came first, raising expectations of Christian discipleship for all, and the clergy by implication. The Tractarian movement followed in the same direction, but also much more clearly stressing the particular and higher expectations upon the ordained. Both looked back on the eighteenth century with disdain as an era of laxity and indifference. Although the period remains firmly the Cinderella of church history in England, the recent study of Jacob demonstrates firmly that in their own terms, the clergy of the eighteenth century were conscientious and dutiful, fulfilling the expectations of the Church of the day.[14] It may be true that their standards owed more to the general norms of gentlemanliness and professionalism rather than a vision of a sacramental priesthood, but it would be wrong to judge them worse because the Victorians aimed higher.

Our concern, though, is with those who did not meet the expected norms, and how the Church dealt with them, given that there was not, unlike today, any procedural distinction now made in the Church's laws between matters of bad conduct and matters of doctrinal error. In the seventeenth century and before the same courts had adjudged clergy inadequate on grounds derived from both sides and sentenced them accordingly. Admittedly, an important precedent was made in the 1665 case of *Slater v Smalebrooke*, when the King's Bench permitted a clergyman to be deprived for forging his Letters of Orders, even though forgery was a secular offence, and this was in effect a conduct case. "This distinction between correcting a sinner *pro salute animae* and getting rid of an unfit minister was long overdue; it was unknown to the medieval canon law."[15] But this precedent lurked around in the lawbooks until *Burgoyne v Free* in the 1820s, about which much more below.

The significant point is that through the eighteenth century the only use of the courts by bishops against their clergy were in fact over what we would now call matters of conduct: Rodes is unable to find any formal proceedings save for incontinence, drunkenness or non-residence.[16] Jacob gives a number of cases, all likewise involving sex, drink or complete failure of duty, and notes the varied methods in which bishops tried to resolve them.[17] This was in part because if court proceedings were to be brought, the costs had to be found from the bishop's own income. This is less personal than it sounds, for the substantial revenues of the episcopate were understood to sustain them in their roles, but it was nonetheless a disincentive. The courts were not being used to enforce standards of teaching or doctrinal orthodoxy, and so their justice was not controversial. Jacob finds a few examples where bishops had to resist the enthusiasm of good-living parishioners for eccentric clergy, but this would not seem quite the issue. The Stone case of 1808, which does consider doctrine and will be discussed in the next chapter, had to look back to Whiston in 1714 for a precedent,[18] and so reopened ground that had lain quiet for most of the Georgian century.

Further evidence that the courts fell into desuetude as regards the doctrinal discipline of the Church can be seen from the mid-eighteenth century, when controversies did rage, in a civilised and literary way, over Deism, Socinianism and the use of the Athanasian Creed, and in response to the rise of Methodism and Wesley's decision to defy the parochial system with his national ministry. But they do not seem to have brought forth cases to the church courts. Particular examples can be given from the career of Archbishop Thomas Secker, who was thought in his time to be a particularly keen defender of orthodoxy, but whose strongest efforts to restrain those he disapproved of still only involved the power of patronage.

In the 1760s Secker found himself concerned by the opinions of Peter Peckard, the Rector of Fletton, near Peterborough. Peckard was suspected of believing in 'soul-sleep.' This is the (highly speculative) doctrine that after death the soul does not (as in traditional orthodoxy) come into an immediate consciousness of judgment but sleeps unknowing until the General Resurrection. For some reason (possibly because it came close to denying a future state at all) this was known as the 'mortalist heresy,' and certainly also suspected because it was associated with the anti-Trinitarian theology known as Socinianism. However, Secker only acquired the means to attempt to bring Peckard to heel when the latter wished to hold a second benefice in plurality, which required a dispensation from the Archbishop. This Secker refused to do until he had received both writings from Peckard explaining his beliefs and renouncing any unorthodoxy and interrogated him at length in person. "Only after all this did Secker grant Peckard his dispensation, and the latter never again published in support of the mortalist heresy. Bullying could work."[19]

Alternatively, of course, Peckard could have defied the Archbishop, and simply endured the inconvenience of remaining in possession of only one living. Similarly, Francis Blackburne offended Secker with his 1766 work *The Confessional*, arguing against any subscription beyond that to Scripture, and Secker organised a published rebuttal, and got word through to Blackburne that he would have no chance of further preferment. Since he was already Archdeacon of Cleveland, this was presumably a bearable cross. Secker had a greater zeal to resist heresy than most eighteenth century Archbishops, but even he felt the courts would not be any help to him. And similarly, the slow estrangement of the Methodists from the Church of England came from refusal to support their structures rather than because disciplinary devices were used to exclude them.

The case of Dr Free

From this eighteenth-century perspective, with the church courts losing their coercive power over the morals of the laity, and with a clergy largely able to think and write as they please, can be viewed a case which stands among the most spectacular examples of clerical misconduct in English history, Dr Edward Drax Free. The significance of Dr Free is considerable in the history of ecclesiastical discipline, if obscured by the scandalous details of his story. The nature of his misconduct meant that he was tried by courts and procedures which were accustomed to the half-hearted prosecution of lay sin, and his vexatious obstinacy all but obstructed their working. As the case progressed, the courts had recourse to precedents and principles which mark the beginning of a distinctive concept of enforceable professional standards, as opposed to all-round moral quality, among the clergy. His case was widely reported and discussed, including in Parliament, and had an impact on the subsequent Church Discipline Act 1840. Finally (and very like that of Mr Bland a century and a half later) the reputation of the case was burnished with each retelling, giving to all the bishops and leading commentators of the following generation a persistent sense that dealing with errant clergy was difficult, slow and above all very expensive under the laws in place. The costs to the bishops were estimated at over £1,500. No-one could forget the case of Dr Free, and it is told most fully in the biography by Brian Outhwaite.[20]

Dr Free is memorable because of the tabloid nature of his story, and it is necessary to recount this concisely before considering the legal and disciplinary implications. Edward Drax Free was born into a clergy family in 1764, and took a conventional route of Oxford and holy orders, spending over 20 years as a Fellow of St John's and obtaining the degrees of MA, BD and DD in due order. Given that many made a connection between a better educated clergy and higher standards, we may note that Oxford's highest degree was no preventative against his decline. However, towards the end of his time at St John's there are records of substantial fallings-out and Free's refusal to attend disciplinary meetings, until his acceptance of the vacant college living of Sutton in Bedfordshire in 1808. The generous disbursements from the College for improvements to Sutton Rectory suggest enthusiastic endorsement of his move.

The account of Free's incumbency suggests a man of enormous self-importance and self-indulgence: it is worth describing his supposed enormities by category and note how they may possibly have seemed to him in the context of his times, as well as how they were each difficult to deal with legally. Although indisputably a bad man, Free had the fate to live at a time when standards of both gentlemanly and clerical conduct were rising, and so for pious early Victorians he could be remembered as a sort of hangover from the lax old days of Georgian England. The three categories to consider are property, behaviour and sex.

Dr Free regarded the emoluments of his parsonage as possessions to be enjoyed, even exploited, rather than a patrimony to be conserved. One of his first acts on arriving in Sutton was to fell a fine stand of trees for quick cash. His management of agricultural business on the glebe with his parishioners was characterised by profiteering and wrangling. He exacted his tithes determinedly, even on the allotment potatoes and vegetable gardens of the poor. Most significant in his trials was his readiness to treat the church and churchyard themselves as part of his earning and farming capacity without restraint. He replaced the lead roof of the church with tiles in order to sell the lead. He kept pigeons in the tower, repeatedly allowed his pigs to root in the churchyard, and folded his sheep in the porch. Many cases (considered further below) concern his zeal in extracting fees for baptisms, weddings and funerals.

The reporting of all these issues as a matter of scandal in the courts demonstrates that they were clearly regarded as of concern to parishioners. However, one should note that Free's behaviour only constituted a very selfish interpretation of the traditional and in some cases ill-defined rights of the clergy. All clergy needed to be supported financially. Both tithe and glebe income often involved a good deal of deal-making, and there are centuries of clerical comment about how difficult this was to do with the very parishioners to whom one was expected to be a source of Christian charity at all times. The church building and churchyard were his legal possession, and the taking of hay off and careful grazing of churchyards were accepted benefits which also kept the ground maintained. As late as the 1840s, antiquary John Martin lamented the use of Bedfordshire churchyards for the grazing of clerical cattle to the exclusion of parishioners.[21] In respect of fees, these were considered at the time (and for long after) as customary rights, in defiance of the ancient tradition against simony, embodied in Canon 40 of 1604, but there was no authoritative guide to what fees could or should be charged. The property rights of the early nineteenth century parson required good understanding and tact to make them work, and Edward Free did not have these. But that did not mean he necessarily committed any offence under ecclesiastical law.

Free's general behaviour is simpler to describe but harder to put to trial. All accounts make it clear he was a rude, aggressive, argumentative person, these traits worsened by frequent heavy drinking. He was capable of conducting a decent service, but was sometimes hasty, and more often entirely absent due to disinclination or hangover. The witness accounts of his demands for fees, notably those for funerals of children, display contempt for the pastoral needs of his parishioners. And every verbal attempt to challenge his behaviour, like those that came later by law, was met with immediate defensive anger. But again, it is impossible to make a man polite by law.

Fortunately for his longsuffering parishioners, Dr Free had a further weakness which provided strong evidence for the purposes of trial, and prolonged titillation to contemporary readers of *The Times*. His domestic requirements through his incumbency were consistently simple. He employed one female housekeeper, who was provided with a bedroom adjacent to his own with a connecting door and expected to act as his mistress for the duration of her employment. Six successive housekeepers testified to this pattern, and at least five pregnancies resulted between them. Reports were also made that his manner towards his young housekeepers was essentially sexual harassment, 'assisted' by books of indecent prints, until they succumbed or left his employment. Clearly this looks like a textbook example of 'unbecoming conduct' in almost every period, but again it proved difficult to define and convict.

It seems likely that, amongst the thousands of clergy in England at the time, there were others as difficult. Free comes to occupy a place in legal history because he brought upon himself, by invoking one of the obsolete matters of church discipline which have been discussed, the prolonged and eventually successful vengeance of the principal landowning family in his parish, the Burgoynes. In 1817, Free prosecuted Sir Montagu Roger Burgoyne for non-attendance at church. (This Sir Montagu, 8th Baronet, who died later in 1817, was the nephew of the Montagu Burgoyne who was Free's chief adversary in his subsequent trials).

Sir Montagu was therefore tried for non-attendance at Bedford Assizes, under the 1581 statute, with Dr Free aiming to extract £380 in fines from him for nineteen months' absence. Free's then housekeeper was duly presented as a witness. The 1581 statute had never been repealed, but it had been rendered increasingly ineffective since the passing of the Toleration Act, and was by this time a dead letter. It is possible that this is the last prosecution attempted in England for non-attendance. At any rate, the case failed, chiefly because the disgruntled churchwardens were quite ready to confirm that the church had been shut up for months at a time during the period concerned due to Dr Free's disinclination to take any services. His erratic timing of services and readiness to put Sir Montagu off coming to church by preaching personal abuse were also aired. A year later, Free had not learnt any lessons in tact, and charged Sir Montagu's uncle, Montagu Burgoyne, £100 for the burial of his daughter in a vault in the church.

It was therefore to be this Montagu Burgoyne who would take the lead, gathering evidence against Free and in 1824 taking rooms in the parish in order to be himself elected churchwarden to make it easier to pursue the case. However, "Doubt and indecision characterised the prosecution of Dr Free from the outset."[22] The presentments were first laid before the Archdeacon's court in late 1823, and both the Archdeacon and Chancellor seem to have agreed rapidly that they did not have the expertise to cope with the case, and recommended transfer to the Court of Arches. Here Free found his first legal help – Lushington and Fox sent back the opinion from Doctor's Commons that the main charge, of incontinency with the successive housekeepers, be it ever so serious, could not be sustained because all the offences occurred before the eight-month limit introduced by Mr Bastard's act of 1787. The other matters of rudeness and venality should be dealt with by admonition from the Bishop.

Outhwaite records a lack in the evidence as to how this was received in Sutton, but Burgoyne must have secured the support of the diocesan authorities for the question to return, because in October 1824 the case proper opened at the Court of Arches. What is significant is that there had come a recognition that even though the general laws of ecclesiastical discipline (as for both non-attendance and incontinency) had decayed to an ineffective level, this man was so bad something had to be done. A further short legal delay resulted from the complaint that the case had never come before the Chancellor of Lincoln, who was jealous of his jurisdiction, but was overruled.

The Court of Arches, having struck out some of the articles presented which seemed to lean to generalisation or dependence on hearsay, faced the problem of how to deal with the out-of-time incontinence. Argument was given for or against the view that the 1787 Act was only intended to prevent 'frivolous' suits, and Dr Free's case was clearly anything but frivolous. Sir John Nicholl, presiding, expressed the view that the Statute of Limitations had been intended to save the laity from vexatious presentment, not protect immoral clergy. As far as the canonical tradition was concerned, this was a prosecution *pro salute animae*, and Dr Free as a clergyman could be held to a higher standard than that expected of the laity. However, he welcomed an appeal to another court to test his argument.

In May 1826, the King's Bench duly delivered their verdict, noting their need to consider

> that by the ecclesiastical laws, canons and constitutions of the Church of England, all clerks and ministers in holy orders are particularly enjoined and required to be grave, decent, reverend and orderly in their general deportment, abstain from fornication or incontinence, profaneness etc.[23]

They found, subtly differently from Nicholl, that the 1787 Act only limited prosecutions "where the object of the suit is reformation of manners or the soul's health" and that this case was in fact seeking not Dr Free's penitence but his deprivation from his living. (Such a case could not by definition be brought against the laity, for they would have nothing to be deprived from.) This depended in turn on the 1665 precedent of *Slater v Smalebrooke* (for some reason spelled *Slader v Smallbrooke* in the law report).[24] Free appealed to the House of Lords, who upheld King's Bench.

In his argument against Free, Dr Lushington (later Dean of the Arches) cited the significant 1736 case of *Middleton v Crofts*, which had established that the 1604 Canons could bind the clergy but not the laity.[25]

Even before the Lords had replied Nicholl resumed the case. This gave Free the opportunity for an opportunistic appeal from the Arches to the High Court of Delegates, on the grounds that Nicholl was prejudiced against him. He also introduced the argument that if there was no case *pro salute animae*, there could be no case at all, for that was the only basis of the Arches' criminal jurisdiction. The Court of Delegates "did not meet this argument head-on. It simply said that a church court could hear a case with the limitations the lay courts had put on it, even though there was no canonical basis for such limitations."[26] Rodes observes this as a 'businesslike' relationship between the jurisdictions, with the distinctive (and in earlier periods, defiant) character of the church courts as having been eroded. The ecclesiastical lawyers by now had far more in common with their common law counterparts than they did with the ecclesiastical hierarchy they supposedly served. For our purposes, what is significant is the continuing erosion of the idea that the church courts existed to punish or amend sin, rather than deal with disputes arising in the specialised forum of the Church of England.

The Free case resumed in the Arches at last in 1828, with exasperation showing all round. Montagu Burgoyne had in the meantime petitioned Parliament, Free was writing to St John's and elsewhere for money, and Addams, Free's proctor, was understandably trying to be released from the case. The many witnesses assembled by Burgoyne were duly examined and written depositions taken, against which Free offered a barrage of attempted character assassination but no witnesses to defend his own good name. Nicholl in judgment took full opportunity to make it clear that the enormous delay and expense of the case was entirely Free's fault before describing enough of the "disgusting and profligate history"[27] necessary to justify the sentence of deprivation. Free naturally appealed again, to the High Court of Delegates, who affirmed the deprivation in February 1830. In the end Burgoyne and the archdeacon had to starve him out of his rectory.

Consequences of the Free case – the 1840 Act

Dr Free's case may on review look to be somewhat distant from the main object of this study. He certainly falls firmly into the category of 'I didn't do it' rather than 'it isn't wrong,' and he was, of course, eventually convicted. But in the process the courts can be seen coming to realise that the need to deal with clergy simply unfit to hold office, as Free clearly was, required new methods rather than the old prosecutions *pro salute animae*, and which would also not be liable to endless delay by prohibition from the secular courts. Such thoughts lurked in the back of the mind of those who worked on the Royal Commission into the practice of the church courts from 1830, notably Stephen Lushington, who had prosecuted Free, and amongst the parliamentarians who debated various bills until one finally became the Church Discipline Act 1840. "This dog's dinner of a statute was, perhaps fittingly, Dr Free's legacy to posterity."[28]

The 1840 Act provided new procedures for bishops to bring their errant clergy to trial. They were given the choice upon hearing of an alleged offence of either convening a five-man commission to hear evidence and recommend whether there was a case or not, or send the case by the traditional letters of request to the provincial court. If the suspect were their own appointee, the archbishop was empowered to act in the bishop's place (as occurred in the Denison case). A two-year limit was placed on serving articles after the alleged offence, or within six months of a secular conviction regardless of the date of offence.[29] What the 1840 Act did not clarify was the categories of offence of which a clergyman could be found guilty. There was a particular problem about whether or not simply behaving in a way as to cause scandalous report (without being proven to be guilty of e.g. drunkenness) was itself grounds for deprivation.

What the CDA 1840 represents, in conjunction with the final abolition of the criminal jurisdiction of the church courts over the laity in the 1850s, is the working-out of the distinction between the Church's disciplinary role over its clergy and the abandonment of one over its laity, which the courts wrestled with in Free's case. In the 1840s, it might have seemed that everything was set fair for a very sensible modernisation. A new Act provided (albeit by cumbersome procedures) for the raising of clerical standards by the investigation of the negligent or incompetent, whereas the laity were on the cusp of complete religious freedom. Lushington and his contemporaries reckoned, however, without the storms of controversy which were to rock the Victorian church, covered in the next three chapters. The discipline of the clergy was once again to involve, as it had in previous eras of controversy, the attempt to discipline those who were quite capable of ministering, but not in the ways or with the teaching accepted by their contemporaries.

Changing expectations of the clergy

Even though Dr Free was in the end deprived, he was still held up from 1830 onward as an example of the sort of abuse tolerated too much in the Church of England. As noted, the Evangelical and Tractarian movements are both manifestations of a wider spirit of revival, striving, among other things, to better clergy standards in every way. One aspect of this was a readiness to look back with disdain, sometimes selecting stories of uncertain provenance to assert the bad character of the previous generation. A memorable example is R. D Blackmore's character 'Parson Chowne,' said to be closely based on John Froude, incumbent of Knowstone on the edge of Exmoor for much of the early nineteenth century. Froude, besides being a keen hunter like so many Devon parsons of his day, is supposed to have maintained a collection of village ruffians who would extort and threaten on his behalf, and innumerable stories exist of his hard-living and extremely unclerical life. In particular, he is said to have evaded the attempt of Bishop Henry Philpotts to bring him to heel by feigning illness. The veracity of the stories is firmly asserted in the 1870s diaries of another Devonshire parson,[30] and can be seen as part of an overall picture whereby "the Church of England's ministry was believed to have become seriously compromised, because it still possessed no adequate means for disciplining its clergy."[31]

The aspirations of the 1830s and 40s for higher and more precise standards in the Diocese of Lincoln (Free's diocese) continued to be combined with an acknowledgement that the legal means seldom existed to secure compliance. In 1833, charges were brought against John Bewicke, the Rector of Hallaton, who was alleged to have failed to wear a gown or kneel for prayer, and more seriously, to have paid visits to a certain lady by a ladder to her bedroom window. It might have been thought that the precedent of Dr Free offered encouragement for a proceeding for incontinence and incompetence, but the Bishop, John Kaye, remembered more that Dr Free had cost the diocese £1,500, and by persuasive letters induced Bewicke to cease regular duty and appoint a curate instead.[32] In his charge to the Lincoln clergy in 1839, Archdeacon Goddard noted how the bishop had little beyond admonishment and censure available to keep order.

Such discipline as was achieved in Lincoln continues to be of the limited kind we see again and again down the centuries. Patronage offered a means to keep out trouble – in 1837 John Missing was refused a curate's licence in Buckinghamshire on the grounds that he was reported to depart from the Prayer Book text, in a manner sympathetic to Dissent. He protested crossly to the bishop that a fox-hunter and gambler willing to read the service correctly would not have had such trouble (no doubt thinking of other clergy he knew). A successful prosecution under the CDA 1840 was achieved against John Willis, the rector of Haddenham, who was found guilty of "having frequented a brothel in Aylesbury and of having been intoxicated in the pulpit and later in a hayrick … etc"[33] However, he pleaded guilty, and was in the event only suspended for a year.

In the end, Knight concludes that perhaps the most significant effect of the 1840 Act was to give a distinct jurisdiction to rural deans, then lately revived in most places. If so, this does not say much for the greater ease of prosecuting the errant clergy. What is true is that the period 1830–1870 saw a continuous rise in expectations of clergy behaviour, and with improved communication, awareness of realities that might often have been ignored before. This culture change meant that whereas the Georgian parson was simply expected to behave with the good manners of any gentleman, there were certain things his Victorian successor could expect to be sniffed at for doing. Put simply, hunting, drinking, dancing and gambling remained entirely normal, even normative, social activities for the nineteenth century gentleman, whereas the clergy became expected to hold themselves apart from something like this arbitrary list of enjoyments, unless they were content to be thought disreputable rakes. The irony is that those within the Church who inveighed most against such good-living clergy were those who were at the heart of the liturgical disobedience of Chapter 4.

The last years of the disciplinary jurisdiction

Even as the stage was being set for the titanic battles to come, the jurisdiction of the church courts was holding on as an increasingly quaint relic, in the end to be swept away just in time to be largely forgotten by those who came later to yearn for the restoration of a disciplined Church. Following Mr Bastard's Act of 1787, proceedings for fornication and incontinence dropped away, leaving the main area of penitential work (besides the courts' busy and profitable probate work) to judgments over defamation. For as long as the jurisdiction lasted (until 1855) recourse to the church courts was still a realistic route for anyone concerned to defend their reputation against verbal slurs.

Waddams's study of defamation[34] in the last 40 years from 1815 found that the vast majority of cases involved accusations of defamation by women against women, and a large proportion from the poorer classes. Many seem to fall into the category of 'fishwife A alleges that fishwife B did call her a whore, which she denies' – they were cases where the courts were attempting as best they could to adjudicate matters of gossip and reputation, and in some cases what we would now call harassment. Waddams argues that there is little evidence, as others have suggested, that the women concerned were seeking to avoid prosecution for fornication (by getting a denial of the rumour in first), but that it was simply the accepted way of responding to offence of this sort.

What the defamation cases really were not was any attempt to impose Christian law upon those found guilty. This was partly because of the complete detachment of the courts and their officials from the parish clergy, especially as the latter looked increasingly to party literature or deanery organisation for their loyalty and inspiration rather than the old court-based administration. They "did not usually perceive ecclesiastical law as an instrument of their own policies,"[35] and likewise "those making use of the ecclesiastical courts did not usually perceive their function as closely relating to the interests or activities of the church."[36] It must also have been an ineffective response to unkind gossip in the many cases where the exact defamatory words were included in the penance to be read out in public. It was simply a peculiar old corner of English law, ripe for reform. Two of the very last known cases of public penance following a conviction for defamation show, however, a subtly different spirit, in which on the verge of its abolition in an era of growing religious pluralism the jurisdiction of the courts was again perceived as an oppressive manifestation of the Church of England over the land.

Fen Ditton, Cambridgeshire, was the venue for one of the last attempts to use the ecclesiastical jurisdiction to defend the privilege of the Church of England. Edward Smith, the village fiddler, was ordered to do penance for calling Martha James, the rector's wife, a "blasted whore,"[37] and it appears that it was at the strong insistence of Mr James that he was ordered to the church in the white sheet to confess his sin. A crowd estimated at 3,000 assembled in the village to witness the penance on 6 May 1849, with about 1,000 getting inside the church. The penance was done, but "amid cat-calls and riot and hassock-throwing and pew-breaking, and [Smith] was carried shoulder-high for drinks at the Plough after service."[38] Both church and rectory were damaged, and at least some of those present regarded this as due revenge for the clerical high-handedness of the Jameses.

Possibly the last case of all occurred at Wakefield in 1850, reported in the Bury and Norwich Herald of 11 September, a week or so later. A Mr Horner was convicted of having defamed a Miss Fernandez, who had recently broken off a prospective marriage in the town, by stating that she had "gone away *enceinte*" (I do not know whether this use of French is Mr Horner's or the newspaper's euphemism). Richmond Ecclesiastical Court (the archdeaconry court) duly ordered penance in the parish vestry, a punishment of which the paper comments, "Mr Horner is an Independent in religion and a strenuous oppose of church rates. Hence to him this submission in the Episcopal church [sic] as peculiarly galling."[39] Like Smith at Fen Ditton, he was supported in his penance by a sympathetic crowd of thousands, although in this case they stood quietly outside in the rain rather than wrecking the church.

The defamation jurisdiction was abolished in 1855, bringing to an effective end the practice of public penance in England. The numerically and financially important probate and marriage jurisdictions followed in 1857, and finally in 1860 brawling and defamation in Ireland were the last to go,[40] although it was not possible to find any cases after 1850. These reforms, and the replacement of the church courts by secular courts to judge equivalent matters, had been discussed for over a decade before their final enactment. The delay was principally due to the need to find Parliamentary time, and the concern about the loss of earnings of the small but committed body of ecclesiastical lawyers. The Tractarian movement brought about a new desire for ecclesiastical discipline, but not even there was the pure conservatism of keeping the existing courts in their decayed state to be found. "Neither the reformers nor the conservatives of the nineteenth century thought that the administration of the ecclesiastical courts would be improved by the addition of religious zeal."[41]

Early aspirations to discipline among the Tractarians

The appearance of the *Tracts for the Times* from 1833 onward indisputably represents a new start in ecclesiology in England, reviving the distinct theme of the apostolic succession and all its consequences, and generating controversy from the start. The originality of the Tractarians' thinking should not obscure the extent to which they were reacting with concern to the state of the Church and society in their own time, and in particular to the exertions of the Whig government to bring the ancient institutions and endowments of the Church into some sort of defensible shape. An aspect of this is the concern that the Church was being remodelled without any opportunity to agree, and in time this would lead to the demands for a revived Convocation able to debate and shape the laws under which the Church lived.

A matter for debate is the extent to which the specific theme of discipline, or rather, lack thereof, was of concern to the Tractarian movement, given that this was undoubtedly part of the ancient structures of the Church being subjected to rationalising Whig legislation. Russell Dewhurst notes that the journals seen as the voice of the new High Church movement, the *British Magazine* and *The British Critic*, give scant attention to the courts question.

> We do *not* wish to revive prosecutions for immorality and public penance. But we do wish to impress both upon individuals and upon government the propriety and even the necessity of paying increased attention to the morals of the people.[42]

Dewhurst describes this as a traditional high church view, and indeed it echoes back in this form throughout the eighteenth century. Perhaps even more strikingly, not one of the 90 *Tracts* themselves discusses the courts or the need for church discipline.

Yet Dewhurst also feels able to claim:

> The Tractarian priority, on the other hand, was the restoration of an effective church discipline. They wanted a doctrinally pure church, which could censure and expel the immoral and the heretic. For Tractarians, the aim of ecclesiastical court reform had to be a revival of church discipline.[43]

In fact, it is difficult to identify a broad range of interest in the question of church discipline in the way that there is for example for Eucharistic doctrine or apostolic succession. Rather the idea of church discipline appears like a will-o-the-wisp, yearned for but seldom seriously sought. Yet because when church law comes to be formed, those who are already interested in the idea stand forth with disproportionate expertise, this tradition has had a strong influence on the ongoing development of the law of the Church of England, even when as so often that law has been out of step with ecclesiastical reality.

A single major writer stands out for his passionate advocacy of ecclesiastical discipline, Archdeacon Robert Wilberforce, son of the abolitionist and whose brother Samuel became Bishop of Oxford in 1845. His 1843 work *Church Courts and Church Discipline* is a furious denunciation of the decayed state of the courts and represents the solid aspiration to discipline which Dewhurst optimistically attributes to all the Tractarians. Wilberforce is clear in his principles, "The neglect of Church Discipline is the Church's sin"[44] and bookmarks the Homily for Whitsunday for its recognition of "the right use of ecclesiastical discipline"[45] as a mark of a true church (although the Homily does not in fact elaborate this, discoursing rather on the evils of 'Popedom'). Above all, for Wilberforce, church discipline, like the apostolic succession and other aspects of the Church acclaimed by the Tractarians, was of Divine Origin, even if brought down by time and secular abuse.

Particularly interesting is Wilberforce's survey of the decline of the courts, indicating his wholesale regret at every stage. He yearns for the restoration of the Court of High Commission and the oath of compurgation. Noting that Gibson referred to the latter as a discipline too wholesome to be digested, he defends it awkwardly from the charge of abuse of process, claiming this applied only because of the civil penalties wrongly attached to it. Wilberforce also regrets, with considerable passion, the passing of the Statute of Limitations 1787, which as far as he is concerned simply allowed the flourishing of sexual vice. His text overflows with the sentiment (which can be found in every period of Christian history regardless of the actual state of society at the time) that sin is abounding on all sides.

In response to the reforms, Wilberforce acknowledges the inadequacy of the church courts, reduced largely to a minor jurisdiction over marriages and wills. He would have them restored to power, and above all exercising their ancient power of excommunication which "is their inalienable duty to inflict as a punishment for sin."[46] In his vision the church courts would also be purged of their lay personnel and instead staffed by clergy, whose holy calling would befit their work of holy discipline. Looking to that pure Church of Tractarian aspiration, he is able to scoff at the Whig reformers as they reform the Church: "Its enemies may fancy that they are stripping it of the gilded trappings essential to its dignity, but they will find that they are only removing those shackles, which concealed the fair dimensions of the ordinance of GOD."[47]

Yes, he does use GOD throughout, and it says a great deal about his theology. Wilberforce did just about notice some complications – what would it be like for a parson if many of his parishioners died excommunicate, and had to be denied church funerals and churchyard burials, for example? But, on the whole, his zeal for disciplinary excommunication dominates, as when he notes with approval the Scottish system of only permitting communion to those in possession of a 'token' for good behaviour. So it was very much in character that after the death of his second wife in 1854 he converted to Rome.[48] There he presumably found for a few years before his death in 1857 the pure and disciplined church for which he had yearned.

Other Tractarian witnesses to a desire for discipline besides Robert Wilberforce are limited. Henry Manning, when still also an Anglican Archdeacon before he too converted to Rome, is noted by Dewhurst as agreeing with the overall view that "lay discipline had fallen into desuetude because of the overly cumbrous court processes"[49] but nonetheless using his archidiaconal charges to encourage churchwardens to present cases of immorality. The young Gladstone wrote to Lushington in 1843 expressing his view that he wanted "dissenters free to dissent, but churchmen bound by discipline,"[50] but he does not seem to have said much more on the subject.

Further incidental evidence may be found in the choice of works for the *Library of Anglo-Catholic Theology*, envisaged by its Tractarian editors as a grounding for their position by selections from High Church sources from Elizabeth I through to the early eighteenth century. As already noted, the very first volumes are the works of the disciplinarian Bishop Thomas Wilson of Sodor and Man, prefaced by his *Life* written up by Keble. A later inclusion was *The Penitential Discipline of the Primitive Church* of Nathaniel Marshall, originally published in 1714. Marshall unhesitatingly accepts the primitive conception of Christian discipline, and presents a Tory vision of renewed jurisdiction, albeit with caution about what the times will bear. Wilberforce picked up with approval Marshall's proposal to replace the archdeacons' 'bawdy' courts with deanery *chorepiscopi*, disciplinary local bishops exercising the power of excommunication.[51] Nonetheless, especially if we accept Wilson's inclusion as largely a tribute to his pastoral diligence, ecclesiastical discipline can hardly be called a central concern of the 20-author *Library*.

Conclusion to the decline

The structures of ecclesiastical discipline stood at a tipping point in 1850. On the one hand, in respect of the laity, the punitive jurisdiction of the church courts was on the verge of abolition, and its continuing exercise had become an embarrassment. Yet, at the same time, a slender thread of argument, not very widely aired but equally not disavowed among the new Tractarian movement, posited that part of the proper function of the Church belonging to her of ancient times was the right to correct the morals of her members, high or lowly. And this was to be done by reviving the practice of excommunication, and its use by the Church as punishment for sin or exclusion of the heretical.

As far as the clergy were concerned, the enormous freedom they had enjoyed in the eighteenth century was being constrained as much by social expectation as the increased effectiveness of the church courts to discipline them. The Church Discipline Act 1840 had introduced a clearer procedure, but the laws, canons and constitutions against which they might be tried remained contradictory and, in many places, obsolete. Fatefully, in 1833, as part of the wider modernisation of the courts, the Judicial Committee of the Privy Council had been set up as the final court of appeal, eliminating the need for the *ad hoc* summoning of the High Court of Delegates. "In 1833, no one had thought of its having doctrinal or liturgical questions to decide. Most ecclesiastical appeals had involved the probate and matrimonial jurisdiction (abolished in 1857) with a few drunk or incontinent clergymen for variety."[52] Little did the bishops realise it was to be their own faithful clergy they would be attempting to discipline in the following generation.

Notes

1 Robert E. Rodes Jr., *Law and Modernisation in the Church of England* (Notre Dame 1991) 26ff.
2 Smith, M. G. *Pastoral Discipline and the Church Courts: the Hexham Court 1680–1730* (Borthwick Papers No.62, 1982) 3.
3 Rodes, *Modernisation*, 28.
4 Smith, *Pastoral Discipline*, 27.
5 W. M. Jacob, *Lay People and Religion in the Early Eighteenth Century* (CUP 1996) 140.
6 R. Ussher, *Notes on White Sheet Confessions in Churches and Market Places* (privately published 1934), 8–9.
7 James Woodforde, *The Diary of a Country Parson 1758–1802. Passages selected and edited by John Beresford* (OUP 1949) 474.
8 S. M. Waddams, *Sexual Slander in Nineteenth-Century England. Defamation in the Ecclesiastical Courts 1815–1855* (University of Toronto Press 2000) 111–12.
9 William Gibson and Joanna Begiato, *Sex and the Church in the Long Eighteenth Century. Religion, Enlightenment and the Sexual Revolution* (I. B. Tauris 2017) 105–6.
10 R. B. Outhwaite, *The Rise and Fall of the English Ecclesiastical Courts* (CUP 2006) Ch. 12.
11 Ibid., 13.
12 Harry Potter, *Hanging in Judgment. Religion and the Death Penalty in England* (Continuum 1993) Ch. 1.
13 Rodes, *Modernisation*, 63.

14 W. M. Jacob, *The Clerical Profession in the Long Eighteenth Century 1680–1840* (OUP 2007).
15 Rodes, *Modernisation*, 11.
16 Ibid., 63.
17 Jacob, *Clerical Profession*, 282–90.
18 *King's Proctor v Stone* [1808] 1 Hag Con 424.
19 Robert Ingram, "'The Clergy who affect to call themselves Orthodox': Thomas Secker and the defence of Anglican orthodoxy, 1758–68" in Cooper and Gregory (eds) *Discipline and Diversity – Studies in Church History 43* (Boydell 2007) 348.
20 R. B. Outhwaite, *Scandal in the Church. Dr Edward Drax Free 1764–1843* (Hambledon 1997).
21 William Whyte, *Unlocking the Church* (OUP 2017) 107–8.
22 Outhwaite, *Scandal*, 75.
23 *Free DD v Burgoyne* [1826] 5 B & C 401.
24 *Free* (1826) 405.
25 *Middleton v Crofts* [1736] Ridg t.H 109.
26 Rodes, *Modernisation*, 12.
27 *Burgoyne v Free* [1829] 2 Hagg. Ecc 491–2.
28 Outhwaite, *Scandal*, 138.
29 Rodes, *Modernisation*, 212–17.
30 W. H. Thornton, *Reminiscences of an Old West Country Clergyman*, Duff Hart-Davis (ed.) (Excellent Press 2010) 164–8.
31 Frances Knight "Ministering to the Ministers: The Discipline of Recalcitrant Clergy in the Diocese of Lincoln 1830–1845" in *Studies in Church History 26. The Ministry: Clerical and Lay* (Blackwell 1989) 351.
32 Ibid., 362.
33 Ibid., 364.
34 Waddams, *Slander* Ch. 8–10.
35 Ibid., 168.
36 Ibid., 65.
37 Ibid., 113.
38 Owen Chadwick, *The Victorian Church. Part 1 1829–1859* 3rd ed. (SCM Press 1971), 489.
39 Bury and Norwich Herald, 11 September 1850.
40 Outhwaite, *Decline and Fall*, Ch. 15.
41 Waddams, *Slander*, 56.
42 The British Critic 1832, Vol 12 p465, cited in Russell Dewhurst *The High Church Reactions to the Reforms of the English Ecclesiastical Courts 1830–1861* (unpublished Cardiff LLM thesis 2010) 23.
43 Dewhurst, *Reactions*, 23.
44 R. I. Wilberforce, *Church Court and Church Discipline* (John Murray, London 1843) 4.
45 *Certain Sermons or Homilies Appointed to be Read in Churches in the Time of Queen Elizabeth of Famous Memory* (SPCK 1938) 495.
46 Wilberforce, *Discipline*, 51.
47 Ibid., 57.
48 Chadwick, *Victorian Church, Part 1*, 495.
49 Dewhurst, *Reactions*, 24.
50 Ibid., 24.
51 Marshall, Nathaniel, *The Penitential Discipline of the Primitive Church* (New Edition Oxford 1844) Ch. IV.
52 Rodes, *Modernisation*, 258.

3. A century of doctrine trials 1775–1871

Georgian antecedents to the Victorian controversies

Just as the story of the old church courts can be continued until the bitter end in Fen Ditton and Wakefield, so the question of the Church's disciplinary jurisdiction over those defined as heretics needs to be extended back from the very public cases of the 1850s and 60s to gain a better perspective. This will tend to confirm the underlying thesis that trial for heresy is at best an intermittent success for the Church in terms of disciplining the wayward. There is no simple reason why the trial of Voysey in 1871 is the last successful trial for heresy in the history of the Church of England. What becomes apparent, however, is that both the unpredictability of outcome and the challenge of defining wrong doctrine in court have played their part in the abandonment of judicial proceedings as a response to overambitious intellectual enquiry.

We have noted the case of Whiston in the days of Queen Anne, and it might be thought that the clergy of England were at liberty to indulge in theological speculation for the duration of the long eighteenth century thereafter. As seen above, even the diligent Archbishop Secker used only the pressure of patronage on the alleged mortalist Peckard in the 1760s. There are however two cases, Evanson in 1775 and Stone in 1808, the former especially little known, where clergy were tried for heresy by the church courts between Whiston and the era of Victorian controversy. Since Evanson was not convicted but Stone was, they set the pattern early of intermittent success in prosecution, and so support the view that the difficulty of prosecuting heresy was not a wholly new phenomenon in the mid-nineteenth century.

Edward Evanson had become Vicar of Tewkesbury in 1769 and caused controversy by his willingness to preach and minister in accordance with his heterodox views. His studies had led him to doubt about the doctrine of the Trinity, the traditional conception of the general resurrection and the authority of large parts of the Scriptures. These were comparatively new opinions for his time, although not necessarily original and certainly entertained in academic circles in every period since. Evanson stood out, however, both in his readiness to preach and publish his views, and to alter those parts of the Prayer Book services which he felt unable in conscience to read as printed. He is reported, for example, to have stopped in mid-recitation of the Nicene Creed, at 'invisible,' and by prior arrangement, left the clerk (the lay officer who in the eighteenth century Church of England typically led congregational responses and sometimes singing, in addition to parochial administration) to lead the congregation in the remainder of the text.[1]

The response of the concerned parishioners was led by Mr Neast Havard, the Town Clerk, based upon articles drawing attention to Evanson's omissions from the liturgy, thereby identifying his heterodoxy in terms of his emendations of the Prayer Book. They do not seem to have been able to identify teaching in print or sermons against, for example, the 39 Articles, as grounds for the proceedings. However, they reckoned without the determination of Evanson's legal team, who were able to identify three grounds on which the proceedings were at fault, and on the basis of these, to secure the dismissal of the case by the Consistory Court in Gloucester, and on appeal to the Court of Arches and the High Court of Delegates in succession.

None of the three grounds are directly relevant to the question of heresy but are of legal interest. First, an inconsistency was pointed out between the citation of Evanson as Vicar of Tewkesbury *and* Curate of Tredington, whereas in the articles he is only referred to as Vicar of Tewkesbury. This reflected the fact that the alleged offences had all only occurred at Tewkesbury but could be counted as an unjust difference of description invalidating the suit. Second, it was noted that Havard and his supporters had engaged a Mr Stock as their proctor, but Stock was an apparitor of Gloucester Consistory Court and therefore forbidden to act as a proctor under Canon 138 of the canons of 1603.[2] More seriously, the employment of an officer of the court to act could be seen as an obvious case of conflict of interest, as well as reflecting on the miniscule size of the local ecclesiastical law profession available to a gentleman from Tewkesbury. Finally, it was objected that the case was prejudiced by the publication of all the articles in advance, preventing the fair examination of any witnesses. The second and third of these objections were decisive in securing the dismissal of the suit.

Also interesting in the defence is the deployment of the argument that this was a criminal case, and so demanded the highest standards of proof and correctness of procedure before visiting punishment on Evanson, as would be expected in a secular criminal trial. The Solicitor General, speaking before the Delegates at the second appeal, stressed (italics original):

> the object of this suit is as *severe* and *punishable* as any that can possibly be carried on against a clergyman – I say, as severe as any suit that attacks his moral conduct, the purity of his life and conversation, or in any degree affects the character and situation of the object of the suit, as a man. – As a beneficed clergyman, the object of the suit is to take *from him everything.* [3]

There is obvious rhetorical indulgence by Alexander Wedderburn here, but underlying it is an argument which clearly appealed in an age when a gentleman's property and status were his all.

There is a wider significance. The church courts had functioned under the customs of the civil law, assessing written evidence rather than witnesses, and concepts developed under the common law like evidence and proof were not automatically applicable. In terms of issues of controversy like heresy, it could be said that the work of the church courts had been much more to identify the common mind of the church, based on Scripture, canon and precedent, and judge whether or not the accused was at fault by those lights. But, in Evanson's case, long before the much-maligned introduction of appeals to the Privy Council, we see very much common law principles being argued before the ecclesiastical High Court of Delegates, to the effect that a man should not be penalised without a scrupulous case being brought with proof of his misdeeds. Richard Helmholz has also drawn attention recently to the assimilation of the practice of the church courts to the common law by the mid-eighteenth century.[4] Among the few who noted Evanson later was Edward Pusey, who bemoaned him as an example of the lack of doctrinal discipline in the Church in an 1881 open letter to Liddon.[5]

The 1808 case of Francis Stone, which was to be regularly cited in the cases later in the century, is more straightforward, and shows how if there was no strong defence the courts could still act effectively against an indisputable heretic. Stone was rector of Cold Norton in Essex, and a public and published Unitarian, and a suit was promoted by the royal proctor in London Consistory Court. Stone only offered "a loose verbal protestation"[6] which Sir William Scott dismissed robustly in his judgment:

> It is quite repugnant … that the construction of the articles should be left to the private persuasion of individuals … the preaching diversity of opinions shall not be fed out of the appointments of the Established Church.… For what would be the state and condition of public worship if every man was at liberty to preach from the pulpit of the church whatever doctrines he may think proper to hold?[7]

Scott went on to deny that the court was being "minute or rigid" but that the only possible response to a plain denial of the first and second of the 39 Articles, i. e. the doctrine of the Trinity and the divinity of Christ, was to sentence Stone to deprivation.[8] A belated and half-hearted attempt at revocation from Stone (in fact an apology for unintended offence and a promise of future good behaviour) was dismissed, as was a subsequent appeal. If the case was sufficiently plain in 1808 it was still possible to enforce at least the basics of Christian doctrine against those who would publicly reinterpret them.

A case of heresy in the laity

The vast majority of heresy trials were conducted against clergy; they were more likely to publish heterodox theology and also to be considered to be at fault for doing so, when they should have been preaching according to the Church's teaching. It would also have been difficult, certainly after the effective end of public penance in the 1850s, to identify how to punish a heretical layperson. One case from 1838, however, does illustrate that alleged lay heresy was treated in much the same way as clerical, and was cited in the much better-known 1863 case of Williams and Wilson, and others.

Mary Woolfrey, a Roman Catholic from the Isle of Wight, was prosecuted by her vicar, John Breeks, for erecting a headstone in the churchyard for her late husband which asked passers-by to pray for the dead, and also quoted 2 Maccabees 12 in support. The Court of Arches noted, as in other cases before and after, "This being a criminal proceeding the burthen of proving the charge lies on the promoter"[9] and went on to consider the theology. Sir Herbert Jenner defined the issue as to whether prayer for the dead necessarily implied the 'Romish doctrine of purgatory' and found numerous evidences that it did not, notwithstanding the Roman Catholic faith of the respondent (which had not been pleaded in evidence). Significantly for later cases, he also minimised the authority of the Elizabethan *Homilies*,[10] and dismissed the case. Although not strictly relevant to the decline of discipline within the Church of England, this case contributes to the record of courts being unwilling to enforce particular teaching inasmuch as it affected what went on in churches, upon the laity as much as the clergy.

General aspects of the period of Victorian controversy

The heyday of heresy trials in the Church of England was surprisingly brief, opening with the 1843 case of *Sanders v Head* and concluding with those of *Noble v Voysey* in 1871 and *Sheppard v Bennett* in 1871–72. The outbreak of controversy in the courts was natural outcome of controversy in the Church at large, fanned by the vast output of theological writing, serious or ephemeral, since the beginning of the Tractarian movement. In its attempt to redefine the nature and calling of the Church of England, all manner of debates, mostly of Reformation origin like the nature of the sacraments, were given new life as controversies internal to the Church of England. The sixteenth-century formulae of the 39 Articles and Book of Common Prayer were turned over in attempts to settle the questions again. Then at a later stage the effects of the first theological modernisers, asking critical questions of both Scripture and tradition, opened a new front in the conflicts.

Three significant elements of interest in the cases of the period make them relevant to a study of the church's discipline: the how, the who, and the aftermath. The attempt to adjudge matters of doctrinal controversy tended strongly to push the courts in the direction of liberty for a range of opinions. This tendency is most pronounced in the final court of appeal, the Judicial Committee of the Privy Council. Whilst these judgments were a matter of fierce controversy at the time for proceeding from an apparently secular court, the most important such as that of Gorham took place with the endorsement of the Archbishops sitting as judges, and can be viewed as much as the judgments of the Established Church as those of the Court of Arches.

The who is significant because each case required, as had the office cases for lay discipline of old, a promoter to bring the case. In the 1863 case of Williams, the promoter was his diocesan bishop, Walter Hamilton, and in the Gorham case (although there Gorham was the promoter) it was contested with his bishop, Henry Phillpotts. Both bishops were considered High Church, and so, perhaps, more likely to believe it to be their personal duty to discipline their clergy. In the majority of cases, however, it was not a representative of diocesan or episcopal authority, seeking to use the court to discipline an erring clerk, but a controversialist from the opposing side in theological debate, seeking the endorsement of the law for the condemnation they wished for their opponent. Only the painful history of the following decades, as seen below, succeeded in dimming the litigious enthusiasm of Victorian church controversialists. Bishops seem to have acquiesced in this tendency, contributing to the feeling that what was happening was not a keeping of disciplined order but the Church airing its controversies. This in turn increased disapproval of the whole process, and specifically the reluctance of the bishops (as can be seen directly in some cases) to become involved or let the cases come to court.

Sometimes bishops were felt to have allowed complainants to act in the hope of securing a conviction for the purported heretic, but this is still not quite the same as themselves exercising discipline over their charges. Both bishops and courts were undoubtedly at times frustrated by the zeal of some, such as Archdeacon Denison, to bring cases to court in the hope of securing the satisfaction of a legal victory over their opponents. Fierce religious movements in Christianity tend to look for moments of truth, however artificially conceived, and the Evangelicals and Tractarians were no different, with some of the most revered characters equally responsible. "In 1842 the supposedly saintly John Keble unsuccessfully tried to persuade C. R. Sumner to prosecute him after the bishop had refused to ordain his curate."[11]

Finally, there is the aftermath, in some ways difficult to explain, that *Noble v Voysey* in 1870–71 remains the last case brought before a court in England in which a clergyman was tried and deprived simply for the expression of theological views outside the accepted limits. It would not have seemed so at the time, not least because of the flood of ritual cases both before and after the passing of the Public Worship Regulation Act in 1874, to be considered in the next chapter. Yet given the theological speculation and the expression of controversial opinion certainly did not stop in 1870, this is a very important moment in the development of the Church of England's indiscipline.

Early cases in the Victorian period

The two most important cases, both in terms of the literature they have generated and the extent to which they attracted contemporary controversy, are those of Mr Gorham and Archdeacon Denison, and both are very well known. Helpfully, there are considerable parallels between the two cases, and so whilst it will be necessary to retell the stories of the cases to some extent, it will be attempted to note first what the doctrinal issues were, recount the cases, and then provide some commentary upon the cases from a disciplinary perspective.

Before grappling with Gorham and Denison, one notes briefly that these cases did not come to an ecclesiastical jurisdiction entirely without experience in dealing with doctrinal controversy. In 1843, the Court of Arches heard the case of Henry Erskine Head, rector of Fenistone in Devon, who was accused of the traditional offence of "derogation and depraving of the Book of Common Prayer"[12] in that in argument with his bishop he had attacked the Prayer Book's understanding of baptism and confirmation. The bishop was the combative Henry Phillpotts, who was greatly concerned to uphold a High Church view of baptism and confirmation and found Head at fault accordingly. This will not be the last case which someone holding views currently controversial only ends up in court in the diocese with a bishop strong both in opposing views and his own legal dignity.

Phillpotts features repeatedly in this study, and it is worth remembering that he was such a celebrated character of the Church in his own time to merit the brilliant parody of Trollope as the second son of Archdeacon Grantly in *The Warden*. To understand the parody, it is necessary to know that Phillpotts as a young Tory magistrate had campaigned very flexibly against and then for Catholic emancipation, and been rewarded by Wellington as Prime Minister with both a controversially rich living and then the see of Exeter, besides his well-known pugnacity:

> Henry was indeed a brilliant boy. The versatility of his genius was surprising, and the visitors at Plumstead Episcopi were often amazed at the marvellous manner in which he would, when called on, adapt his capacity to apparently the most uncongenial pursuits. He appeared once before a large circle as Luther the reformer, and delighted them with the perfect manner in which he assumed the character; and within three days he again astonished them by acting the part of a Capuchin friar to the very life. For this last exploit his father gave him a golden guinea, and his brothers said the reward had been promised beforehand.... He was also sent on a tour into Devonshire.
>
> It was soon known ... that young Henry could box well and would never own himself beat; other boys would fight while they had a leg to stand on, but he would fight with no leg at all. Those backing him would sometimes think him crushed with the weight of blows and faint with loss of blood, and his friends would endeavour to withdraw him from the context; but no, Henry never gave in, was never weary of the battle. The ring was the only element in which he seemed to enjoy himself; and while other boys were happy in the number of their friends, he rejoiced most in the multitude of his foes.[13]

In this case, the pugnacious Phillpotts was to be victorious, but not before Sir Herbert Jenner-Fust, in his judgment, had set out at some length the authority of the court, derived from the general ecclesiastical law, in order to sentence Head for his heterodox views. Head's proctors had attempted a defence based upon the technicalities of the Elizabethan Act of Uniformity, which they argued was both superseded by that of 1662 and referred only to preaching and speaking against the Prayer Book. However, Jenner-Fust had no difficulty in identifying, in lengthy quotations from Head's published works, the necessary heresy.

Notably, though, Head begins to open up the argument which would come to grow in support, that the constraint of the canons "seeks to deprive me of … freedom of thought, speech, inquiry and discussion" and "cherish withal the vital principles of that popery of which they would be thought opponents."[14] In this he echoes Foster's opposition to Gibson just over a century before, that the laws of the church represented the very unjust power from which the Reformation had occurred to deliver England,[15] and which many nineteenth century churchmen felt looming again in the form of a revived Roman Catholic Church in England. Head was suspended for three years as it was a first offence,[16] and lost his appeal to the Privy Council.

Only a couple of years later, Jenner-Fust displayed judicial balance between the warring factions of the Church of England by depriving Frederick Oakeley from his cure at the Margaret Chapel. Oakeley had written a pamphlet in support of William Ward, a fellow-follower of Newman whom he had supported in his trials within the university at Oxford. Oakeley adopted the peculiar position that he held "all Roman doctrines"[17] and would encourage anyone else to do so, but that he would not teach them, and would encourage fellow Roman-believers to remain part of the Church of England. Unhindered by any defence, for Oakeley did not attend, Jenner-Fust was able to examine the doctrines of the Council of Trent and other suitable sources, find that they contradicted the 6th Article of Religion, cite in full the Stone case of 1808, and condemned Oakeley accordingly on 30 June 1845.[18] By the end of the year he, with Newman and Ward, had converted to Rome.

So, by the time of Gorham and Denison the church courts had managed successfully to assert a degree of disciplinary jurisdiction over apparently erring clergy. The Privy Council had upheld the Court of Arches, and not produced controversy. The courts were playing their modest part in keeping order in an increasingly fractious church. It completes the set to notice a case not brought which testifies to the deep-seated reluctance of those in highest authority to use the courts to hold a line. In 1847, amid great controversy at his alleged heterodoxy, Dr Renn Hampden was nominated as Bishop of Hereford. Samuel Wilberforce as Bishop of Oxford allowed a suit for heresy under the Clergy Discipline Act 1840 to be commenced, but then stopped it following a quasi-withdrawal from Hampden and advice against from Archbishop Howley.[19]

Sacramental controversy in the 1850s

The major cases of Gorham and Denison both hinged on controversies over the sacraments, and although it was a different sacrament, baptism and Holy Communion respectively (and the individuals concerned represented opposite sides in the church), the divisions of opinion were closely related. Within the theology of baptism, the shibboleth was one's view of the concept of *regeneration*. This technical term refers to the belief that an essential part of being a true Christian, personally redeemed and destined for eternal salvation, is new birth, in some sense. The difference occurs as to what that new birth is. For the High Church, the focus was on the new birth effected by baptism administered by the Church, regardless of the age or (for an infant) awareness of the person concerned. For the Low Church, the focus was on the individual experience of spiritual rebirth, with baptism seen as only the public manifestation or the necessary precondition of this. To use the conventional terminology, the first was a belief in *baptismal regeneration*, the second a denial of that belief.

In relation to Holy Communion, for baptismal regeneration, read *real presence*. In other words, the High belief was in an objective presence of Christ in the Eucharistic elements, whereas the Low tendency was to deny this. These crude simplifications serve to identify the similarity of the arguments in the Gorham and Denison cases. At worst, the High saw the Low as rationalist, individualist and secularising, belittling the spiritual and miraculous inheritance of Christianity, aided by a modernising liberal Parliament. Likewise, the Low could present the High as quasi-papists, importing the meaningless superstitions of the Middle Ages or the resurgent English Roman Catholic Church to the good Protestant Church of England, and worse, seeking to impose them by means of church law.

There were of course a great many shades of opinion on both questions. Although, according to Chadwick, Stephen Lushington, for example, could not understand the subtleties of Gorham's teaching,[20] what comes across from the reports is the distinctive Calvinist teaching that the real source of spiritual regeneration must be a free act of God's grace (which is 'prevenient,' and in a sense timeless because it occurs in God's eternity) and not any human action such as baptism. More important is that, unlike the eccentrically expressed disdain for confirmation expressed by Head or the extreme Romanism of Oakeley, the issues of baptismal regeneration and the real presence divided the Church of England, and were felt to be matters of major concern to thousands. The resultant petitioning and pamphleteering contributed to the mood that the courts were not the right place to settle such questions. However, these in turn led to the practical result that they could not be settled at all, and remain open questions in the Church of England to this day.

Charles Gorham and baptismal regeneration

The Gorham Case, as it is usually known, arose from a dispute between a bishop and one of his clergy – and therefore from the outset can be seen as a question of discipline, although it is over an appointment, unlike most in this study. The bishop, predictably Henry Phillpotts of Exeter, objected to the views of Charles Gorham on the question of baptismal regeneration, and Gorham's presentation to the parish of Bramford Speke in 1847 offered Phillpotts an opportunity to act, although he had not done so when Gorham first came to his diocese less than two years before. Phillpotts examined Gorham in person at extraordinary length, determined him unsound, and refused to institute him to the living. He had, he felt, fulfilled his episcopal duty to maintain doctrinal discipline in the church.

Gorham therefore sought the remedy known to the ecclesiastical law as *duplex querela*, that Phillpotts had wronged him by refusing to carry out the institution for which he had been presented by the Lord Chancellor on behalf of the Crown. A lengthy case in the Court of Arches ensued in which all the relevant texts about baptism were duly debated as they were being in the pamphlet war outside the court. This exposed very fully the tension between the language of the Prayer Book, more sympathetic to the High, regenerationist, viewpoint, and that of the Articles supporting more the Low. Jenner-Fust delivered the judgment of the Court of Arches on 2 August 1849, to the effect that Gorham's views fell outside the doctrines of the Church of England and so Phillpotts had been right to refuse to institute. The Church's own court, it might be argued, upheld the Church's own discipline.

It should be noted by those keen to view it from that angle, though, that Jenner-Fust expressed considerable frustration at the nature of the case he was obliged to decide.

> the evidence which has been produced, if evidence it may be called, is most unsatisfactory. It consists merely of one short affidavit by Mr. Gorham; no affidavit on the part of the bishop at all, but a book is annexed to his act on petition, containing upward of 250 pages of introduction, correspondence, and 149 questions addressed to Mr. Gorham, with his answers to those questions: upon this so-called evidence the whole case turns, and the Court is left to find its way, as well as it can.... I say this is not a convenient mode of proceeding, nor is it the correct mode according to the practice of the Court.[21]

He also noted that the task of the Court was not theological enquiry but ascertaining what the Church had defined in her written teachings. Gorham's counsel had offered an extensive exploration into Reformation writings which were supposed, in accordance with the Articles, to support Gorham's views, but these did not impress the Dean of the Arches. He cited in an earlier opinion of the Privy Council (on *Escott v Mastin* (1843), discussed in Chapter 5) that "the question is not to be decided by a reference to the opinions, however respectable, of individuals eminent for their learning, or distinguished by their station in the Church."[22] Any idea that the purpose of a spiritual court was to identify some sort of wider *sensus fidelium* was firmly rejected.

Gorham, supported by a surge of Evangelicals horrified at Phillpotts's success in excluding him from his diocese, appealed to the Judicial Committee of the Privy Council. Chadwick gives a picture of the committee meeting in somewhat informal circumstances,[23] and these may have contributed to the High Church barrage of complaint that the Judicial Committee was a secular court unfit to judge a matter of such spiritual delicacy as the doctrine of baptism. The Judicial Committee shared, in even more forthright terms, the Dean of the Arches' dissatisfaction at the way in which the case had been put before them:

> it was to be expected that both parties would require a strict and formal proceeding, in which the particular unsound doctrine imputed to Mr. Gorham would have been distinctly alleged. Unfortunately this course was not adopted.... The book published by Mr. Gorham was the only evidence adduced on either side ... with no statement on the part of the Bishop of what was, in his Lordship's view, the true doctrine of the Church of England in respect of the efficacy of Baptism either of adults or of infants; nor any specification of the doctrine imputed to Mr. Gorham, except the general charge before stated; and no distinct statement on the part of Mr. Gorham, of what, in his view, is the true doctrine of the Church of England.[24]

Having accepted reluctantly that the use of Gorham's book could not be refused, as this course of action was acceptable to both parties, the committee nonetheless felt the need to point out that it was most unsatisfactory for them to be obliged to work through all Phillpotts's questions and Gorham's answers,

> questions upon a subject of a very abstruse nature, intricate, perplexing, entangling, and many of them not admitting of distinct and explicit answers – of answers not given plainly and directly, but in a guarded and cautious manner, with the apparent view of escaping from some apprehended consequence of plain and direct answers.[25]

The judgment goes on to endorse Jenner-Fust's principle that they were not to investigate theologically, but to judge based upon the Church's recognised formularies, construed in the long-established legal manner of all written instruments.

The argument (endorsed by both Archbishops) proceeds to note that the 39 Articles of 1562 step back from some of the clarity of their predecessors of 1536, and this is taken as evidence of a degree of freedom of interpretation. The more ingenious argument responds to and relativises the texts of the Prayer Book, which the Arches' judgment had found more decisive for Phillpotts. It is noted that the Prayer Book often makes optimistic, charitable, spiritual claims for individuals, most strikingly talking of the 'sure and certain hope' of resurrection to life eternal, used indiscriminately in the burial service, regardless of the known or suspected spiritual state of the deceased.[26] Extending the analogy to the baptism service, the expectation there that every infant is regenerate can be seen to be no more theologically decisive than the supposition of the burial service that everyone buried is saved.

The outcome was that the Judicial Committee were not satisfied that Gorham's doctrine was contrary or repugnant to that of the Church, and so there could be no legal grounds for Phillpotts to refuse to institute him. "They applied the usual canons of statutory construction because the meaning of a term to theological specialists was irrelevant. What mattered was how it would have been read by the peers and Members of Parliament who approved it [in 1571 and 1662]."[27] Strikingly, the whole judgment is a refusal to define Gorham as a heretic, a defiance of the voices decrying his teaching as unsound – and in that it is a lasting marker of the Church of England's move to greater freedom. There is no acknowledgement of any particular rights for Phillpotts as bishop (indeed, Chadwick suggests the committee tactfully agreed at Blomfield's request not to refer to his views at all). This had the effect of confirming the established principle in English ecclesiastical law that the episcopate has no inherent privileges other than those conferred by the law.

Archdeacon Denison and the Real Presence

If Gorham's case arose chiefly because of the strong views of his bishop, that of Archdeacon Denison came to court through his own yearning for a fight, and in spite of the embarrassed efforts of the episcopacy to stave it off. Denison had already made a name as a controversialist by writing and speaking for the High side in the Gorham period, as a leading member of the National Society defending (as he saw it) Church schools from state interference, and participating in the revived Convocation of Canterbury.[28] In addition to being vicar of East Brent and Archdeacon of Taunton, he acted as examining chaplain, and in 1852 told those preparing for Advent ordinations that he expected them to believe in the Real Presence in the sacrament received by all, worthy or not. This led to complaints and the resignation of the assistant bishop, but Bagot, the Bishop of Bath and Wells, did not want a court case.

Knowing that if his teaching were to receive a trial it needed to be set out clearly, Denison first preached and then had published three sermons in Wells cathedral in 1853–54, and these were to be the substance of his case. A neighbouring vicar, Joseph Ditcher, sought a prosecution by Bishop Bagot. "And now began a comedy of the English legal system; cross-fire of jurisdiction, gold-mine of barristers, ineffective church courts and effective state courts. Denison revelled like a Hercules in these serpentine coils."[29] Analysing the comedy, the predominant theme is the great reluctance of the bishops to act, which contributed to the eventual conclusion.

Two diocesan bishops (Bagot died in 1854) refused to allow the suit against Denison to proceed, but Ditcher discovered the clause in the Church Discipline Act 1840 which reserved to the *archbishop* the duty of acting against clergy who were nominees of their diocesan bishop, as Denison was. Archbishop Sumner did act, first by convening a commission of enquiry, then delayed responding to its recommendation that there was a case to answer. Finally, he was compelled by *mandamus* from the Queen's Bench, obtained by Ditcher, to try the case, which he did acting *pro hac vice* for the Bishop of Bath and Wells, assisted by Stephen Lushington as Dean of Arches, George Johnson, Dean of Wells and Charles Abel Heurtley, Oxford Lady Margaret Professor of Divinity.[30]

No doubt considerably frustrated by both the time taken and the obligation to sit in the diocese (at the Guildhall in Bath), Sumner duly listened to Denison's defence by his brother-in-law Robert Phillimore. Or not, if we believe the story that he slept throughout and left the conduct of proceedings to Lushington.[31] The plea that the case was out of time was raised but dismissed, before the court sat through a lengthy defence from historical sources. All this was to no avail, for the very short Bath Judgment, as it was known, simply picks up Denison's published view that even 'the wicked' receive the Body and Blood of Christ, and defines it as contrary to the 28th and 29th Articles.

Denison refused to recant but allowed his lawyers to appeal to the Court of Arches on the grounds that the judgment was void, over two years having elapsed between the preaching of the controversial sermons and the Bath trial. The Arches ruled for Denison in April 1857 and their judgment was affirmed by the Privy Council against Ditcher's appeal. Denison returned home in triumph,[32] albeit with his rejoicing tempered by the knowledge he had got off on a technicality. The irony is even greater if one considers that it was his own choice to publish his controversial sermons which got him into court in the first place. Ditcher in frustration published his account of the proceedings, but some measure of his disappointment is captured by his defensive remarks on the Bath Judgment (italics original) that it was

> *the only hearing of the cause upon its merits which it has yet received.* Of the value of such a decision, the Public must be left to judge. To my own mind it is, alone, an ample recompense for all the labor, [sic] expense, inconvenience, and reproach that this attempt to vindicate the doctrine of our Church, as expressly laid down in her authorised Formularies, has occasioned to those engaged in it.

The wider reaction to Denison's case, however, implied that the doctrine of the Real Presence could not be forbidden as part of the teaching of the Church of England. Tracts written in support of him during the case and subsequently extolled a high doctrine of the Eucharist without restraint, and the same High Churchmen who had been appalled at the success of Gorham could now feel that their side was vindicated. Nonetheless, "It is not altogether apparent why people who were content that Catholic Eucharistic doctrine should be *tolerated* within the Church of England were insistent that Catholic baptismal doctrine should be *required*"[33] (my italics).

Reflections on the Gorham and Denison cases

Many accounts of the Gorham and Denison controversies lay stress upon the High or Low leanings of the bishops and lawyers involved, seeking to co-opt them as sympathisers to the rival camps, swayed by their convictions to judge accordingly. The Anglo-Catholic tradition has laid stress upon the secular nature of the Judicial Committee of the Privy Council, and indeed that was the complaint made at the time, and the justification given by Manning and Wilberforce, for example, for their disenchantment with the Church of England.[34] But we have seen above that Wilberforce and Manning in particular already believed, as Anglicans, in an unrealistic and anachronistic conception of a disciplined Church, which was never going to be fulfilled in Victorian England.

A different view would be to see the bishops and lawyers as being fundamentally united as one class of liberal rulers, tried to the utmost by the divisive campaigning of ecclesiastical factions seeking authoritative rulings in their favour (or, and the difference of emotive weight is significant, *against* their enemies) from the courts. Phillpotts wished to be able to exclude Gorham and those of his views from his diocese. Ditcher and his evangelical financiers wished to exclude Denison and his kin from the Church. Both were perhaps campaigning under the illusion that the Church of England could hold only one doctrine in each of the controversies, and it was most vital to the cause that theirs was the right one. But both campaigns failed, not least because those in judgment could not find substance in the laws of the Church of England to sustain the exclusions. Inclusion, although the word would have been foreign to them all, prevailed.

The Gorham and the Denison cases can also be written down as key points in the weakening of doctrinal discipline in the Church of England. Bishop Phillpotts had asserted his rights to question a clergyman at that point of a bishop's greatest power, just before agreeing to an appointment, and the Court of Arches had accepted his right to do so. However, the public exposure of the extreme length of his interrogations, together with his eventual defeat in the courts, for most bishops restored their traditional caution in asking too much of clergy, of generally sound reputation, presented to them for institution. The Dean of the Arches had specifically dismissed some of the controversial claims about Gorham as irrelevant to the case, with an implication that Phillpotts might be showing an excess of zeal:

> It is not my duty to consider whether it is an offence in the diocese of Exeter to allude to the Church as a "National Establishment" or to advertise for a curate "free from Tractarian error." These are matters extremely well suited for declamation, and may be calculated to raise in the minds of some persons a prejudice against the bishop; but they cannot, and ought not, to have any weight in the mind of a judge.[35]

In doctrinal terms, the Gorham judgment did not, as is sometimes alleged, determine that the Church of England does not believe in baptismal regeneration. Rather, it established that it is not outside the bounds of permissible faith in the Church to not so believe. Likewise, although the result of the technical dismissal of the case, the effect of the Denison judgment was to free English church people to believe in the Catholic conception of the Real Presence in the Eucharist, with devotional and liturgical consequences which would have their own place in court in following decades. But again, they are by no means obliged so to believe. The effect of *Denison* was confirmed by the 1870 case of *Sheppard v Bennett*, where Bennett, the Real-Presence-believing vicar of Frome, was successfully defended before both Phillimore at the Arches, who provided extensive theological support for him, and the Privy Council, who criticised such reasoning ("No mode of argument is more fallacious on a subject so abstruse and of so many aspects")[36] but likewise acquitted him. In respect of the doctrinal interpretation of the two dominical sacraments, discipline was abandoned, or at least re-defined in much broader terms.

A twentieth-century coda to Denison

An interesting legal coda to the effects of the Denison case may be found over a century later. Although the ritualist cases to be considered in the next chapter often involved the vigorous contention by the ritualist clergy that the ceremonies they introduced were intended to honour the Real Presence and the sacrificial, Catholic doctrine of the Eucharist, they were in fact fought on the rubrics of the Book of Common Prayer. The one legal case since in which the Church of England's doctrine of the Eucharist could be said to have been at least aired is that of *In re St. Stephen's Walbrook*, which from 1987 constitutes the only case in which the Court of Ecclesiastical Causes Reserved has ever made a decision on a matter of doctrinal controversy. It was in that case prompted by the consideration that the Holy Table being proposed under the contested faculty (a travertine sculpture by Henry Moore) was very much an altar, and that the chancellor at first instance had rejected it for that reason.

The doctrinal part of the judgment was written by the then Bishop of Chichester, Eric Kemp. Kemp had played a significant part in the creation of the Court of Ecclesiastical Causes Reserved, and in particular the insertion of section 45(3) of the Ecclesiastical Jurisdiction Measure 1963, which states that the CECR is not bound by doctrinal, ritual or ceremonial opinions of the Judicial Committee of the Privy Council. It therefore gave him considerable satisfaction to cite the said section in setting aside the 1845 precedent of *Faulkner v Litchfield and Stearn* and proceeding to a judgment based on his own theology.[37] Kemp's undoubted adhesion to the school of Anglo-Catholic history which saw the nineteenth century cases as a pattern of a secular state oppressing the Church may have led him to forget that *Faulkner* was in fact determined at the Court of Arches, and he did not necessarily have the same licence to set it aside. What is perhaps more surprising is that Kemp did not refer to *Sheppard v Bennett*, and set himself up as the heir to Phillimore by adopting his lengthy defence of catholic Eucharistic doctrine, so scorned by the Privy Council.

Kemp in fact reverted to the form of argument condemned by Jenner-Fust in the Gorham trial and by the Privy Council in *Bennett*, of citing selected helpful sources, in this case the Archbishops' 1897 response to Pope Leo XIII's condemnation of Anglican orders, a generalised reference to the ARCIC statements, and a passage from Lancelot Andrews.[38] There is one reference to the Prayer Book and none to the Articles. There is also no reference to the Holy Table Measure 1964 which was a distinct attempt to make a new and impartial start in the doctrine of Anglican altars, which had been contested in a number of faculty cases since the nineteenth century, not covered in this study. However, in spite of the rather weak reasoning, it was clear that Kemp reflected a reasonable possible interpretation of Anglican doctrine for the time, that the language of Eucharistic Sacrifice, and the word 'altar,' were not beyond acceptable bounds, and so further extended the liberty of thought and expression begun by the success of Archdeacon Denison.

Heath – a confused modernist

I have mentioned the Bennett case above out of date as it fits into the pattern of doctrinal controversy between Anglo-Catholic and Evangelical in which neither side won in the sense of gaining a judgment to exclude the other, but in which breadth of thought in the Church of England prevailed, protected by liberal lawyers from the passions of partisan churchmen. The picture is more complicated in respect of the new challenge to the peace of the Church emerging in the nineteenth century, the question of reconciling theology with the development of modern thought, and shows continuities with the earlier cases of Evanson and Stone in that a line could be found beyond which the courts could find grounds to deprive.

The three main cases all dealt with the challenge brought to traditional beliefs by advancing Biblical scholarship; this tended to erode belief in the authority of Scripture both by questioning the authorship and unity of Biblical books, and by developing a theology of progressive revelation. The overall theological trajectory tended to be towards Christian universalism, the disbelief in Hell, or at least that anyone in particular was destined for it. This laid upon those maintaining orthodoxy the uncomfortable duty of insisting that in the teaching of the Church of England someone, even if no-one could say whom, was definitely damned.

The case of Dunbar Heath in 1862, his eventual deprivation notwithstanding, goes some way towards showing the great difficulty the courts were under trying to settle doctrinal cases. Heath, a vicar in the diocese of Winchester, had published a volume of sermons which attracted attention for their heterodoxy. Arguments that he may never have actually preached them, or that the doctrine he propounded was not maintained 'advisedly' (a word used in the Elizabethan statute without much meaning) were dismissed in both the Arches and the Privy Council.[39] However, the Judicial Committee became tangled up in trying to work out Heath's understanding of the doctrine of justification. They noted Article 11, stating that we are justified by the merits of Christ and not our own, that this is consoling, and directing us to the Homily of Justification for further reading. Their Lordships then struggle to pin this down with legal precision:

> The evident meaning of this 11th Article is, that man is accounted righteous, which in the Article is treated as the same thing as being justified before God, not for his own merits, but for the merit of our Saviour by faith in him, *i.e.* that man is admitted to the favour of God, not for his own works or deservings, but for the merit of our Saviour, and by faith in him, i.e. by man's faith in our Saviour (however faith is to be defined).[40]

Wrestling with traditional theology they may have been, the judges still managed to find that Heath's teaching was not it. Heath propounded a rather unusual theology that the faith by which we are justified is Christ's faith in God, and that justification, far from being anything to do with restoring human relations with God as conventionally derived from Romans 5 and other Scriptures, was all about 'putting everyone in his just place.' Heath also quibbled at length over the very word 'merit' as being full of unhelpful obscurity. At length the committee resolved painfully:

> Their Lordships do not feel bound to say that they distinctly comprehend the exact bearing of the whole of Mr Heath's opinions on this mysterious subject. Perhaps his own views are not very distinct or clear even to himself. It is sufficient for the present purpose to say that the doctrine propounded by him is not that contained in the 11th Article; it differs from it fundamentally, and is inconsistent with it.[41]

The judgment goes on to analyse Heath's understanding of redemption, where his sermons set out a challenge to established convention without very clearly setting out an alternative. The sense in which the Articles afforded only a rather vulnerable doctrinal standard is shown up by the judges' remark that "they lay down as clear doctrine that our Saviour suffered and died in order to reconcile the Father to us, *whatever may be the exact import of that phrase*, and to be a sacrifice for sin" (my italics).[42] Still, given lines from Heath's sermons like "I am afraid it is a very common idea that God was propitiated 1,800 years ago by blood. I do not know how to find words strong enough to express my abhorrence of this detestable doctrine"[43] the court was able to judge him guilty of teaching against the Articles and confirming the Arches' sentence of deprivation. Heath was offered an opportunity for a last-minute retraction, which he did not take.

A Unitarian condemned

A similar approach can be found in the trial of Charles Voysey, Vicar of Healaugh in Yorkshire, before the Chancery Court of York and Privy Council in 1870–71. Voysey had gone some way beyond most of his contemporaries in a thorough rejection not only of some of the subtleties of doctrines such as justification and redemption, but of the basic Christian understanding of the Incarnation and the authority of large parts of the Scriptures. It was argued that "Mr Voysey seems to think that if he cannot understand a doctrine set forth by the Articles of the Church, he may not only reject it, but impugn and discredit it."[44] A hint appears of the way in which Voysey's Unitarian tendencies were in response to the authoritarian pretensions of some churchmen:

> They [Ritualist priests] are (most falsely, as it seems to me) convinced that we are all by nature in danger of endless suffering; and that, unless we obey *them* in thought, word, and deed, unless *they* pray and sacrifice for us, and *they* pardon our offences, there is no hope for us beyond the grave [original round brackets and emphases].[45]

Voysey conducted his own defence, on the rather weak grounds that:

> the maintaining, affirming, and promulgating doctrines or opinions contrary to or inconsistent with the passages set forth or referred to in parts of the Book of Common Prayer, other than the Articles of Religion, or other than such of them as are by law made a test of doctrine, was not an offence that could be charged against him in that suit.[46]

Fortunately for their Lordships, Voysey had committed his sermons extensively to print under the title *The Sling and the Stone*, selling over 1,250,000 copies,[47] and they found a wide range of passages totally incompatible with the 39 Articles. They expressed their regret that the broad-minded pattern of legal decisions, taking the minimal approach of relying on the Articles alone, could not encompass Voysey, and appealed to his reason:

> Mr Voysey will, we think, himself feel how impossible it is that any society whatever of worshippers can be held together without some fundamental points of agreement, or can together worship a Being in whom they have no common faith.[48]

Even the liberal judges and the broad-Church Archbishop Tait knew when they were faced with a vicar who was no longer really a Christian, and deprived him accordingly.

Moderate modernism and its acceptance by the courts

In spite of the condemnation of Heath and Voysey, they do contribute to the picture that heresy was perceived increasingly as a matter unsuitable for resolution by legal process. Neither Heath nor Voysey divided the Church, however, being regarded more as embarrassing eccentrics. The same would not be true of modernism in the 1900s, or the 1980s. The case that arguably did make a difference to the acceptability of more modern teaching was that of Williams and Wilson in 1863, two of the authors of *Essays and Reviews.* Because this case has been written up so extensively, what follows must be acknowledged as a sketch, intended to highlight it, with Gorham and Denison, as the third side of a triangle of varied belief which legal exertion could not restrain within the Church of England.

Essays and Reviews had been intended by its seven authors (six clerical) as a cautious attempt to broach the silence around Biblical interpretation in the Church of England, carried out in loyalty to the expectations upon them within the Church.[49] From the controversy that followed, prosecutions emerged against only two of the authors, Rowland Williams and Henry Wilson, apparently because they were the only two who were beneficed parish clergy, arguably more in need of correction and certainly easier to act against. Notably, in comparison with other cases considered here, the promoter of the case against Williams was his own diocesan bishop, the High Church Walter Hamilton. In this, and the pamphlet campaign in support, the double-sidedness of the nineteenth-century High Church movement can be seen: at once radical and defiant of discipline in the revival of Catholic teaching and practice, whilst conservative and invoking discipline against modernists.

The progress of the cases reveals again the reluctance of the courts to condemn opinions, and a willingness to construe controversial writings in a positive light. The first trial, at the Court of Arches, was one of the celebrated encounters between Stephen Lushington as Dean and his successor Robert Phillimore acting for the promoters of the case. In spite of the latter's eloquence, Lushington adopted the procedure of reforming the lengthy articles against Williams and Wilson (22 and 19 respectively) to a minimum by reading their writings as not excluding other interpretations, in order to give them the benefit of the doubt in what was a criminal case. For example, "I do not think that I am justified in holding that Mr Wilson, in representing our Lord as a moral teacher, meant to represent Him as that and nothing more."[50] He also adopted the important principle that simple quotations from Scripture, unsupported by any official teaching of the Church as to their interpretation, could not be used against the authors.

Having reduced the charges to three against each of the respondents, Lushington imposed the mild sentence of a year's suspension and costs upon both. The remaining articles related to the speculative expressions both Williams and Wilson had used about the inspiration of Scripture, Williams's attempt to subjectivize the concept of justification, and Wilson's aspirations towards universalism. Wilson had both expressed a hope of universal salvation and in a particularly unclear passage, the possibility of some sort of ongoing spiritual development "in the bosom of the Universal Parent." The latter was condemned by Wilberforce, Bishop of Oxford, as "a poor Buddhist dream of re-absorption into the Infinite," and "a dreamy vagueness of pantheistic pietism."[51]

The Judicial Committee, however, found it possible to be even more charitable in their interpretation of Williams' and Wilson's writings, although not before attempting to placate the concerned public about the overall merits of *Essays and Reviews:*

> A few short extracts only are before us, and our judgment must by law be confined to the matter which is therein contained. If, therefore, the Book, or these two Essays, or either of them as a whole, be of a mischievous and baneful tendency, as weakening the foundation of Christian belief, and likely to cause many to offend, they will retain that character, and be liable to that condemnation, notwithstanding our judgment.[52]

The resulting final judgment is quite brief and amounts to a declaration that the judges could find nothing in definite contravention of the Articles in the selected passages from Williams and Wilson. Again, the stress is on finding certainty of guilt, and it could not be found, for example "We cannot say, therefore, that it is penal in a Clergyman to speak of merit by transfer as a fiction, however unseemly that word may be when used in connection with such a subject."[53]

As in other Privy Council cases until 1876, the archbishops and the Bishop of London sat on the committee, and in this case the archbishops were sufficiently concerned by the implication that the court had rejected the inspiration of Scripture to dissent publicly from that part of the judgment. Tait, the Bishop of London (and next Archbishop of Canterbury) did not dissent, and indeed had taken a lead in drafting the judgment. The archbishops also published articles explaining that although they had agreed not to condemn Wilson for his universalism, they definitely did not endorse it. Nonetheless, the case was immortalised in the satiric comment on Lord Chancellor Westbury: "He dismissed Hell with costs/And took away from orthodox/ members of the Church of England/ their last hope of everlasting damnation."[54]

The end of doctrinal discipline by legal means

The three great heresy cases of the mid-nineteenth century – Gorham, Denison and Williams and Wilson – were decisive for perceptions of the usefulness of the ecclesiastical courts as a mechanism for doctrinal discipline. Those disappointed by the judgments were not slow to denounce the procedures by which their opponents secured dismissal of their cases, and to attack the secularised nature of the courts, particularly the Judicial Committee of the Privy Council. Some such as Pusey made the explicit observation, "The Gorham judgment impaired the discipline of the Church, such as Bishop Phillpotts wished to enforce it. It did not impair her teaching."[55] However, the prospect for all parties of a stronger discipline which might in fact end up being effective against *them* meant that these were scattered protests.

Two Acts of Parliament, not mentioned by the authors cited, may have been contributory factors to the end of doctrinal cases. The Clerical Subscriptions Act 1865 replaced the requirement of the canons for a subscription to each and every of the 39 Articles with a general statement of assent,[56] perhaps reducing the practicability of accusations of disbelief in individual points. The Clerical Disabilities Act 1870 made it possible for the first time for clergy to resign from Holy Orders, and so may have afforded an escape route for clergy otherwise liable to face trial.

Hansard reveals that one of the situations that provoked the latter Bill was that of a Mr Shore, who had left the regular ministry to operate an independent chapel, and consequently been persecuted by, inevitably, Bishop Phillpotts. Most of the debate concerned whether or not to include a clause providing for those who resigned Holy Orders to return after six months. A presumably satirical speech by Mr Henley suggested that a clergyman could thereby alternate between half the year in a lucrative and fashionable London parish and the other half fox-hunting.[57] In the Lords, the Bishop of Llandaff was concerned that by reducing the absolute commitment of ordination vows there would be "a danger of the introduction of a lower class of minds into the Church"[58] and the reversibility clause was dropped. No-one in either House suggested directly that the Bill would afford relief to clergy no longer able to conform to the Church of England's formularies, but this would have been one of its effects.

It is possible, though, to draw together a much more positive interpretation of the work of the courts. Within both the Court of Arches and the Judicial Committee, the judgments in doctrine cases reflect a settled tradition of jurisprudence, founded in the common law wherein all the major participants had trained, that a criminal case resulting in definite penalties to office or standing could only be sustained on clear evidence against the written doctrine of the Church. By that high standard, most of the important cases fell, to the disgruntlement of their promoters. Reading the arguments, it becomes apparent that speculative theology is of its very nature unsuitable to the sort of judicial proof which the courts required. Whilst it is true that all courts reflect the temper of their times, the fact that these controversies were worked out in court meant that the temper of high-minded Victorian liberalism was helped to prevail against the strong voices of Victorian religious passion.

What is particularly important is that whilst the courts were willing to act against figures with marginal views like Oakeley or Voysey, they were able, through their own procedures, to reflect an establishment view that they should not be the means for one major part of the Church of England to secure the condemnation of another, with the possible consequences of schism or secession. Yes, those who could not bear their opponents to be tolerated would leave, like those who went to Rome after *Gorham*, and many since, but that is not the same thing as being directly excluded, whatever the rhetoric says. Part of the challenge for the Church of England today, as Chapter 7 will note, is to see whether that refusal to exclude can be sustained with the same rigour.

Notes

1 Neast Havard, *A Word at Parting* (London 1778) 21–2.
2 Appendix to Havard, *Parting*, 4.
3 Ibid., 11–12.
4 Richard Helmholz, "Notable Ecclesiastical Lawyers: IX. Sir George Lee (c.1700–1758)" *17EccLJ* 348–54.
5 E. B. Pusey, *UNLAW in the Judgments of the Judicial Committee* (Parker & Sons and Rivingtons, 1881) 15.
6 *King's Proctor v Stone* [1808], 1 Hag Con 426.
7 *Stone*, 1 Hag Con 427–8.
8 *Stone*, 1 Hag Con 433.
9 *Breeks v Woolfrey* [1838], 1 Curt 888.
10 *Breeks*, 1 Curt 900.
11 Arthur Burns, *The Diocesan Revival in the Church of England c.1800–1870* (OUP 1999) 188.
12 *Sanders v Head* [1843] 3 Curt 565.
13 Anthony Trollope, *The Warden* (Everyman's Library, J. M. Dent & Sons 1907) 109–10.
14 *Sanders v Head*, 3 Curt 590–1.
15 Foster, *Examination*, 70–3.
16 *Sanders v Head* 3 Curt 604.
17 *Hodgson v Oakeley*, 1 Rob Ecc 322.
18 *Hodgson*, 1 Rob Ecc 362.

19 Owen Chadwick, *The Victorian Church Part 1 1829–1859* 3rd ed. (SCM Press 1971) 243–4.
20 Ibid., 261.
21 *Gorham v The Bishop of Exeter* [1849], 2 Rob Ecc 37–8.
22 *Escott v Mastin*, 4 Moore PC 137, cited at 2 Rob Ecc 58.
23 Chadwick, *Part 1*, 259.
24 *Gorham v Bishop of Exeter, The Judgment of the Judicial Committee* (Seeleys, London 1850) 3–4.
25 *Gorham* [1850] 5.
26 *Gorham* [1850] 11.
27 Augur Pearce, "Episcopacy and the Common Law" (2003) 7EccLJ 203.
28 Bernard Palmer, *Reverend Rebels* (DLT 1993) Ch. 2.
29 Chadwick, *Part 1*, 493.
30 Although repeated in multiple sources, a lengthy original account of this saga is in Ditcher, J, *A Statement of the Proceedings in the case of Ditcher v Denison* (Hatchard 1858).
31 J. H. Baker, *Monuments of Endlesse Labours* (Hambledon Press 1998) 138.
32 Palmer, *Rebels*, 47.
33 Robert E. Rodes Jr, *Law and Modernisation in the Church of England* (Notre Dame 1991) 271.
34 For example, at Chadwick, *Part 1*, 262.
35 *Gorham v Bishop of Exeter* [1849] 2 Rob Ecc 46–7.
36 *Gorham* [1849] 209.
37 E. W. Kemp, *Shy but not Retiring* (Continuum 2006) 126.
38 *In re St Stephen's Walbrook* [1987] 3 W.L.R. 731–2.
39 *Heath v Burder* [1862] UKPC 10, 3.
40 *Heath* 4.
41 *Heath* 6.
42 *Heath* 8.
43 *Heath* 8.
44 *Voysey v Noble-Noble v Voysey* [1870–71] 7 Moo N.S. 200.
45 *Voysey* 219.
46 *Voysey* 179.
47 Malcolm Johnson, *Victorian Worthies* (Darton, Longman & Todd 2014) 77.
48 *Voysey*, 7 Moo N.S. 234–5.
49 Owen Chadwick, *The Victorian Church Part 2 1860–1901* 3rd ed. (SCM Press 1972) 75ff.
50 Cited in Rodes, *Modernisation*, 272.
51 Cited in Duncan Henderson, "The Devil's Law Cases" (2012), 15EccLJ 36.
52 *Williams v Salisbury (Bishop of)* [1863] 2 Moo N.S. 423.
53 *Williams* 428.
54 Cited in Henderson, *Devil's*, 15EccLJ 42.
55 Pusey, *Unlaw*, 4.
56 The Clerical Subscription Act 1865, §1 and note, *Church Acts and Measures* 334–5.
57 HC Deb 25 May 1870, vol 201, cols 1380–1.
58 HL Deb 28 July 1870, vol 203, col 1068.

4. Law defied – the Ritualists

Introduction to the Ritualist controversies

In the case of the diversity of thought in the Church discussed above, or the freedom of the laity, below, the fairly consistent role of the courts in the nineteenth century and after has been to defend freedom, but it was to be quite different over the question of the way in which the Church's services were conducted. The courts attempted, through a series of controversial and highly-publicised cases, to respond to the Ritualist movement in the Victorian period by reference back to the Prayer Book, Articles and certain other historical texts, largely to constrain innovation. Arguably, they made a fair effort given the resources at their disposal. However, they were faced with a distinctive response of civil disobedience which rendered their decisions ineffective, and in time inhibited promoters from bringing cases.

As noted in the Introduction, the movement towards greater use of Catholic ceremonial in the Church of England in the mid to late nineteenth century, and the loud legal controversy it generated, has been the subject of extensive study. In the first generations of the early twentieth century, memory of the Ritualists was coloured by their veneration as confessors by the growing Anglo-Catholic movement, heroes who defied unjust law in the name of freedom of worship. The less sympathetic parties of the Church do not seem to have fundamentally disagreed with the analysis, but rather lamented the fact that the defiance of the ritualist priests had gone to show that law was no use in putting down bad practice.

A balance between these, with vast evidence for the basic thesis, is provided by the records of the Royal Commission on Ecclesiastical Discipline 1906 with its famous conclusions that "the law of public worship in the Church of England is too narrow" and "the machinery for discipline has broken down."[1] More recent studies, by for example John Shelton Reed[2] and Dominic Janes,[3] have moved away from the disciplinary cases to the underlying culture of the era and the many fascinating influences, conscious and subconscious, on the Ritualists, their supporters and opponents. We are now much more able to see them in their social and cultural context, and this is an area for ongoing work. This study, however, returns to the legal and disciplinary situation.

It will be argued that there were aspects of the legal process which contributed significantly to this disobedience. Amongst the 'what if's' of Anglican history would be to ask what if the archbishops and bishops, rather than cooperating with the popular mood of alarm at ritualism and seeking to use the courts to prosecute and strengthening them by the Public Worship Regulation Act 1874, had instead managed to use Convocation as a source of authority, passing Acts declaring the opinion of both Houses on ritual questions. In practice on any questions of discipline, "consensus was almost impossible to obtain within Convocation. Further, while some saw the consultation of Convocation as the best hope for securing peace and agreement within the church, its detractors derided its claims to be either representative or useful."[4] The limited representation of the parish clergy until 1920 in particular raised doubts about its legitimacy;[5] possibly ritualist clergy would have carried on regardless. But the belief that they were defying *wrongly-constituted* authority, as will be apparent in the cases which follow, undoubtedly added to the boldness with which ritualist clergy ignored the sanctions brought against them.

Nonetheless, as this whole study has sought to show, far from being an isolated phenomenon of a particular part of the Church of England in the 1870s and 1880s, the failure to stamp out Ritualism fits with tendencies deeply seated in the Church's nature and identity. As stated in the introduction, among my intentions was to show that far from having 'broken down,' the Church of England was already without an effective 'machinery of discipline' and that this conclusion is of much wider and more important application to her whole life. The basic shape of the Ritualist story is sketched out, without elaborating all the details of each individual case under the Public Worship Regulation Act as several other authors have done already.[6] For economy's sake, the cases which arose as a result of Faculty petitions to introduce the furniture of Ritualist worship into parishes have been omitted, as whilst these were often bitterly contested between the same parties as the cases of clergy, they did not constitute attempts at spiritual discipline of individuals in the same way.[7]

There are two elements in the story of particular relevance. The first is to put the Public Worship Regulation Act 1874 clearly into the context of the long-term challenge of church discipline, and to show how its well-documented failure stemmed in part from a fundamental misjudgment by those who introduced it about what is possible in the field of Christian discipline in a free society. The other is to take seriously the legal arguments put forward amongst the Ritualists themselves, that they were not merely wrongly on trial by bad courts, but that their understanding of the law of the Church obliged them to undertake their ritual practices. There may have been a dialogue of the deaf between these and the Privy Council, but both sides fed, as we shall see below, into the development of canon law study in the twentieth century.

There is also a theological lens through which the Ritualist cases can be and sometimes were seen, even if only implicitly. In every case where a Christian is persecuted, he or she, and those who follow the story, will be drawn to identify them with the early martyrs and with Christ himself before his judges – the trope of Christian history is that to be persecuted is to be right, however implausible the reason. In England this understanding was strengthened by the generations for whom Foxe's *Book of Martyrs* was standard reading, aligning the Protestant victims at the Reformation firmly with the martyrs of the Early Church. We have seen how for the critics of the Church in the early eighteenth century the fear of 'popish tyranny' was alive and well then, and it was revived for Protestants by the re-establishment of the Roman Catholic hierarchy in England in 1850.

Although the Ritualist clergy were personally out of sympathy with the Reformation, there is a sense, so obvious as to not need to be always publicly stated, that they too were righteous victims. And the Gospels also provide ample opportunity to identify one's internal opponents with the 'wrong religion' of Jesus' Jewish adversaries. For example, a broadsheet posted to Archbishop Tait's annoyance near Lambeth Palace in 1880 declared that "history repeats itself," and listing with dates among other sufferers "for conscience sake" the prophet Daniel, John the Baptist, Cranmer and Arthur Tooth.[8] Only the slightest hint was needed to remind pious readers of campaigning tracts that as far as they need be concerned, Father Mackonochie or Father Tooth, or Bishop King, were Christ to them; the worldly and Erastian episcopate were the Pharisees, and Lord Penzance was Pontius Pilate *redivivus* to the Victorian Church.

An earlier case of liturgical indiscipline

Before moving on to the excitements of imprisoned priests and Kensitite agitation, one much earlier case shows how the courts responded more calmly to liturgical development in the Church of England. The development of hymnody has sometimes been credited to the Tractarian movement, popularising translations of medieval hymns and publishing *Hymns Ancient & Modern*. However, Thomas McCart shows that hymns were becoming popular as far back as the later eighteenth century, first with the Methodists, and played a major part in the Evangelical revival within the Church of England. However, within the Church there was prolonged unease at the legitimacy of hymns as adjuncts to the legal liturgy. Two metrical editions of the Psalms, the Old Version by Sternhold and Hopkins and the New Version by Tate and Brady, were considered more acceptable, and in some places hymn-singing confined to institutions like hospital and school chapels which were outside the parish structure and so the law might be held not to apply in the same way. In a 1787 treatise William Vincent, the Dean of Westminster, laid down that there was no legal authority for the use of hymns in church.[9]

In spite of the supposed legal prohibition, the use of hymns in the services gradually spread across the Church of England in parishes where there were Evangelical clergy. It was one such, St Paul's, Sheffield, a chapel of ease to the parish church, from which a case came to court to settle the matter. The curate, Thomas Cotterill, was an enthusiast for hymnody, and was promoting an established custom to the extent that the hymnbook he edited had reached its 8th edition by 1819; it was this he wished to introduce to St Paul's. The churchwardens, Daniel Holy and Samuel Broomhead Ward, objected to the hymnbook, and their objection was heard as a disciplinary case against Cotterill by G. V. Vernon, the Vicar General of York, on 6 July 1820.

Vernon noted the conflict between the fact that hymns were now used by "a majority of the Established Clergy,"[10] but were illegal as interpolations by a plain reading of the Act of Uniformity 1662. However, he came down on the side of established usage, so long as it did not impede the liturgy. The Archbishop of York was asked to mediate between the parties and appears to have done so successfully. It was not the end of controversy, with the Bishop of Peterborough, for example, issuing a more conservative Charge[11] to his clergy upholding the narrow legal line, but the use of hymnody became gradually established without further attempts to discipline its practitioners. As with Ritualism, law was no restraint on changing fashions.

The buildup to the Public Worship Regulation Act

Controversy over details of liturgical performance began at least as early as the 1840s, when Bishop Phillpotts of Exeter had waded in to defend the curate of Helston, Walter Blunt, for his wearing of the surplice, and ended up rebuffed by his Archbishop in turn, and when the stone altar at St Sepulchre's, Cambridge, had been condemned by the Court of Arches.[12] However, two factors conspired to generate a greater sense of crisis by the 1870s. The first, progress of theological liberation by the courts charted in the previous chapter, left observers concerned that such Catholic beliefs as the Real Presence were now unchallenged within the Church of England. The second was that an increasing number of clergy had moved far beyond the modesty of surplices and gothic-looking church furniture, largely now accepted, to chasubles, incense and candles. Although usually claiming inspiration from the English Middle Ages, it was obvious that these were also the contemporary practices of Rome.

The movement to resist such introduction was led by the broadly evangelical Church Association, crucially providing the funds to pay the legal costs necessary to sustain the complex cases. Two early landmark cases, the first of many titled *Martin v Mackonochie* in 1868, and the Purchas case of 1870–71, may serve to demonstrate how before the Public Worship Regulation Act 1874 (hereafter 'PWRA') there was great difficulty bringing cases and enforcing judgments, besides the underlying difficulty of determining the legally correct answer to ritual disputes at all. Significantly, both cases were heard first at the Arches by Sir Robert Phillimore, who consistently showed greater sympathy to many details of Ritualist practice, before being partly reversed by the Privy Council, crystallising for many Ritualists their views (derived from the Gorham case) about the illegitimacy of the final court of appeal.

Alexander Mackonochie took charge of the new parish of St Alban, Holborn, in 1862 after cautious negotiation with the patron, John Hubbard, as to how ritualist he would be.[13] Once instituted, however, he turned out to be either "heroically stubborn or merely pig-headed"[14] and adopted without compromise all the current liturgical innovations. The first of a long stream of cases was brought by the Church Association's man, John Martin, in 1867, being adjudged first by Phillimore at the Arches in March 1868 and then on appeal by the Privy Council in

November. Phillimore's judgment was mixed, rejecting as unlawful the elevation, incense and mixed chalice, but accepting the "kneeling or prostrating" and lighted candles.[15] However, the Privy Council ruled against the kneeling and the candles as well, leaving Mackonochie forbidden from all his desired ceremonies.

The significance of the case, like most of those in the Ritualist controversy, lies not in the lengthy perorations of the courts into Edwardine Injunctions and medieval customs, but in the great difficulty which then ensued in making Mackonochie obey the decision of the courts. Palmer cites George Russell's account of his cases:

> If he might not elevate the paten above his head, he would elevate it to his chin. If he might not prostrate himself, he would bow. If he might not have two candles on the Altar, he would have seven lamps above it.[16]

Palmer gives more detail of the 'Scots logic' by which Mackonochie attempted to defy the spirit of the judgment whilst not disobeying its letter. The Church Association was naturally less impressed, and returned to court to secure, eventually, a three-month suspension, during which Mackonochie occupied his stall in church in silence whilst his curates carried on the ritual around him. His story was to continue until 1883 and in time "the litigation was heard by 25 judges – including three Lord Chancellors – and provided work for 20 different counsel at different stages in its history,"[17] but even the earliest defiance contributed to the campaign for stronger legislation than the slow Church Discipline Act 1840.

The other most important case before the PWRA was the judgment over the ritual activities of John Purchas at St James's, Brighton, memorable for including among the 35 allegedly illegal activities the suspension of a stuffed dove over the altar at Pentecost, the rare union of the two Victorian interests of ritualism and taxidermy.[18] Once again, Phillimore as Dean of the Arches delivered a mixed judgment, accepting as legitimate vestments, the eastward position, wafer bread and a mixed chalice (so long as not mixed ceremonially). These he judged to be justified by the appeal, general among the Ritualists, to the Ornaments Rubric in the Book of Common Prayer, which seems to require (though much-debated) a return to the ceremonial of the First Prayer Book of Edward VI, and other key rubrics. In this Phillimore not only made an arguable construction of the rubrics, but reflected the practice of a number of other clergy besides Purchas.

The Church Association, however, took the case to the Privy Council. Purchas refused to appear, but the appellant counsel responded indirectly to Phillimore by entering at considerable length into the history of the Ornaments Rubric, noting its apparent contradiction in the Prayer Book of Elizabeth I (where it refers to the appended Act of Uniformity 1559, which in turn refers firmly to the *Second* Prayer Book of Edward VI). It is then argued that whatever ambiguity existed there is set aside by the Elizabethan Advertisements of 1564 and the 1604 Canons, decisively outlawing vestments.[19] The obvious rubric that the bread is 'such as is usual to be eaten' is appealed to against wafers[20] and that no water is mentioned against the mixed chalice. Finally, the need for the congregation to see the 'manual acts' during the consecration, citing *Martin v Mackonochie*, is invoked against the eastward position. Throughout there are allusions to the need to avoid the Catholic, sacrificial, implications of the various ceremonies.

The Lord Chancellor felt it necessary to include in his judgment a kindred display of learning, citing among other things Puritan tracts of some obscurity from the reign of Elizabeth I in support of the utter disuse of vestments.[21] This was to refute the case put by Phillimore that the Elizabethan Advertisements were possibly invalid because not provably endorsed by the Queen. He ruled against all Purchas's vestments, except that carrying a biretta was allowed because there was no evidence he had ever worn it.[22] The judgment proceeds on similar lines, also advancing repeatedly the obvious point that the law seemed to have been settled without controversy from 1662 until about 1840, and that antiquarian pedantry could not set aside centuries of accepted Protestant reading of the texts.

Purchas himself made a sad appeal including the defence that he had been too poor to be represented, which the Privy Council dismissed, and he died the following year. However, Phillimore's arguments had given strength to the Ritualists, and in the early 1870s the pamphlet talk was of the Six Points, i.e. vestments, the mixed chalice, eastward position and wafer bread allowed by the Arches, and also incense and altar candles, which were not,[23] with the argument made that the courts should be defied on these points. It is worth noting that, in the process, elements of modern Anglicanism developed – the appeal to medieval practice and contested Reformation rubrics gave a subtler character to Ritualism than would have occurred by straightforward adoption of contemporary Roman Catholic practice – but this is a study of the effects of the legal system on discipline, not on liturgy.

Exactly who decided first that 'something must be done' seems to be lost in the private conversations of Disraeli, Archbishop Tait and Queen Victoria, none of whom were enthusiasts for ritualism. But it was Tait who brought a Bill to Parliament whose "aim was to increase the power of the bishops"[24] and discomfited the clergy by first revealing his aims in *The Times*. Bentley describes the progress of the Bill through Parliament, with Lord Chancellor Cairns introducing the single lay judge who would unite the Court of the Arches and the Chancery Court of York, and also on its next vacancy become Master of the Faculties. However, with the support of Lord Shaftesbury, the Bishops defeated the efforts of the Commons to remove their discretion over whether a prosecution should be brought (often described as the 'episcopal veto'). Whatever the details, "by far the strongest consideration in Parliament was the notion that ritualists were romanisers,"[25] summarised by Disraeli's motto that he wished to outlaw the Mass in masquerade, and Tait's modified Bill became law as the Public Worship Regulation Act 1874.

Before exploring the failure of the PWRA in the face of organised resistance, two aspects of the Act should be noted. The first is that the PWRA provided for a bishop to invite the complainant and the clergyman, if both were willing, to submit to his episcopal judgment rather than go to the court. Rodes dismisses this unrealistic provision:

> In the wildly unlikely event that both parties were so willing, the bishop could hear the matter any way he thought fit, and enter a binding judgment. His judgment, however, was not to be taken as finally deciding any question of law. I know of no case in which the parties chose this route.[26]

However, it is possible that the existence of such a provision encouraged more widespread compromise than is often acknowledged by the hagiologists of the Ritualist martyrs. Reed argues that in many cases where the bishops refused to proceed against clergy, they nonetheless ordered at least some ritualism to cease, and secured consent. He cites as an example from among the first 17 cases, in the four years after 1874, Horace Chapman at Donhead St Andrew, who was armed with a strong counter-petition in support from his parishioners (italics original):

> The bishop vetoed the prosecution, but asked the rector to give up the candles and the mixed chalice. Chapman defended the practices, but submitted. The bishop acknowledged his submission, and, significantly, added that the mixed chalice was in his opinion a good practice and that it was a "grave misfortune and wrong" that it was forbidden. *Most* of the PWRA cases were resolved by this sort of negotiation.[27]

It was the willingness of only a few clergy, encouraged as we shall see below by their membership of the Society of the Holy Cross (hence 'SSC') to face prison that undermined such understandings, and left the PWRA a dead letter within a couple of decades.

The second feature of the Act apparent in practice was the inadequacy of the penalties provided – monition at the first instance and three months' suspension at the second, with deprivation available only after a disobedience lasting three years from the initial complaint. It is difficult to understand such leniency when priests like Mackonochie were already setting an example of defiance of the law, except by presuming that the bishops and other parliamentarians really did think of the ritualist clergy as naughty and silly boys (as Purchas was depicted by *Punch*), who would respond meekly to a sound telling-off by stopping doing the naughty things. It may also be that the nineteenth century reverence for property rights amplified the traditional sanctity of the clergy freehold in the minds of legislators, making them most unwilling to provide the means for gentlemen to be deprived of their livings.

A Ritualist in a dilemma

The belief that the PWRA could be an effective tool for bringing the ritualist clergy back into line was ironically strengthened by the first case, of Charles Ridsdale of St Peter's, Folkestone, which was brought by the Church Association soon after the Act had passed. In his new court, Baron Penzance (of whom more below) ruled against Ridsdale on all 12 of the charges in early 1876, and Ridsdale appealed to the Privy Council on four (all notably part of the Six Points, viz.

wafers, vestments, altar candles and the eastward position). The Privy Council judged against on 12 May 1877 on all points except a partial acceptance of the eastward position. Suspicion of the courts was increased by an attempt to hide the fact that Penzance's predecessor, Sir Robert Phillimore, now himself a member of the Judicial Committee, was among the minority in Ridsdale's favour,[28] and by an ongoing controversy about the propriety of including episcopal assessors on the Judicial Committee.[29]

Ridsdale now found himself in a dilemma which illustrates the peculiar complexity of legal opinion amongst the Ritualists. From a personal point of view,

> poor Ridsdale had had enough. He had recently married, and was unwilling to risk the possible loss of his livelihood by carrying on a campaign of civil disobedience – even though such a course would at once have turned him into a martyr in the eyes of the *Church Times* and its more militant supporters.[30]

However, although his ritual was condemned by the courts of Church and State, Ridsdale believed in the theory, expounded within the SSC and sometimes by the *Church Times*, that not only were those courts illegitimate, but that the clergy of the Church of England were *obliged* by the Ornaments Rubric to carry out their ritual. If he defied the courts, he could be suspended or eventually deprived, but if he obeyed them, he believed himself to be disobeying the law of the Church, paying no heed to the obvious argument that that law (in the 1662 Prayer Book) had been laid down by Parliament neither more nor less than the loathed Public Worship Regulation Act.

Ridsdale's method of escape was to argue (mainly, it seems, to himself) that it was in the power of his bishop (perhaps fortunately, also his metropolitan) to release him from the obligation of the Ornaments Rubric in order to obey the compulsion of the courts, and accordingly he sought what he called a 'dispensation' from Archbishop Tait. Although resisting the force of Ridsdale's peculiar reasoning, Tait had not become Archbishop without mastering the art of Anglican compromise, and wrote back stating ambiguously that although he could not accept his argument, "I am ready to use all authority I possess as Diocesan and Archbishop to relieve you from any such supposed obligation, and I gladly take upon myself the whole responsibility of directing that you [give up the ritual]."[31] Ridsdale therefore felt able in good conscience to conform to the judgment of the courts, and his new wife was no doubt thankful too.

This manoeuvre, however, caused considerable heart-searching amongst ritualist clergy. This has not always been clearly understood, not least because their principal forum of the SSC maintained strict secrecy in order to allow free discussion of such trying situations. Nigel Yates reports:

> The Society of the Holy Cross, of which Ridsdale was a member, was appalled at his decision and referred the matter to its Canon Law Committee to consider "whether a Dispensation is of any value which avowedly does not

> recognise the obligation from which it professes to dispense … whether the Bishops have power to dispense … from … the Law of the Church … [and] whether it is advisable for Brethren of the Society to act upon such a Dispensation."[32]

This must also be the background to an 1877 pamphlet found at Pusey House by Reed, asking "whether an English *parochus* is at liberty at the present moment to act upon a dispensation releasing him from the rubrical obligation of wearing the eucharistic vestments."[33]

Reed misses this context, and simply notes the pamphlet as an example of odd clerical reasoning, but it illustrates the remarkable fact that the ritualists did not in fact believe they were defying the law but obeying what they felt to be a higher law, in the interests of a greater truth. Whilst in the case of Ridsdale this reaches an obscure complexity, it follows a line of reasoning going back to the Tractarians, who had found their key conceptions of the Apostolic Succession and the importance of the Holy Communion in the Prayer Book and the history of the Church of England rather than anywhere else. The specific provision in the Shortened Services Act 1872 that the morning services could legitimately be used separately suggests strongly that there were still many churches in England at this time whose morning service followed what now seems the unlikely pattern of Mattins, Litany and Ante-Communion rolled into one. For the Ritualists, who gladly agreed to this return of the Prayer Book services to their original shape long neglected, it seemed a natural further step to return them to their supposed original ceremonial richness.

The victory of the martyrs

The response of the SSC to Ridsdale's surrender has already been noted. This falls into the context of a Ritualist clergy, meeting as the SSC and supported by the English Church Union (hereafter ECU), with a strong sense of purpose and self-belief. Bentley observes "the ritualists had already developed a tradition of resistance to the law, and they drew upon it now," citing as example an 1874 pamphlet by the prominent Brighton Ritualist, A. D. Wagner, on *Reasons for Disobeying in Principle.* [34] In addition to their theory that the Ornaments Rubric justified their ceremonial, the Ritualists attacked the legitimacy of the courts. The Judicial Committee of the Privy Council had been suspect since the Gorham case, but it could now be argued that the PWRA had removed the historic legitimacy of the ancient Court of Arches in favour of a new court which could not be respected. This viewpoint was strengthened by the appointment of a judge, Lord Penzance, whose main career had been in the divorce courts, and by his refusal (having been appointed by statute) to take the customary ecclesiastical oaths on taking office.[35] Mackonochie's patron, John Hubbard, for example, subjected Lambeth Palace to "an avalanche of impassioned letters"[36] seeking confirmation that he had taken the oaths, and not obtaining such, he "stated his conviction that Lord Penzance did not possess the historic and spiritual authority which allowed a true Dean of Arches to bind the consciences of offenders."[37] Nonetheless, working through the judgments of the most significant Deans of Arches of the nineteenth and early twentieth century, Jenner-Fust, Lushington, Phillimore, Penzance and Dibdin, Phillimore looks the odd man out in his unusual willingness to depart from the Erastian conventions of his office and entertain Anglo-Catholic theories.

Underlying this non-recognition of Lord Penzance's court was an outworking of the wider Tractarian contention about the uncertain place of authority in the nineteenth century Church of England, following the repeal of the Test Acts in 1828, opening Parliament to dissenters and indeed atheists. According to this theology, inherent from Keble's 1833 Assize Sermon onwards, the unreformed Parliament which had made the Reformation and passed the Act of Uniformity 1662 was (as an exclusively Anglican institution with the Church represented directly through the bishops) a legitimate body to define the will of the National Church. The unbroken use of the 1662 Prayer Book assisted the Tractarians in skipping over the reality of the Toleration and building the Anglican forgetfulness that the 1662 Parliament was not only exclusively Anglican, but was drawn from a nation in which non-Anglicans were actively persecuted as we have seen above. During the 1870s at least, this view of Parliamentary authority, as once right but now illegitimate, was the dominant explanation among the Ritualists, combined with the widespread desire to see the recently revived Convocation as the mechanism to give the Church its own voice. However, in time the strongest Ritualists came to develop a further theory of authority, still with influence in the Church of England, as we shall see below.

A number of studies of the Ritualists such as those of Bentley, Reed and Yates provide the detail of the 'five martyrs' who suffered imprisonment under the PWRA (presumably they have come to be thought of as *martyrs* simply because that word is better known and ironically evokes the Reformation martyrs who actually died; there was no shortage of pamphlets at the time invoking their historically correct designation as *confessors*). Before providing brief accounts of the cases, it is useful to note the several common factors in each case. The five who were imprisoned were Fathers Tooth, Dale, Enraght, Green and Cox. The cases of the first four all took place in the narrow period 1876–82, with overlaps between their various trials and imprisonments, which has contributed to the sense of them being a group with a common cause and a common fate. All refused to appear before Lord Penzance, and all were therefore subject to the 1813 writ *de contumace capiendo* and imprisoned for contempt (rather than directly for their ritualism, though this was obscured by both contemporary media coverage and subsequent Anglo-Catholic legend).

Arthur Tooth had become vicar of St James's, Hatcham, in 1868, and combined vigorous pastoral work with the usual ritual. Preliminary controversy by complaint and letters to the Bishop of Rochester escalated to legal proceedings once the PWRA had been passed, and his case came before Lord Penzance in 1876, Tooth refusing to appear.[38] He was, however, "supported by a carefully orchestrated press campaign"[39] and refused to obey Penzance's suspension or allow the bishop's nominated locum into his church.[40] After riots and other disorder, Tooth was arrested for contempt and sent to Horsemonger Lane Gaol in January 1877. "Tooth's committal to jail changed him in a flash, in the eyes of many, from rebel priest to Christian martyr"[41] even if the Protestant *Rock* newspaper could still sneer at his comfortable imprisonment. More significantly, though, the complainants, embarrassed by the publicity, sought to have Tooth released. This Penzance did, only to have the whole prosecution quashed by the Queen's Bench on the grounds that his court had sat in the library at Lambeth Palace, and that this was not, as Tait had ordered, within "the diocese of Rochester, or in London or Westminster."[42] Tooth himself, after a brief attempt to wrest back his parish, resigned and spent the rest of his life in ministry that did not require episcopal support. Nonetheless, the "case enraged his would-be prosecutors, and at the same time forced them to proceed with extreme caution."[43]

T. P. Dale of St Vedast, Foster Lane in the City of London and R. W. Enraght of Bordesley, Birmingham, offered two more "embarrassing case[s] involving imprisonment"[44] although both imprisonments were short as the clergy were both released on another technicality of some obscurity, that under *de contumace capiendo* the writs to the sheriffs who seized them should have been opened before the justices of the Queen's Bench under an act of 1563, and had not been.[45] The latter case was memorable mainly for the 'Bordesley Sacrilege' when a consecrated wafer, pocketed by a Church Association spy at the altar rail, was produced as evidence of Enraght's use of wafer bread, and stamped as court evidence. Archbishop Tait managed eventually to obtain the specimen and was able to assure alarmed Anglo-Catholics that he had personally and reverently consumed it. Such incidents did nothing to enhance the idea that legal process could resolve spiritual and liturgical disagreement. Bishop Jackson of London acknowledged that "Imprisonment as the result of an ecclesiastical suit *looks* like persecution for religious opinions"[46] (italics original) and Bentley estimates that by 1878 seven-eighths of suits were being vetoed by the bishops.[47] The power to veto was upheld in the 'Clewer case' where the Bishop of Oxford refused to allow the suit against Thomas Carter for ritualism to proceed. The complainant, Frederic Julius, successfully obtained *mandamus* from the Queen's Bench ordering the bishop to proceed, but it was taken to the Court of Appeal and then the House of Lords, both of whom confirmed the bishop's statutory right to veto.[48]

The case of S. F. Green, of Miles Platting in Manchester, was marked by the most prolonged imprisonment, for over a year and a half. The difficulty arose because "Green was determined to use his imprisonment to humiliate his prosecutors"[49] and he succeeded. By refusing to appear, Green exposed the weakness of the PWRA that three years had to elapse from the original offence until he could be lawfully deprived of his benefice, and thence released as having no charge remaining to answer. The technicality about failing to open the writs before the Queen's Bench was not available to spare his bishop's embarrassment, since that requirement did not apply in the County Palatine of Lancaster wherein Miles Platting is located.[50] Ironically, many of the complaints about worship in the parish were directed at things done by the curate, Cowgill, under Green's authority – whilst Green was imprisoned, Cowgill continued the ritual, and was nominated as the next incumbent once Green had been deprived, although the bishop managed to resist this.[51] Once again, ritual was not really getting 'put down' at all, and the *Church Times* supported the legal theories of the ritualists with a standing advert throughout Green's imprisonment reading "ARRESTED MARCH 19 1881. The Prayers of the Church are desired for SIDNEY FAITH-HORN GREEN, Priest. IN PRISON FOR OBEDIENCE TO THE CHURCH'S LAW."[52]

The decline in cases after Green followed a meeting of the Upper House of Convocation in April 1881 which "unanimously passed a motion stating that litigation in matters of ritual is to be deprecated and deplored, and, if possible, avoided."[53] Will Adam says this decision has been widely overlooked by historians because the crucial record is a near-indecipherable marginal note by one of the bishops present, preserved at Lambeth.[54]

A final case of imprisonment, however, involved J. B. Cox at St Margaret's, Toxteth, after he had unsuccessfully defended his ritual in correspondence with his strongly Evangelical bishop, Ryle, before being brought to court in 1885. Ryle defied his brother bishops (possibly in part because it is not clear whether the Province of York was represented at the 1881 meeting?) and a shift in public mood around such prosecutions, resulting in considerable pressure put on Ryle to veto, including a petition from a third of diocesan clergy, and the Church Association was reluctant to support the case.[55] In the event, Cox was for some reason not inhibited under the PWRA, but suspended under the Church Discipline Act 1840 for three months, and when he refused to comply, imprisoned during 1887. But after the three months he was released by *habeas corpus*, and his case to be so released defended up to the House of Lords.[56] This had the effect of closing off his prosecution altogether, and so

> this was the only case under the [PWRA] where the defendant won a complete victory, since it was now impossible for Cox to be forced to abandon the use of any illegal ritual without a totally new suit being instigated.[57]

When in 1892 his prosecutors attempted such a new suit, Penzance offered Ryle a fresh veto, which he is assumed to have used.[58]

The ritualists were supported by a vigorous press campaign, led by the *Church Times*, identifying them as persecuted martyrs for the sake of religious conscience, and presenting them as heroes to other Anglo-Catholics. Bentley summarises the effect of the cases:

> The four imprisonments had changed public opinion. Particularly horrifying had seemed the enforced sale of Green's goods and chattels to pay the legal costs of his opponents (especially as this apparently involved turning onto the streets his wife and six children, the eldest of whom was only six).[59]

In fact, the ECU looked after the Green family, but it made good press to tell the story of their suffering. The other notable feature of most of the cases was that they simply did not 'put down ritualism,' even in the parishes of the clergy concerned, where curates continued to carry out the ritual for which the incumbent was indirectly imprisoned.

Nigel Yates, however, in a relatively recent study of the period, cautions against the simplistic approach that the ritualists defied the law and won, which he finds in contemporary sources who followed Archbishop Tait's own observations. But he points out that as individuals, those prosecuted did suffer and were mostly not the same again (my italics):

> If one looks in detail at the cases ... then the measure of success was considerable: Ridsdale capitulated; Mackonochie, Edwards, Tooth, Enraght and Green were compelled to resign their benefices; Dale was persuaded to accept another benefice in a remote part of Lincolnshire and removed from the parish he had disrupted; only Cox, through intelligent manipulation of legal loopholes, had managed to retain his benefice whilst failing to make any concessions whatsoever.... If the [PWRA] failed it did not do so because it was badly drafted, or impossible to implement, but because there was an unwillingness to implement it. Some bishops, who had never made any secret of the fact that they disliked the Act, were determined to frustrate its implementation by deliberately vetoing prosecutions. Other bishops simply lost their nerve.... The press did not help. It had campaigned, or much of it had, for the suppression of ritualism. Then, when ritualist clergy went out of their way to become martyrs, the press decided, *in the interests of fairness and justice*, the law should not be allowed to pursue its course. It was indeed the case that it was panic that had led to the introduction of the [PWRA] but equally it was panic about its consequences that ultimately led to its being viewed as inoperable.[60]

I note within Yates's summary the line about the perceived objectives of the press as revealing. In the period leading up to the PWRA, the Ritualist clergy were viewed as the enemies of fairness and justice because they were perceived as leading the Church of England towards Rome, and it remained a tenet of Englishness in the mid-nineteenth century that Rome stood for opposition to fairness, justice and freedom. Through their martyrdom, the ritualist clergy won their freedom, but in the process became subtly dissociated from the adherence to Rome which nonetheless continued to inspire them.

Further developments in Ritualist amateur canonism

As noted above in the case of Ridsdale, part of the interest of the period is the way the ritualists, debating together in fora such as the SSC, developed their own legal and canonical theories, which for them proved the illegitimacy of the prosecutions against them and the rightness, even the obligation, of their own conduct. Rodes notes "a variety of sermons, pamphlets, and open letters"[61] setting out the overall position that the ecclesiastical courts in the late nineteenth century could not be regarded as legitimate sources of authority, since they were both established by a secularised state, and crucially, subordinate to the appellate jurisdiction of the Privy Council. As also observed above, this viewpoint was given added strength by the appointment of Lord Penzance and the way in which the PWRA was enacted.

Rodes sets out the competing argument (which he attributes especially to Lewis Dibdin) that as a matter of history, the Church has never had any juridical form other than that given by the state (Rodes refers to English history, but in reality this inconvenient fact goes back to Constantine) and that it is an illusion to see the Reformation in England as the willing act of the Church, instead being the decisive taking of authority by the State.[62] The Anglo-Catholics anticipated this response, and the inconvenient reality that even with their ritual, the 1662 Book of Common Prayer was not quite what they believed in, with a different and ingenious theory of church authority. In doing so, it is vital to perceive the particular dilemma of Anglo-Catholics (then, and to some degree, now) of needing to defend most of the practices of the Roman Catholic Church whilst also defending their own continuing adherence to the Church of England rather than converting.

The key figure was Edmund Wood, curate and then vicar of St Clement's, Cambridge, who published *The Regal Power of the Church* in 1888[63] and became Master of the SSC in 1902.[64] *Regal Power* picks up the tradition of Wilberforce and Chambers in asserting boldly the authority of the Church, as "the representative of Christ on earth, his vice-gerent and instrument in regard to the spiritual and moral government of mankind,'[65] and convinced that 'the canon law itself is a very holy thing."[66] The greater part of the work, however, is an exposition of a purely Catholic conception of canonical authority, with scarcely a sign that the author is a priest of the Church of England. Wood does follow the deceptive tendency of many Anglo-Catholic writers with his assertion that "[i]t is only in a limited sense that ecclesiastical jurisdiction is coercive. The only sanctions it possesses are spiritual ones, the only penalties it can inflict are spiritual."[67] This is a fair retort when his friends had been sent to gaol for their ritualism, but it is poor theology. Punishment in spiritual matters, deeply important to the one punished and held to be of eternal significance, is every bit as coercive as whips and chains for a Christian.

The ingenuity of Wood's position is hinted at in one place where he states "in the absence of properly constituted and properly acting diocesan synods, the provincial synod cannot command obedience to its decrees."[68] The meaning of this cryptic assertion is revealed in Alan Wilson's 1988 study of the Church Crisis of 1898–1904, when Wood was a leading Anglo-Catholic involved in fierce public conflict with the Church Association led by John Kensit to disrupt services in London, with the longsuffering Bishop Mandell Creighton, who felt that "liberty is a tender plant, and needs jealous watching"[69] trying to keep the peace. Wilson explains how Wood taught his fellow Anglo-Catholics that they were defending 'œcumenical custom,' drawing particular attention to his addressing a meeting in Holborn Town Hall on 13 January 1899.[70] This theory accepts as true the contention made above by Rodes and Dibdin that the Reformation in England had indeed been carried out basically by State authority, through Parliament.

Wood's ingenuity, however, was to argue that this meant that because throughout the Reformation, Convocation had been deprived of its proper authority as the 'provincial synod' referred to, all the liturgical changes of the Reformation had been done without authority. Therefore, he was able to claim, the liturgical and canonical situation in place before the Reformation was still the right and valid source of authority for the English Church, and the English clergy could and indeed should regard themselves as obliged to follow all pre-Reformation custom and ceremony. This, of course, also carried the helpful corollary that no English court at all could be accepted capable of judging any ecclesiastical case, unless and until the Church of England should gain complete independence from the State to determine its own affairs.

This argument has had considerable appeal to Anglo-Catholics throughout the twentieth century. It leaves the question of Papal jurisdiction hanging awkwardly, but the usual response is to say that the Papacy has been itself fatally compromised by the adoption of the doctrine of Infallibility. It also meant that even the most advanced Anglo-Catholics hesitated to support the introduction of Benediction, which was generally agreed to be a post-Reformation development, and this affected two later cases recounted below. The whole thing is less implausible if one remembers that, at least until recently, the Orthodox churches held the sequence of Ecumenical Councils closed for the simple reason that they cannot be legitimately convened except by an Emperor in Constantinople, inconveniently now unavailable.

Wood's argument, framed to defend extreme ritualism when reliance on the Ornaments Rubric was wearing thin, played a role in reintroducing to the Church of England the idea that she ought to have her own mechanism for defining her own laws, which could then be enforced upon her members. This viewpoint supported both the ongoing revival of the Convocations, and the eventual arrival of the Church Assembly as we shall see below. *Regal Power* was republished in 1948 by Eric Kemp, who regarded Wood as "one of the really learned Anglican canonists of recent years."[71] Kemp noted that Wood was "inspired by an authoritarianism theologically unacceptable to us"[72] but was able to conclude, "[w]e do not wish to rebuild the medieval system, but we must be careful that in avoiding authoritarianism we do not slip into anarchy both in faith and morals."[73] As we see below, Kemp played a leading role in attempting this balance in the twentieth century Church of England, with distinctly debatable results. The essence of Wood's argument, mediated by Kemp among others, also formed a key plank of Anglo-Catholic opposition to women's ordination at the end of the twentieth century.

The Lincoln Judgment

The story of the case brought in 1888 against Bishop Edward King of Lincoln, resulting in the 1890 'Lincoln Judgment,' is frequently depicted as the final act in the Ritualist story. It was not, as seen below, the last case against the clergy for their ritual, but occurring only a few years after the main PWRA cases it has tended to be recounted with them. It is more helpful to see it as a decisive example of the response to the main Ritualist cases above, in which those in authority in the Church were increasingly looking to find means to prevent liturgical questions being settled in court. It is also a legal one-off as a trial of a bishop, and it was precisely that which enabled it to take a different course from the others.

Historians of the period agree that the Church Association had reached a point of frustration with the vetoing of their cases against clergy by bishops, and so concluded that the response was to try to prosecute a bishop. Edward King was both the best and the worst choice; he was the first bishop to follow the ritual of ritualist parishes he visited, and the first to wear a mitre or vestments since the Reformation, and so a good candidate to accuse. But he was also revered as a gentle and saintly man, at least in the terms of his era. The prosecution was led from within his diocese by a Cleethorpes solicitor, Ernest de Lacy Reed, who was alleged to have obtained the witnesses to King's ritualism (when visiting the Lincoln church of St-Peter-at-Gowts) by bribery.[74]

When the case came to Archbishop Benson, a scholar by temperament sympathetic to King, he is reported to have been uncertain whether he had the right to try the case himself, no such case having arisen since 1698.[75] He passed the case to the Judicial Committee, which confirmed that he did have the right to try it, and Benson then took it as an opportunity to make a decisive intervention in the Ritualist saga. Benson therefore sat at Lambeth, supported by four other bishops as assessors, but himself judging, and referring to himself as 'the Court.' This is said to have drawn the repeated criticism from one of the assessors, Stubbs of Oxford, that "it is not a court. It is an archbishop sitting in his library,"[76] although this may simply have been another of Stubbs's many witticisms.[77] From the Lambeth viewpoint, though, this was the same library in which Lord Penzance had also sat, even if with unfortunate consequences, in the case of Tooth and others.

Benson's judgment found King innocent of the majority of the charges, disapproving only the sign of the cross, the mixing of the chalice during the service, and the concealment of the manual acts by the eastward position (although not the eastward position itself). King was not present, but his counsel, Walter Phillimore (son of Sir Robert) telegraphed him, detailing (in Latin) the above points, but "*omnia altera pro te.*"[78] The judgment was widely felt to have drawn a line under the Ritualist controversy, and King himself accepted the judgment with thanks. Certainly, it is true that no further prosecutions were brought under the PWRA, although it remained on the statute books until 1963. "Most High Churchmen, and those within the Church of England who wanted peace at any price over matters of ritual, welcomed the Lincoln judgment. Some Evangelicals, including Bishop Ryle of Liverpool, were in despair."[79]

It can be noted that Benson "took pleasure in continually correcting and lecturing the lawyers"[80] and Rodes examines carefully his in-depth historical approach to the issues at question, noting how these contrast with the much briefer analysis by Lord Halsbury in his judgment of the subsequent unsuccessful appeal to the Judicial Committee. Benson developed lines of reasoning as to why certain ceremonies (Rodes looks at the mixed chalice at length) could be justified, whilst Halsbury mostly dismissed the history as inconclusive and therefore irrelevant. Over lighted candles the contrast was very clear

> [T]he archbishop devoted fifteen pages of opinion and thirteen of appendix to justifying [use of lit candles] on historical and doctrinal grounds. Halsbury said merely that if the candles were lighted before the service started they were not an illegal ceremony because they were not a ceremony at all, and that if they were an illegal ornament the bishop was not responsible for them because it was not his church.[81]

What can be seen in the contrast, though, are the two different approaches to judgment in ecclesiastical causes seen throughout this study. Archbishop Benson embodied the approach rooted in the ancient *jus commune,* taken at times by Sir Robert Phillimore and in *re. St Stephen's, Walbrook* by Eric Kemp, that the purpose of a church court is to examine the tradition of faith and practice and judge whether or not the controversial practice before it accords with that *sensus fidelium* embodied in law and canon. Halsbury spoke for the narrow and technical tradition of judgment based with precision upon text and fair procedure, which has been dominant in the formation of the undisciplined and broad Church of England.

Indiscipline after King – late exceptions to the veto

After King, many accounts suggest that all cases against clergy were vetoed, and the attempts to restrain ritual by law ceased. This was not in fact the case but may perhaps be viewed as an example of the historical reality that periods of activity characteristic to one era tend not to begin and end neatly at the climactic dates but overlap messily. Chapter 6 will note how the Church Crisis of 1898–1904 displayed the clear desire of the hierarchy to avoid the use of prosecution, and contributed to the diversion of the energy of controversy into different areas for most of the twentieth century.

It is no accident that the last cases of deprivations that did occur involve clergy whose enthusiasm for ritual led them beyond the standards of 'œcumenical custom,' i.e. the real or supposed practices of the pre-Reformation church in England, as defended by Wood, and specifically to introduce to their parishes the ceremony of Benediction, because that step deprived them of the financial support of the ECU and the moral support of many of their peers. However, the first of these cases illustrates yet again the difficulties of a successful prosecution where those eager to put down ritual had failed to do their homework.

Oliver Henly, vicar of St Mary's, Wolverton, in the diocese of Oxford, discomfited the Bishop of Reading on a visit to his church for a funeral in December 1905 by instructing him to genuflect before the reserved sacrament.[82] In subsequent correspondence with Paget, the Bishop of Oxford, Henly confirmed that the sacrament had been reserved since the previous Easter, and in response to the experience of his visitor stated "the choir was trained to genuflect before it, the only person occupying a position in the choir who on that occasion neglected this act of reverence was the Bishop of Reading himself."[83] In ongoing correspondence Henly refused utterly to give up reservation, and a suit was brought under the CDA 1840 to the Court of Arches, Henly refusing to appear.

In judgment, however, Sir Lewis Dibdin felt constrained by the weakness of the case. He was content at length to explore the history of reservation in the Church of England and conclude that it was unlawful. However, the specific charges laid were that Henly had failed to consume the consecrated elements as required by rubric on 27 December 1905 (the day of the Bishop of Reading's visit) and on Sundays following, and had kept the sacrament reserved between certain specified dates. But as the prosecution had failed to obtain any independent witnesses to the alleged reservation, not even summoning the churchwardens, but relied on Henly's own letters, Dibdin was able to note that "it is perfectly consistent with his letters that during part or even the whole of the period ... he for some reason suspended the practice."[84] In the absence of evidence, the only charge which Dibdin would accept was that the sacrament was indeed illegally reserved on the day the Bishop of Reading had visited, but for this single offence he simply issued Henly with a monition not to reserve it in future.

Henly now had an opportunity to amend his practice, but characteristically he did not do so. Presumably in this knowledge the Archdeacon of Buckingham and the bishop's chaplain attended Wolverton church on 10 January 1909, in order to obtain reliable evidence of his enormities. They were entirely successful, as shown by the following description given in Dibdin's judgment, revealing the diocesan spies picking up every detail of suspect Popery:

> A tabernacle was still placed above the altar, with a lamp burning before it, just as it had been before the former proceedings were begun. The defendant preached a sermon in which he made very grave statements as to the change effected, as he said, by "transubstantiation," in consequence of which the bread and wine after consecration were no longer bread and wine, but the body and blood of Christ, and so proper objects of worship wherever present. Both witnesses are certain that the word "transubstantiation" was used, but in other respects do not profess to quote the defendant's exact words, which, it would seem, were not read from a manuscript, but spoken. [After] ordinary evening service....The defendant ... reappeared vested in a cope and attended by two acolytes and a thurifer. He advanced to the altar, on and around which many lights had been placed, and, standing before it, opened the tabernacle and appeared to transfer something from it to a vessel with glass sides, called a monstrance. He then placed the monstrance on top of the tabernacle, so that it was in the full view of the congregation (who were now kneeling), and the witnesses clearly saw through the glass sides of the monstrance a round white object, which they supposed to be a wafer.[85]

The judgment then noted the texts of the service, all suspect 'translations' from Roman sources, summing up in a telling sentence and continuing:

> The only part of the service to be found in the Prayer Book was the collect for the Annunciation. When these prayers were ended, a large gold-coloured cloth or humeral was placed over the shoulders and arms of the defendant, still kneeling before the altar. Thus vested, he rose, and taking the monstrance into both his hands, turned and held it up, facing the people. Next, lowering it, he presented it first toward the south, then towards the north, and finally, turning to the altar, placed the monstrance thereon. The defendant was seen to open the tabernacle, and the witnesses inferred from his movements that he took the wafer out from the monstrance and replaced it in the tabernacle, which, when he moved away, was seen to be closed. The defendant then retired and the congregation dispersed."[86]

It comes as something of a relief after such forensic description when Dibdin cuts to the chase and admits that this event was a service of Benediction, and that this is a step on from Henly's illegal reservation, for "he is now employing the reserved sacrament for quite other purposes – purposes not only illegal, but also alien to the ritual and subversive to the teachings of the Church of England."[87]

The report of the service, combined with the existence of the previous monition and Henly's persistent refusal, resulted in a complete change in Dibdin's tone from the weary grumbling at the poor evidence in 1907. Finding in the defendant "the absence of any withdrawal from the attitude of self-will and obstinate contumacy"[88] he agreed with the promoters that "the incorrigible persistence of the delinquent"[89] demanded that he be deprived from his benefice. The case was adjourned for a fortnight to give Henly a final chance of repentance, and then in the absence of this, sentence was duly and solemnly passed, citing still the ancient expression that he had been cited to answer "certain articles heads positions or interrogatories touching and concerning his *soul's health* and the lawful correction and *reformation of his manners* and excesses" (my italics).[90]

Rodes believed in 1991 that Henly had the distinction of being "the last clergyman to be prosecuted for his liturgical practices"[91] but I have had the satisfaction of identifying at least one, possibly two, later cases. Sandys Wason's life appears to have been full of character and eccentricity as he pursued his extreme Anglo-Catholicism.[92] His interest for our purposes is his incumbency at Cury with Gunwalloe from 1905, in the diocese of Truro. Brown's centenary history of the diocese summarises "he introduced a great deal of purely Latin ceremony and services, adorning his church with tawdry furnishings."[93] Gunwalloe church is "virtually on the beach,"[94] and it was perhaps this which prompted Wason to the imaginative idea of casting a wreath into the sea on All Souls' Day, in memory of those lost at sea. A photo in Brown shows the scene, with Wason standing on a rock in cope and biretta attended by his servers[95] - it could be taken for a scene from Brittany or indeed Sicily, where anthropologists might speculate that it represented the perpetuation of pagan sacrifices to Neptune.

The response of Bishop Stubbs in 1910 was to place Wason "under discipline"[96] an ambiguous concept we shall see again, but which in his case meant he was not supposed to visit other parishes or attend synods, and the Bishop would not visit the parish. Perhaps more significant, as Yelton records from the memoirs of the visiting Compton Mackenzie, is that most of the congregation had been driven away. This meant that when J. A. Kensit discovered about Wason's activity in about 1916, he had little local support to draw on. Once again it was benediction, introduced by Wason in 1918, which brought matters to a head. Wisely following the pattern of the successful prosecution of Henly, Bishop Burrows of Truro sent his archdeacon to witness the offence for himself before bringing an action under the CDA 1840. Both because Wason refused to appear and because the ECU refused to provide any defence for benediction, he was duly deprived at Truro on 27 May 1919.[97] A mob of local farmers, agitated by Kensit, removed his furnishings from the church and then (in a curious echo of the case of Dr Free) hounded him from his vicarage.[98]

Wason is probably therefore the last parson in England to have been deprived for ritual offences, although Yelton records that "at about the same time Revd Reginald Wynter of Taunton was also ejected"[99] so he may have been later. There is no clear account of his case, but another Anglo-Catholic history states that he "persisted in using the service of benediction when instructed not to do so."[100] This last gasp of ritual prosecution did however bring reaction. "The Cury controversy was widely discussed and Burrows was strongly criticised over several months for his supposedly harsh action and its indefensible outcome."[101] A deputation from the Federation of Catholic Priests, led by Darwell Stone and H. P. Bull, visited Archbishop Davidson to protest at what they perceived as a resumption of legal persecution, which could usher in a new period of strife. Davidson managed to combine sympathy at the difficult state of the law with defence of episcopal authority, but his acknowledgement that "[a]t no time have we had Bishops less willing to go to the Courts than now"[102] suggests that the protest contributed to Wason and Wynter being as far as can be ascertained the true and final coda to the era of Ritualist Martyrdom. The Public Worship Regulation Act and the others under which cases were brought, however remained on the statue book until repealed with the passage of the Ecclesiastical Jurisdiction Measure 1963.

Notes

1 *Royal Commission on Ecclesiastical Discipline* (HMSO 1906) both quotes from the Conclusion.
2 John Shelton Reed, *Glorious Battle. The Cultural Politics of Victorian Anglo-Catholicism* (Tufton Books 1998).
3 e.g. Dominic Janes, *The Victorian Persecution: Anglo-Catholics & Martyrdom* (Anglo-Catholic History Society 2010).
4 Charlotte Smith, "The Quest for an Authoritative Court of Final Appeal in Ecclesiastical Causes: A Study of the Difficulties, c.1830–76," *The Journal of Legal History*, 32.2 (2011) 205.

5 Eric Waldram Kemp, *Counsel and Consent* (SPCK 1960) 182–5.
6 See Owen Chadwick, *The Victorian Church. Part II 1860–1901* 3rd ed. (SCM Press 1972) large parts of section VI; James Bentley, *Ritualism and Politics in Victorian Britain: The attempt to legislate for belief* (OUP 1978); Nigel Yates, *Anglican Ritualism in Victorian Britain 1830–1910* (OUP 1999), Ch. 5.
7 For example, *Liddell v Westerton (1857), Liddell v Beal (1860), Boyd v Phillpotts (1874), Durst v Masters (1876), St Augustine Faculty Case (1877), St Ethelburga Faculty Case (1878).*
8 Dominic Janes, *The Victorian Persecution: Anglo-Catholics & Martyrdom* (Anglo-Catholic History Society 2010) 7.
9 Thomas K McCart, *The Matter and Manner of Praise. The Controversial Evolution of Hymnody in the Church of England 1760–1820.* Drew Studies in Liturgy Series, No. 5. (The Scarecrow Press 1998) 78–80.
10 Ibid., 99.
11 Ibid., 104–5.
12 Owen Chadwick, *The Victorian Church. Part 1 1829–1859* 3rd ed. (SCM Press 1971) 218–21.
13 Bernard Palmer, *Reverend Rebels, Five Victorian Clerics and their Fight Against Authority* (Darton, Longman & Todd 1993) 77–80.
14 Ibid., 66.
15 *Martin v Mackonochie (1)* [1868] 5 Moo N.S. 506.
16 Palmer, *Rebels*, 93, citing G. W. E. Russell, *St Alban the Martyr: A History of Fifty Years* (George Allen 1913).
17 Charlotte Smith, "*Martin v Mackonochie/Mackonochie v Penzance*: A Crisis of Character and Identity in the Court of Arches?" *The Journal of Legal History*, 24:3 (2003) 37.
18 Palmer, *Rebels*, 9.
19 *Hebert v Purchas* [1871], L.R.3 P.C. 606–25.
20 *Hebert* 626–8.
21 *Hebert* 639–40.
22 *Hebert* 651.
23 Palmer, *Rebels*, 11.
24 Bentley, *Ritualism*, 46.
25 Ibid., 75.
26 Robert E. Rodes Jr., *Law and Modernisation in the Church of England* (Notre Dame 1991) 256.
27 John Shelton Reed, *Glorious Battle. The Cultural Politics of Victorian Anglo-Catholicism* (Tufton Books 1998) 242.
28 Bentley, *Ritualism*, 98.
29 See Charlotte Smith, "*Ridsdale v Clifton*: Representations of the Judicial Committee of the Privy Council in Ecclesiastical Appeals." (2008) King's Law Journal 19.3 551–74.
30 Bernard Palmer, *Gadfly for God* (Hodder & Stoughton 1991) 56.
31 Letter of Tait to Ridsdale, 30/05/1877, quoted in Will Adam, *Legal Flexibility and the Mission of the Church* (Ashgate 2011) 105–6.
32 Yates, *Ritualism*, 253.
33 Reed, *Battle*, 106.
34 Bentley, *Ritualism*, 81.
35 Rodes, *Modernisation*, 257.
36 Smith, *Martin v Mackonochie*, 53.
37 Smith, *Martin v Mackonochie*, 53
38 Palmer, *Rebels*, 120–5.
39 Yates, *Ritualism*, 254.
40 Palmer, *Rebels*, 126–9.

41 Ibid., 138.
42 Rodes, *Modernisation*, 257.
43 Bentley, *Ritualism*, 102.
44 Ibid., 103.
45 Rodes, *Modernisation*, 302.
46 Quoted in Reed, *Battle*, 243.
47 Bentley, *Ritualism*, 103.
48 *Julius v Bishop of Oxford* [1880] H.L.(E.) 214–16.
49 Bentley, *Ritualism,* 110.
50 Rodes, *Modernisation*, 303.
51 Yates, *Ritualism*, 262–7.
52 Palmer, *Gadfly*, 59.
53 Adam, *Legal Flexibility*, 107.
54 In conversation with the author, 9 November 2017.
55 Yates, *Ritualism*, 271–2.
56 Rodes, *Modernisation*, 302–3.
57 Yates, *Ritualism*, 272–3.
58 Rodes, *Modernisation*, 305–6.
59 Bentley, *Ritualism*, 112.
60 Yates, *Ritualism*, 275–6.
61 Rodes, *Modernisation*, 294.
62 Ibid., 295–6.
63 E. G. Wood, *The Regal Power of the Church. The Fundamentals of Canon Law by the late Canon E. G. Wood. Preface by the Rev E. W, Kemp, Fellow of Exeter College Oxford* (Dacre Press 1948).
64 Wilson, Alan, *The authority of church and party among London Anglo-Catholics, 1880–1914, with special reference to the Church Crisis, 1898–1904* (unpublished Oxford DPhil thesis, 1988) 112.
65 Wood, *Regal Power*, 1.
66 Ibid., 8.
67 Ibid., 48.
68 Ibid., 53.
69 Mandell Creighton, *Persecution and Tolerance* (Longmans, Green & Co 1895) 140.
70 Wilson, *Authority*, 78.
71 Wood, *Regal Power*, preface by Kemp, vi.
72 Ibid., vi.
73 Ibid., vii.
74 Bentley, *Ritualism,* 118.
75 Rodes, *Modernisation*, 307.
76 Ibid., 308.
77 See P. H. Ditchfield, *The Old-Time Parson* (Methuen & Co 1908) 76–80.
78 Bentley, *Ritualism,* 119.
79 Yates, *Ritualism*, 274.
80 Bentley, *Ritualism,* 120.
81 Rodes, *Modernisation*, 311.
82 *Bishop of Oxford v Henly*, [1907] P 92.
83 Letter of Henly to the Bishop of Oxford, 02/01/1906, quoted at [1907] P 102.
84 *Henly* [1907] 104.
85 *Bishop of Oxford v Henly* [1909] P 327.
86 *Henly* [1909] 328.
87 *Henly* [1909] 328.
88 *Henly* [1909] 329.
89 *Henly* [1909] 329.
90 *Henly* [1909] 331.

91 Rodes, *Modernisation,* 312.
92 Michael Yelton, *Anglican Papalism* (Canterbury Press 2005) 169–70.
93 H. Miles Brown, *A Century for Cornwall* (Oscar Blackford Ltd 1976) 66.
94 Yelton, *Papalism,* 172.
95 Brown, *Cornwall,* Plate 4.
96 Ibid., 67.
97 Ibid., 80.
98 Yelton, *Papalism,* 172–3.
99 Ibid., 172.
100 John Gunstone, *Lift High the Cross. Anglo-Catholics and the Congress Movement* (Canterbury Press 2010) 87.
101 Brown, *Cornwall,* 80–1.
102 G. K. A. Bell, *Randall Davidson* (OUP 1935) 1026.

5. The yearning to fence the altar

The principles of repulsion

As noted in Chapter 2, the end of the moral discipline of the Church of England over the laity was accepted by most as the inevitable outcome of long decline and the only reasonable response to a society of religious tolerance. However, it was resisted in principle by a small number, often Anglo-Catholics, who regarded the ancient concept of excommunication as a right part of the Church's life and aspired to use it to restore spiritual discipline. What they frequently failed to acknowledge, however, was that in medieval Christendom, excommunication by the institutional Church could realistically be regarded as exclusion from the Church of Christ, and so a powerful tool of correction of sin, however controversial on occasions. Whereas in a pluralist society the effect was simply exclude them from the institutional Church of England, as one denomination among many, in favour of some other religious body or none.

It is necessary to note the terminology carefully. Excommunication in the proper sense could only in the Middle Ages and later occur by due sentence of a court acting on behalf of the bishop; it was never the prerogative of the parish clergy to excommunicate their erring parishioners on their own authority. Although in theory this sanction remained available to the church courts until the Ecclesiastical Jurisdiction Measure 1963 removed all means of imposing it, in practice the end of the defamation jurisdiction in the 1850s had signalled the end of excommunication as an ecclesiastical sentence in England. As noted above, it is possible that had the Ritualist clergy been formally excommunicated for their defiance of the courts rather than imprisoned under *de contumace capiendo* they may have been slightly more respectful of the jurisdiction.

In ecclesiastical controversy there are a few instances where High Church bishops invoked the language of excommunication in a blatantly political sense, summoning up the anathemas of the Middle Ages in a way more theatrical than legal. After losing the Gorham case, Bishop Phillpotts of Exeter declared that he would withhold communion from anyone who attempted to institute Gorham to his parish (by implication including the Archbishop of Canterbury) although oddly not Gorham himself, causing "amusement, indignation and alarm."[1] Similarly, in 1914 when Bishop Percival of Hereford declared his hand for modernism by appointing the liberal academic B. H. Streeter to a canonry, Bishop Frank Weston of Zanzibar responded by posting a solemn excommunication, "couched in the heraldic language of ancient ecclesiastical courts"[2] on the door of his cathedral. Neither of these forms of 'excommunication' can really be considered attempts to keep up the discipline of the Church.

What we are therefore concerned with is the practice of parish clergy refusing to give communion to their own parishioners whom they believe to have sinned in some important way, in an autonomous effort to exercise spiritual discipline over them. Although this is sometimes referred to as 'lesser excommunication'[3] I shall refer to it instead as 'repulsion' from Holy Communion, this being the expression used in the principal court cases. There was some precedent for this in the medieval Canon Law, but Rodes states that he could find no English example.[4] It is a practice in a degree of limbo to this day. The legal framework within which it exists was and remains ambiguous and all the relevant cases determined that the clergyman in question had been wrong to repel. Nonetheless, it remains in theory a possibility, defined in Canon B16, and so a paradigm of the disciplinary state of the Church of England. A survey by Thomas Culver in the 1990s concluded that "some people are still repulsed from the communion table"[5] but that "One can perhaps venture to say that the indication is that the use of Canon B16 is very unusual."[6]

This chapter is of necessity a limited perspective on the subject, derived from the known cases and other sources making reference to repulsion. References to repulsion tend to be passing, for example that in "William Whiston was excluded from receiving the Eucharist in his parish church"[7] or how in his study of Mackonochie, Bernard Palmer comments of Mackonochie's Rector in the slum parish of St George's-in-the-East, that "he attempted to discipline his congregation by refusing to communicate 'notorious evil-livers.'"[8] The eccentric would-be reviver of Benedictinism within the Church of England, Father Ignatius, was known for imposing 'excommunication' (in fact from his communities rather than from communion) and bizarre disciplinary penances.[9]

Although the idea of refusing communion seems to be on the whole more talked about than practiced amongst clergy of strong views (Anglo-Catholic or Evangelical), there will undoubtedly have been churches throughout the period of this study where clergy have, on the strength of personality or their priestly office, refused communion to individuals over moral issues. In his early ministry as Vicar of Barking, a recent biography records that Herbert Hensley Henson "formally excommunicated a husband who beat his wife; imposed a period of penance on a boy who got a housemaid with child; and publicly denounced a thief"[10] but unfortunately without giving the source (probably Henson's own journals) that might define these actions more precisely. In his later ministry as a bishop, Henson's encounters with excommunication involved repudiating the actions of his clergy, as when his journal for 1930 records "There has been a strange episode in Pelton, where the Vicar has excommunicated three of his parishioners. I made him recant, and he resigned."[11] Natural reluctance to challenge the clergy combined with tacit support for them from the wider congregation will have left alleged sinners without redress, and such cases therefore leave little public record.

The particular and undocumented example is divorce, where the presumption of many clergy in the mid-twentieth century was that those divorced and remarried would be refused communion, at least initially. A rare and again uninformative reference in Henson's own memoirs tells us:

> That pragmatical goose, H. B., has repelled from Communion a young woman who has married an "innocent Divorcé". Her husband, a seafaring man, writes to me in justifiable indignation. The whole discipline of the Church on the subject of Marriage and Divorce is chaotic, and the way of reason and equity is hard to trace. In any case, this foolish parson is wrong in not reporting his action to me.[12]

The response of the Convocations of Canterbury and York in 1937–38 (following the Matrimonial Causes Act 1937 which had made divorce more accessible) was to provide a procedure whereby clergy could seek the support of their bishop to *not repel* those divorced and remarried, after due examination of the circumstances.[13] According to Rupert Bursell there is no reported case of a remarried couple seeking redress through the courts for their repulsion from communion,[14] even though such repulsion rested on no good legal basis.

The legal framework for repulsion is ambiguous because it depended on two historic texts, both of which presumed the operation of church courts able to both impose and lift excommunication as necessary, which no longer happens. The rubric before Holy Communion in the Prayer Book (prior to amendment in 1965 to conform to the new Canon B16) ordered the clergy to repel anyone who was 'an open and notorious evil liver' unless they were penitent, and to inform the Ordinary (i.e. in practice the bishop's or other appropriate court) within 14 days in order that they may respond accordingly. However, the Sacrament Act 1547 provided of communion that:

> everie man maye trye and examyn his owne conscience before he shall receive the same, the saide minister shall not without laufull cawse denye the same to any parsone that wool devoutelie and humblie desire it, anny lawe statue orden^{a}nce or custome contrarie thereunto in any wise notwithstanding.[15]

The only 'laufull cawse' available to a parish priest in the absence of a sentence of excommunication from a church court was provided by the Prayer Book rubric, but none ever managed to prove in court that they had identified an 'open and notorious evil liver.'

Minor cases related to nonconformity

Although the cases are very few, the repulsion movement, if it is coherent enough to be described as such, was anticipated by two cases in which Anglican clergy tried and failed to deny the Church's funeral rites to parishioners on the grounds that they were Dissenters. In 1808, John Wickes, the rector of

Warlby cum Belton in Rutland, refused to read the burial service over the infant daughter of Mr and Mrs Swingler. The grounds were that both were Calvinistic Independents, and that as their daughter had not been baptised by him or any other ordained Anglican, he was correct to treat her as 'dying unbaptized' and refuse the Burial service, as the Prayer Book rubric states. Creditably, given what one might imagine to be the pastoral circumstances, the judgment notes:

> a spirit of candour actuates both the parties, they wishing merely to ascertain by a judicial decision what the law is upon the subject, in order to set the question at rest generally, and in order that these particular parties may live in charity and kindness with each other.[16]

The Court of Arches adopted a notably broad view of the rites of the Church, saying "burial is to be refused to no person. This is the law, not only of the English Church, it is the law, not only of Christian Churches; but it seems to be the law of common humanity."[17] The greater part of the decision is simply a careful reiteration of the solid ancient tradition that baptism by lay people (as the Calvinistic Independent minister who had baptised the child was considered) was considered valid, even if irregular and/or undesirable, and so the deceased could not be considered 'unbaptized.' In the process the court also drew the distinct and important conclusion that the effect of the Toleration Act was that dissenters were definitely Christians – something very obvious to us today, but which arguably the whole of the religious divisions of the nineteenth century were about resisting.

Interestingly, whereas the Roman Catholic Church continues to maintain, at least in principle, that church funerals should be refused to "notorious apostates, heretics and schismatics; those who for anti-Christian motives chose their bodies to be cremated; other manifest sinners to whom a funeral [cannot] be granted without public scandal,"[18] Doe's magisterial comparative study of ecclesiastical laws across the churches notes that "Anglican churches have the most rudimentary of principles applicable to funerals" and "[t]here is not a great deal of material on funerals in the Protestant juridical instruments"[19] suggesting that the benign universalism of *Kemp v Wickes* remains widely honoured.

In 1809, however, the Arches could say that it was advantageous that dissenters should be recognised as Christians with valid baptisms, with ministers recognised as lawful by the Toleration Act, and concluding (before passing no sentence on Mr Wickes) with the impressive sentiment:

> the generality of the clergy, it may be presumed, will rejoice that in this last office of Christian charity there is no separation between the Church and their Protestant dissenting brethren. It is by a lenient and liberal interpretation of the laws of disability and exclusion, and not by a captious and vexatious construction and application of them, that the true interests and the true dignity of the Church establishment are best supported.[20]

It took until 1839 before a clergyman of captious and vexatious tendencies could be found to revive the issue: Thomas Escott of Gedney in Lincolnshire, who had refused to bury another infant daughter, this time of two Methodists, Mr and Mrs Cliff. Given the importance of affirming the reality of Dissenting baptism, the Court of Arches was willing to work over all the arguments again, including dismissing the idea that Methodists were *ipso facto* excommunicates, incapable of bringing a suit, as they had been relieved of this penalty by the Toleration Act. Greater historic depth was brought to the judgment (a particular highlight being the overruling of St Cyprian and St Firmilian by the Council of Arles) and the court reaffirmed the seventeenth-century resistance to the Puritan demand that baptism by women be absolutely prohibited.[21] At length Sir Herbert Jenner (later Jenner-Fust) adopted the argument of *Wickes* and Mr Escott was suspended for three months under Canon 68, which prescribes that penalty for any minister who shall "refuse or delay to christen any child ... that is brought to him ... to be christened"[22]. Characteristically, Bishop Phillpotts was displeased, and referred to the case in his 1842 visitation Charge, defending his own belief that excommunication remained a valid response to heresy and blasphemy.[23]

Arguably, these cases were not matters of the discipline of the Church of England, since they involved dissenters. But the very fact that those dissenters sought the ministrations of the Church of England (albeit because this would be normal to enable their children to be buried in the parish churchyard) is a reminder that the boundary of the Church of England is a matter of definition, and this lack of fixity is in itself a contributing factor to the weakness of discipline. The law of burial remained a matter of controversy throughout the nineteenth and early twentieth century, as the Church of England only reluctantly conceded the right of nonconformists to be buried in parish churchyards by their own ministers, notably by the Burial Laws Amendment Act 1880.[24]

A sample flashpoint which did reach court was provided by the suit for libel brought in 1878 by George Drury, Vicar of Akenham, against the *East Anglian Daily Times* for reporting the argument which had taken place when he tried to reprimand Wickham Tozer, a Baptist minister, for taking a service for a Baptist child outside his churchyard gate.[25] As well as alleging the disagreeable language used, the paper had suggested hypocrisy on his part: "this staunch upholder of ecclesiastical law is already under admonition from his own bishop for lawless proceedings in his own church."[26] In other words, Drury was a ritualist, and indeed had also previously hosted Brother Ignatius and his attempted Anglican Benedictine community in his parsonage. The court found for Drury but awarded only token damages to show how needless it thought the proceedings.

A later disciplinary case involving Dissent, but not burial, is *Swayne v Benson*, which was heard before the Court of Arches in 1889. Mr Benson was vicar of the parish of St Werburgh, Hoo, in the diocese of Rochester, and Mrs Swayne was a parishioner who also occasionally attended the local Methodist chapel. It is possible, unrecorded by the court papers, that there was some more personal antagonism between them, but the basic account seems to be that Benson regarded

Mrs Swayne's occasional nonconformity as a breach of Church discipline and resolved to punish her by exclusion from communion.

Benson refused to appear before Lord Penzance in the Court of Arches, unwilling to recognise "the usurped authority of a temporal Court to pass spiritual censures for spiritual offences."[27] However, the court was left in no doubt as to his views, evidenced by production of a letter from him to the *Rochester and Chatham Journal and Mid-Kent Advertiser* of 9 February 1889, as follows:

> It is worse than idle nonsense to pretend that "schism" and its mischievous fruits are something quite invisible, intangible or undefinable. They are as "open and notorious" as the fruits of any fleshly sin – "gross as a mountain, open, palpable." And nothing will induce me, with my eyes open, to give the Holy Communion to one who expresses no sorrow for these sins, and gives no promise of abandoning them (punctuation as original)[28]

The Bishop of Rochester attempted to suspend Benson, but he refused to relinquish his post, writing to the nominated locum, Frederick LeLievre, with the perverse argument that he regarded his institution (as incumbent) by the bishop as if from God, and so unable to be revoked. Given his unwillingness to appear, however, even such attempts to summon the spirit of the Medes and Persians were not effective with Lord Penzance, who suspended him for a year.

Amateur canonism on excommunication

In the last chapter we noted the 'amateur canonism' of Wood attempting to provide a legal justification for ritualism. Before considering the two most important repulsion cases, note some Anglo-Catholic thoughts on the concept of discipline by excommunication, representing an equivalent for repulsion. J. C. Chambers in an 1873 essay on *Decay of Discipline* [29] sets out the argument to be used later by Figgis that the Church, like any club, has an inherent right to police the boundaries of her own membership.[30] Like Robert Wilberforce, Chambers affects that occasional capitalisation (JESUS CHRIST and similar) which suggests the desire to defend holy things from the profanities of the age.

Also like Wilberforce, he begins from the penitential discipline of the Early Church, and observes of the fourfold gradation of penitents by St Basil, with no realism whatsoever about life in the 1870s, "what a wonderful care and oversight does this give in regard to lapsed Christians!"[31] He recognises his own era in another sense, bemoaning the feeble attempts to discipline the Ritualists by bishops "more anxious about the quantity than the quality of Churchmen."[32] He proposes the restoration of a Church with clear boundaries defined by a communicant roll with discipline and excommunication of offenders – seemingly quite unaware of the last unhappy phase of legal discipline by the white sheet system only a generation before.

Excommunication is necessary because "in quarters where the more respectable classes live, the mercantile swindler and unexpected drunkard or debauchee may think it well to keep up his character by occasional communicating."[33] The only answer to "the tide of vice and immorality"[34] is for priests to ensure that "every drunkard, every adulterer, every fornicator, every miser, every railer, every extortioner within their parishes is to be brought under discipline."[35] We hear again the voice of the Tory campaigner of the 1710s or the admirer of Bishop Wilson, yearning for a sort of Catholic Puritanism, with power to enforce godliness upon a world gone to the bad. Chambers's sentiments can be found echoed, albeit often quite faintly, throughout Anglo-Catholic writings, even if, like the High Churchmen under Charles II, they dissemble against the rather unattractive suggestion that they yearn to persecute someone.

Jenkins v Cook – the case of the Bristolian devil-denier

This case, although opening up both issues of high metaphysics (the existence of the Devil) and fundamental ecclesiology (the limits of communion) might also be called, more parochially, the Vyvyan Terrace Case, for Mr Jenkins lived at No. 3, and Mr Cook at No. 19, of that respectable Bristol street.[36] The case, as explained clearly by Duncan Henderson[37] contained the classic elements of a parish dispute ending in good fees for ecclesiastical lawyers: an eccentric parishioner, an opinionated vicar, and a bishop reluctant to give clear guidance which might have put an end to the row.

The parishioner was Mr Henry Jenkins, whose spiritual life had moved with the spirit of *Essays and Reviews* towards a more figurative and optimistic interpretation of Scripture, rejecting of the traditional doctrines of eternal punishment of the wicked, and the identity of Satan as a personification of evil. In order to help him exercise his role as Victorian paterfamilias, he had published for domestic use *Selections from the Old and New Testaments* in 1865 (hereafter '*Selections*'), a text of the Authorised Version from which he had removed all the parts with which he disagreed, mostly because they either suggested eternal punishment or the existence of the devil or evil spirits. The Old Testament came in for heavier editing, but he was not averse to omitting even words ascribed to Jesus himself from the New.[38]

Flavel Cook was the new vicar of Jenkins's parish of Christ Church Clifton, who arrived in 1872, and received a copy of *Selections* among probably other unwanted gifts from his new parish but did not look at it. If he had, he would have realised earlier that among his parishioners was one who did not share his firm belief in the eternal punishment of the wicked, and he was only alerted after preaching on the subject. This prompted a letter from Jenkins on the 6 July 1874 in order that he might "protest most emphatically against the irreligious tendency of your sermon last night."[39] Somehow the theological heart of the dispute is captured by the fact that Jenkins, who was the one who did *not* believe the traditional Christian doctrine of Hell, felt that Cook, who did, was acting against right religion. As in almost all the cases in this study, both sides believed they were the true Christians.

An unsatisfactory pastoral visit down Vyvyan Terrace (recalled in evidence by Mrs Jenkins)[40] and a series of letters enabled Mr Jenkins and Mr Cook to reach a fairly quick understanding of each other's conflicting positions. Mr Jenkins did not believe in the devil or eternal punishment but claimed his right to not do so within the breadth of opinion available to members of the Church of England, and to remain as he had been for some years a communicant parishioner at Christ Church (including in Cook's time until that point). Mr Cook regarded Mr Jenkins as having aligned himself with such "perversions and denials"[41] of Scripture that could not be allowed to claim the right to receive communion. The argument is summed up in the remarkable reported line of Cook to Mrs Jenkins "Let him tell me that he believes in the devil and I will give him the Sacrament."[42] However, Jenkins would not, and so Cook, through his curate Mr Thomas, reached the point of directly refusing communion to him.

Both wrote to the Bishop of Gloucester and Bristol, Charles Ellicott, who responded to each separately. He cautioned Cook that his intention to repel Jenkins was probably not supported in law (and unwisely told Jenkins this also) but seems to have struggled to understand exactly what Jenkins's views were, and so whether or not he should be repelled. Eventually the Bishop saw Cook in person on 2 October 1874, and the content of their meeting was embarrassingly contested in court. The Bishop claimed he could not remember what was said, but Cook produced a pencil-written note given him by the Bishop on that day setting out his (Cook's) position clearly, and worst of all, a subsequent letter from Ellicott to Cook telling him that "any part I may have had in drawing up the letter which you wrote to Mr. Jenkins, or even any approval of it, should carefully be suppressed."[43]

After being again refused communion on 4 October Jenkins made a formal complaint to the Bishop, who instituted the required Commission of Enquiry under the CDA 1840, with the result that the case came before the Court of Arches under Sir Robert Phillimore in June–July 1875.[44] Two independent lines of defence for Cook were opened up by his counsel: he had sought and gained the advice of his ordinary (even if his ordinary was reluctant to admit the fact), as required by the rubric, and the views of Mr Jenkins made him an undoubted evil liver because he denied basic doctrines of the Christian faith. Counsel for the promoter sought to draw the distinction between doctrinal speculation and the implied *moral* weight of the expression 'notorious and open evil liver.'[45]

Phillimore found entirely for Cook and accepted both lines of his defence. He was clearly not very impressed with the Bishop, noting how he "in his anxiety to make peace, wavered somewhat … accordingly as he addressed the defendant or the promoter"[46] and wished that the case had been heard at first instance in the Consistory Court of the diocese and not had to come to the Arches. But, in the end, he could say that if the Bishop "did not, as I think he did, actually authorize he action of the defendant, he at least did not forbid it."[47] So Cook had consulted his ordinary and obeyed him, and was innocent, and the case could have rested there.

Fortunately for historians of the disciplinary jurisdiction, Phillimore was unable to resist an extensive foray into the doctrinal question, to state just how and why, in his view, Mr Jenkins was an evil liver, because he could be classified (quoting the rubric of the Prayer Book) as among the "hinderers and slanderers of God's word."[48] More than that, Phillimore gives his view that the law of the Church clearly required an exercise of sacramental discipline by the combined system of parish clergy, bishops and their courts, for it

> placed the exercise of the discretion, according to the principles of ecclesiastical law, under the control and supervision of the ordinary, and upon him it cast the double duty, first, of advising the clergyman, and, secondly, if he agreed with his decision, of taking proceedings in Court pro salute animæ against the parishioner, in order that he might be brought into a state of penitence qualifying him for the reception of the sacrament, from which in his present condition he had been rightly repelled. The notion that a criminous layman as well as a criminous clerk is subject to ecclesiastical discipline has fallen into such comparative desuetude that this statement of the law may create surprise, but it is the law of the land.[49]

Within appropriate limits, Phillimore clearly believed that there was still such a thing as the criminal jurisdiction of the Church over the laity.

In order to cope with the defence that Jenkins had only adopted the same freedom as Wilson (in *Fendall v Wilson*, cf. Ch.3 above) in doubting the existence of Hell, he drew the distinction between Wilson's gentle aspiration that universal salvation might be possible and Jenkins's much more absolute denial of the very existence of the devil and Hell. It was then easy for him to compile references to the devil in Scripture and the Prayer Book to demonstrate that such belief was an indisputable part of the faith of the Church of England. But as Henderson notes, Phillimore exercised remarkable freedom in drawing on his theological bookshelf, without much legal precision, citing various theologians whose authority could only be open to question.[50]

Before moving on to Jenkins's appeal to the Privy Council, it is worth noting that even the *Church Times*, whilst willing to admire "Mr Cook's zeal in 'fencing the table'"[51], was both doubtful about whether Phillimore's judgment would stand, and also somewhat uncertain as to whether faith in the Devil was all that certain a matter, compared to "Baptismal Regeneration, Priestly Absolution and the Real Presence" all of whose "depravers … not only enjoy impunity, but claim monopoly within the Church of England."[52] It appears Mr Cook, appointed to Christ Church, Clifton by the evangelical Simeon's Trustees,[53] was not sufficiently Catholic to enjoy much sympathy at the *Church Times*.

The Judicial Committee of the Privy Council, including for one of the last times the two Archbishops[54] and Phillimore's successor as Dean of the Arches, Lord Penzance, met in January 1876 and as predicted by the *Church Times*, reversed Phillimore's judgment. Significantly, their Lordships began by reference to the Sacrament Act 1547 which defines in statute the right of the laity to receive communion in their parish churches unless there is lawful reason why not. This is not referred to at all by the Arches judgment; it is possible that it simply did not occur to Phillimore to refer to it, but once this key plank of Reformation Protestantism was manifest, it is clear how much more of a challenge it would be to reassert any sort of clerical power to restrict the communicant rights of the laity.

Having by reference to the 1547 Act firmly placed the burden of proof onto Cook as defendant to prove he had lawful cause to repel Jenkins, the Judicial Committee offered a disclaimer not unlike that in *Fendall v Wilson*, that the decision they were about to make to refute Cook and Phillimore's condemnation of Jenkins did not amount to any sort of general endorsement of his heterodox views, because that was not what they were being asked. They asserted, not very convincingly in the light of all the quoted letters and Mrs Jenkins's statements, that "there is not before them any evidence that the Appellant entertains the doctrines attributed to him by the Dean of Arches"[55] before going on to reassure their readers that "they do not mean to decide that those doctrines are otherwise than inconsistent with the formularies of the Church of England."[56] To summarise: we do not endorse Mr Jenkins's questionable views, but we do not think they justify his exclusion from his right to receive communion in his parish church.

Instead, their Lordships returned to the relevant rubric, which required the very strong test that to be refused communion Mr Jenkins had to be not only an evil liver, but an *open and notorious* evil liver, and Canon 27, which required that he be not only a depraver of the Book of Common Prayer, but a *common and notorious* depraver thereof. The core of Jenkins's implied sin was his book *Selections*, with its suspicious editing of the Bible to suit his purported theology. However, the Judicial Committee were able to reason:

> It is assumed that all parts of the Holy Bible not printed in the "Selections" are omitted because they are rejected on the ground of the doctrine which they teach … it is contended that omission is rejection, and rejection depravation.
>
> In none of these propositions, nor in their logical connection, can their Lordships concur. Omission is not rejection. If it were, the Lectionary in the Prayer Book would be open to this grave charge.[57]

Taking full advantage of the characteristically robust sixteenth- and seventeenth-century language of the rubric and canons, the judges determined that the concept of open and notorious evil life could only mean obvious moral turpitude, and common and notorious depravation be public contempt for the liturgy of the Church. Mr Jenkins was accepted by all to be a decent, upright, ethical person, who claimed (seemingly without irony) to revere the Prayer Book "second only to the Bible itself,"[58] and this was not him.

The Judicial Committee also adopted a different response to Bishop Ellicott's fumbling interventions, refusing to see them as legitimation for Cook's actions, even if he had given supportive advice. Rather,

> the Bishop in the present case appears throughout to have expressed the opinion that he ought not himself decide the question between the Appellant

> and the Respondent, but that it should be decided in proceedings such as have been taken.[59]

The judgment concludes by admonishing Cook, and awarding costs to Jenkins.

Lest this be thought a mild rebuke, it is possible that the Judicial Committee anticipated the eventual outcome, which can be seen as a much fuller victory for Jenkins. As a parishioner, he had refused to stop attending Christ Church Clifton, and presenting himself at the altar rail to be denied communion. Flavel Cook was unable to accept the logical outcome of the case, that he should give Jenkins communion after all, and instead resigned the living, preaching his farewell sermon on the Sunday following the Privy Council judgment.[60] Lest anyone should have any doubts about his principles, Cook published in 1878 *Righteous Judgment*, six lectures defending the traditional doctrine of eternal punishment against all its modernising detractors.[61] In spite of the lightness of their sentence and refusal to do much more than overlook his heterodox views, the Judicial Committee had vindicated the right of the laity to receive communion in their own parish church, regardless of the theological disapproval of their clergy.

Banister v Thompson – who defines marriage?

Whilst the great ecclesiastical debates of the nineteenth century were about doctrine or liturgy, it seems appropriate to some of what will follow that the key case concerning repulsion at the start of the twentieth century should be about sex. Or at least, be about marriage, and the always faintly absurd-sounding problem of marriage to a deceased wife's sister. Through the seventeenth and eighteenth centuries marriages to deceased wife's sisters were brought before the church courts to be tried as cases of incest within the prohibited degrees, even including one Somerset clergyman in 1736.[62] However, the Marriage Act 1835 defined such marriages as definitely void, and also thereby removed them from ecclesiastical jurisdiction.[63] But this position was still sustained for churchmen by the principle underlying the Table of Kindred and Affinity in the Prayer Book, which showed how all marriages were outlawed within two degrees of affinity – marriage constituting such a degree as fully as parent/childhood or siblinghood. This principle in turn was understood to have been derived from Scripture, and that marriages within the prohibited degrees constituted incest in the sight of God.

The difficulty was that from time to time a situation arose in which a man had been bereaved of his wife, and if she had an unmarried sister, that lady then occurred as a very obvious possible new wife, being probably also already a friend and (if there were children of the first marriage) a particularly natural stepmother. Through the nineteenth century Bills, "fiercely resisted by the Anglican hierarchy"[64] were introduced to Parliament to make such marriages possible, but did not succeed until 1907, when the Deceased Wife's Sister's Marriage Act (hereafter 'DWSMA') passed, with a proviso (key to this case) exempting clergy from any penalty for their conscientious refusal to conduct such marriages.

One of those who had been hoping for such an Act was Alan Banister, but his need to marry Emily, sister of his late wife, was such that he availed himself of the passage in 1906 of an equivalent Act making such marriages legal in the Colonies by a short stay in Canada. He duly married her at St Giles, Montreal, on 12 August 1907, before returning to their home in the parish of Eaton, Norwich, in September after the passage of the DWSMA into law on 21 August 1907.[65] Their vicar, Henry Thompson, was then faced with the need to respond to what he regarded as an incestuous marriage, a conviction in which he was supported by the Bishop of Norwich.[66] In particular, Thompson believed that as far as the law of the Church and of his own conscience was concerned, the situation with respect to the Banisters' marriage was as if the DWSMA had never passed, relying upon the clause of the Act which stated:

> no clergyman in holy orders in the Church of England shall be liable for any suit, penalty, or censure, whether civil or ecclesiastical, for anything done or omitted to be done by him in the performance of the duties of his office to which suit, penalty, or censure he would not have been liable if this Act had not been passed.[67]

The last part of a correspondence between Mr Banister and Mr Thompson is presented in the court report; it appears that they had already established their respective positions, and after a certain amount of reluctance and invoking the need to consult the Bishop, Mr Thompson confirmed in a letter of 24 October 1907 that if the Banisters were to appear at Communion he would indeed repel them;[68] this letter was sufficient for Mr Banister without, in addition (as Mr Jenkins and Mrs Swayne had done), actually having to kneel at the altar rail and be publicly passed over. The Banisters therefore brought a complaint under the Church Discipline Act to the Bishop of Norwich. The Bishop consulted Archbishop Davidson, who wished that the issue was not being made, but giving the advice followed, that it should go to the Court of Arches.[69]

The particular interest of the case for today is that the argument advanced by Mr Thompson's defence was that the DWSMA had opened up a distinction between marriage in the law of the land and marriage in the eyes of the Church – marriage to a Deceased Wife's Sister being legal in the law of the land but forbidden by the Church. What becomes apparent in the course of the case is that although the Act made some hints in this direction, by special provisions for England (as opposed to the Act of 1906 providing for the Colonies) recognising the need to protect the consciences of the clergy, it did not amount to a sustainable distinction, and it became necessary for Lewis Dibdin as Dean of the Arches to criticise the drafting.

The judgment begins with a clear setting-out of the concept of the discipline of excommunication, as exercised through the centuries, including the important shift in the Middle Ages from public excommunication and restoration to private confession. As far as Dibdin was concerned, though, "the compilers of our Liturgy … in the sixteenth century … proceeded on a very clearly defined principle. They asserted the liberty and the responsibility of the individual."[70] He traces this principle through the effective abolition of private confession, the Exhortations of the Prayer Book, and the Sacrament Act. There remained, of course, judicial excommunication and the possibility of repelling the notorious and open evil liver, but of these Dibdin judged:

> The characteristic common to these causes for repulsion from Holy Communion, and the point to be noticed in regard to them, is that they are, one and all, intended to prevent some public mischief. The clergyman in repelling anyone is not simply, or even chiefly, exercising godly discipline on the person repelled, but he is acting as a public officer for the protection of the whole community.[71]

For the Edwardian judge, educated in the highest ideals of the liberal Bar, it was self-evident that a distinction could be drawn between the Christian discipleship ('godly discipline') of an individual and the public good, but the fearful seventeenth-century, or even twentieth-century, Puritan, might be much less confident in allowing diversity of personal life within the community. And Dibdin goes on to show as much, by citing Mormon polygamy as the sort of thing which is unquestionably "in conflict with the moral code of Christendom"[72] How is one then to distinguish between polygamy and deceased wife's sister's marriage as breaches of Christian morality? The difference is that polygamy was (and is) illegal by the laws of England, and the Banisters' marriage was not.

In order to demolish the proposal that the DSWMA had made such marriages legal but not godly, Dibdin found it necessary, whilst cautiously noting the lack of much useful precedent, to resort to *reductio ad absurdum*. He points out that

> if one of the parties to such a marriage were a Church-man and the other a Nonconformist, that one might be an open and notorious evil liver and the other not.... I feel the gravest doubt whether ... it would be possible to put a construction on these words which would lead to results so anomalous and extraordinary.[73]

We may also note that this extraordinary anomaly is a direct consequence of the Toleration Act and the growth of plural Christian denominations in England. Further, the supposed freedom of the clergy from all penalty meant that a vicar

> could assist a man who had married his deceased wife's sister to contract a bigamous marriage with another woman, by proclaiming his banns, solemnising the marriage in church, and registering it, thus actively aiding and abetting in the commission of a felony[74]

or that

> it will be possible for parties to be married by a clergyman and to receive the Holy Communion from him in accordance with the Act, and subsequently,

> on account of the marriage, to be repelled from the Holy Communion by another clergyman (or by the same clergyman should he happen to change his mind), also in accordance with the Act.[75]

The only possible conclusion was that the proviso exempting clergy from penalty must be related only to the actual conduct of deceased-wife's-sister marriages, and not to a range of possible consequences. So, Thompson had exceeded his powers in repelling the Banisters, and was admonished for so doing, and told not to do so in future.

Canon Thompson did not wish to give in on the principle, but was in danger of imprisonment for contempt (like the Ritualists) if he continued to refuse communion to the Banisters, something in which the ECU, offering financial backing, might have rejoiced as a triumph of principle over law.[76] He therefore instead sought a writ of prohibition against the Court of Arches (the case consequently now becoming known as *Rex v Dibdin*) and it was heard in 1909, but rejected both by the Probate Division King's Bench and thereafter by the Court of Appeal. Admittedly, Canon Thompson gained the sympathy of Mr Justice Bray at the first appeal, who entered a minority opinion that Thompson was protected from penalty by the DWSMA, and that the two-status view of marriage was possible. The majority view though, which prevailed, was that of the Erastian Protestants, represented by the trenchant judgment of Lord Justice Fletcher Moulton:

> There is something to my mind revolting to all reverential or religious feeling that in the case of so sacred a privilege as participation in the Lord's Supper a clergyman should say, or be entitled to say, "I know that you are not in fact living in sin but in lawful wedlock, according to the law of God as declared in the law of the land which is binding on you, and I know, therefore, that in fact the congregation are not and cannot be offended, but I am entitled to hold you to be constructively a notorious evil liver and the congregation will be constructively offended, and I will accordingly drive you from the Lord's Table under colour of applying the rubric." Surely legal subtleties never appeared more odious than in such a connection.... I cannot understand, much less sympathize with, any attempt to pervert the plain and simple meaning of the rubric, which in the clearest language prescribes that only actual and notorious personal unfitness takes away the privilege and even the duty of attendance at the Lord's Table.

Canon Thompson fought on in declining health to lose again in the House of Lords in 1912 when, like Flavel Cook, he preferred to resign his living than give communion to those he had so long repelled.[77] Although the *Church Times* had offered vigorous fighting talk in his support, and looked with enthusiasm to the Bishop of Birmingham (Gore) and "a multitude eager to stand beside him,"[78] the Banister-Thompson case stands alone at the end of the history of repulsion cases. In part this is simply because of the rarity of marriages to deceased wives' sisters by litigious would-be communicants, and also because although fighting talk remained strong in pulpits for decades to come, there was less enthusiasm or resource for court battles of any sort after the Great War. After discussion amongst the bishops, Archbishop Davison provided a "typically soothing minimalist interpretation"[79] in the form of an 8 February 1910 exchange of letters in *The Times*, claiming the courts had not assumed control of the right to communion. Standing as it does towards the end of the era of Church litigation, it is more interesting to look at two specimens of the theology provoked by *Banister v Thompson*, and their differing conceptions of the Church, each unsatisfactory in its own way.

Figgis and Christian freedom

Neville Figgis, a Mirfield father and pupil of bishop and church historian Mandell Creighton, continues to be remembered for his *Churches in the Modern State* [80] of 1913, setting out the dilemma of Christian identity in a state which may no longer be Christian, and in some ways anticipating the dangers of twentieth-century totalitarianism. It can be seen as a siren voice for Christian freedom, and this is how Figgis presents it. However, it is a direct reaction to the Banister-Thompson case and others, and represents both a much less free Christianity, and his rejection of the patient tolerance of his teacher Creighton.

Figgis tells us that he sets out to determine "whether, politically speaking, there is such an entity as a Church."[81] The argument presented is that the courts, in *Rex v Dibdin* and other cases such as that of the Free Church of Scotland (*Bannatyne v Overtoun* [1904]), fail to recognise "the Church as a living social union of men bound together by specific ties, recruited by definite means, and acting by virtue of an inherent spontaneity of life which is not imposed but original."[82] The difficulty is that he never really manages to explain what 'an inherent spontaneity of life' means, nor admit that among other things which he would like the Church to do inherently and spontaneously is exclude the likes of the Banisters. He cites, for example, the Tariff Reform League[83] in support of the idea that the Church is essentially a club, and like all clubs to which one might belong (it does all sound quite Edwardian), those who set it up have a right to determine who is sound enough to be a member.

There are two serious flaws in Figgis's argument. He does not seem to recognise the extent to which he is disastrously relativizing the concept of the Church, even as he cites the Free Church of Scotland as a parallel. If the Church is One and Catholic, as the creeds confess, then the presence of a number of different Christian denominations, all calling themselves the Church (of X) and all enjoying inherent spontaneity, only goes to prove that most, if not all of them, cannot really represent the true Church of Christ. The other is that the Church universal is not a club, in the sense that its membership is determined by the Membership Committee. Rather, it is the community of those called into faith by the living God and determining who those are is the very perilous theological question on which so much else hinges.

Feeling that he has established the nature of the Church as something corporate and distinct from society as a whole, Figgis goes on to defend it as one among many bodies in society adding to the virtue of the whole in a Burkean sense, and enjoying both freedom to define her own life and abjuring any right to dictate to non-members:

> If we are to cry "hands off" to the civil power in regard to such matters as marriage, doctrine, ritual, or the conditions of communion inside the Church – and it is the necessary condition of a free religious society that it should regulate these matters – then we must give up attempting to dictate the policy of the State in relation to the whole mass of its citizens.[84]

This sounds, of course, like very good liberal democracy, and indeed represents the position adopted by most churches in the twentieth century. But theologically it sidesteps entirely the real question of what membership of the Church is. Either it is the condition of eternal salvation, in which case this represents the abandonment of concern with the rest of society except as potential recruits, or it is not, in which case what is the point of exclusion at all? But by 1911 it was much easier to talk fiercely about the Church and what it stood for if one did not make any troubling claims about eternity.

Although he manages to maintain the predominant emphasis on the freedom of the Church from the State, he is unable eventually to conceal his disdain for the society in which he lives, and identify the source:

> we can most of us see the evils of the intellectual anarchy of our time, and the lack of all directing ideals in the Western World except those vulgarly materialistic. Is not all this the direct consequence of the religious toleration and the breaking down of the old doctrine of a homogenous State?[85]

Tellingly for a celibate, among the materialistic evils he goes on to identify is the tendency of capitalist fathers to spend too much on clothes for their daughters.

If toleration is regrettable, it offers the possible mercy of enabling the purification of the Church by letting go of nominal believers, a view found occasionally throughout Anglo-Catholic sources. He resists the many churchmen of his time who still sought a repeal of the 1857 divorce legislation, "demanding the enforcement upon a population no longer even nominally Christian of the whole series of taboos and exclusions which Christians themselves find so difficult"[86] because he accepts the Gladstonian premise that the Church is no longer the nation. Nonetheless, within the Church he hopes for "every safeguard … left to us as a society for enforcing our own discipline."[87] In other words, let the Banisters marry, so long as they can be expelled from the Church of England. But as to whether the Banisters are damned for their unchristian marriage, Figgis does not care to speculate.

Fremantle and Christian liberalism

A striking sample of the theology Figgis opposed, but did not necessarily confute, within the Church of England, can be found in the work of William Fremantle,

Dean of Ripon, who published *Natural Christianity* in 1911[88] to expound his distinctly Latitudinarian perspective. Much of the work serves to identify him firmly with the Modernism of the period, particularly his views on the Biblical miracles, but for this study the interest is found in his willingness to continue, with Hooker, to regard the whole nation of England as the real Church of England, and not merely that body in which he served. He denounces the clericalism of the Middle Ages:

> the Church was started on its voyage through the Dark Ages, not as a comprehensive and expansive institution leading mankind in the path of righteousness, but as a clerical sect occupied primarily with public worship and the forms of doctrine and observances, at time enjoying the protection of the secular power, at times opposing it.[89]

The happy solution to this, gifted by God to England, was the Reformation, logically followed in his view by the Toleration. Fremantle's particular perspective is to see in the latter that "the fact that the nation, acting as a Church, allowed its members to worship according to their own consciences, does not imply that they ceased to be members of the English branch of Christ's Church."[90]

In this optimistic view of the Church in England, no-one is excluded, but those who choose worship in others than in the national Church (or none at all) are by right just as much members of the invisible Church of Christ, simply exercising their consciences to be different. And he lambasts his own Church of England for her persistent conservatism and failure to see God at work:

> the great acts which have banished persecution, emancipated slaves, softened the criminal law, made education universal, raised class after class to the full rights of citizenship, have been, though often resisted by those who are called the Church, great acts of the Spirit of God. The nation itself, not a section of it, has shown itself to be the true Church of Christ.[91]

This argument, that the nation as a whole is more Christian than the sectarian so-called Church, is expanded with reference to the role of the monarchy, and in an attack on the growing pressure to give legislative power to the Church Assembly, as would happen in 1919.

Particularly relevant for this study is the way he rejoices in the effectiveness of the ecclesiastical courts, including the Privy Council, enforcing the rule of law in the face of clericalist yearning for narrowness and persecution. Selective choice of cases enables him to claim:

> Each of the great ecclesiastical parties has by turns had its liberty vindicated by the Privy Council Court, when the ecclesiastical court would have condemned it: the evangelical section in the Gorham case in 1850, the liberal section in that of the Essays and Reviews in 1864, and a few years later the Sacramentalists in the Bennett case.[92]

Fremantle offers his most trenchant remarks in an aside:

> In each of these cases the Court which represented "the Church" in its narrower and clericalist sense gave a wrong, that is an unchristian judgment; the Court which represented the national power gave a just and Christian one. It was the national power, not the sectarian and clerical, which spoke the word of righteousness, which is the voice of God and of His true Church.[93]

In contrast to Figgis's dispiriting conception of the Church as a self-defining club, able to set her own terms of membership and (seemingly) define her own God, Fremantle offers a breadth of vision which in many ways presents more impressively the Christian faith as a message for all people, and which none can claim the right to define for themselves. His weaknesses are obvious; naïve about the flimsy reality of Christianity in the mass of the nation, and (apart from his ecclesiology) an extreme liberalism in relation to the historic revelation which threatens to undermine the faith altogether.

Commentary on both

I present the theologies of Figgis and Fremantle in succession because together they reveal the shortcomings of both. Figgis, having accepted (unlike many less thoughtful reactionaries) the inability of the Church to rule national life, aspires instead to a Church which is a holy community standing against the nation. But because he cannot adopt the straightforward Roman Catholic position of being *the* holy community against which all else can be judged, he seems to suggest the contradiction of plural such communities, each maintaining their own discipline. In the practical life of the Edwardian Church of England, this aspiration was confounded by the reality of judges, including the Church's own Dean of the Arches, who worked with the Reformation ecclesiastical law before them to provide for an equally universalistic Church in a pluralist age. Fremantle's ecclesiology envisaged and even celebrated such a Church, even if his wider theology stood in danger of abandoning meaningful Christianity altogether.

Although the law had given much support to Broad Churchmanship in the Fremantle mould, it was Figgis who had the greater impact, not least in feeding into the Life and Liberty movement for the self-government of the Church of England. The era of extensive ecclesiastical litigation appears to have faded even before the First World War, but there is probably some sense in which the Enabling Act of 1919, giving legislative powers to the Church Assembly, diverted energies which had formerly been bent to proving theological or liturgical points in court against the standards of the Reformation texts into the new possibility of changing those texts in a way favourable to the campaigner.

What the next chapter will observe, however, is how the broad and formally liberal legal character of the Church of England, determined by the great court battles of 1850–1912, showed remarkable strength through most of the twentieth century. Among other reasons, it can be noted in the words of a contemporary commentator that for all that it gave legislative power to the Church's own Assembly, the "autonomy secured by the Enabling Act was essentially fictional."[94] This was because Parliament retained the power to strike down any Church measure, as happened most notably with the revised Prayer Books in 1927 and 1928. It is perhaps no accident that a guiding hand, under Archbishop Davidson, in the creation of the Enabling Act 1919, which has been described as "a masterpiece of compromise between the points of view of the high episcopalians and of the common lawyers"[95] was that cautious defender of the rule of law in the Church, Sir Lewis Dibdin.

Notes

1 Owen Chadwick, *The Victorian Church. Part 1 1829–1859* 3rd ed. (SCM Press 1971) 263.
2 Keith W. Clements, *Lovers of Discord. Twentieth Century Theological Controversies in the Church of England* (SPCK 1988) 69.
3 As in Rupert Bursell, *Liturgy, Order and the Law* (Clarendon Press 1996) 239–44.
4 Robert E. Rodes Jr., *Law and Modernisation in the Church of England* (Notre Dame 1991) 291.
5 Thomas Culver, *Excommunication in the Church of England* (unpublished LLM thesis, 1996) 29.
6 Ibid., 28.
7 William Gibson, *Enlightenment Prelate: Benjamin Hoadly, 1676–1761* (James Clarke & Co 2004) 123, citing Maurice Wiles, *Archetypal Heresy, Arianism Through the Centuries* (Oxford 2001).
8 Bernard Palmer, *Reverend Rebels, Five Victorian Clerics and their Fight Against Authority* (Darton, Longman & Todd 1993) 71.
9 Ibid., 217, 231.
10 John Peart-Binns, *Herbert Hensley Henson. A Biography* (Lutterworth Press 2013) 39.
11 Ibid., 133.
12 H. Hensley Henson, *Retrospect of an Unimportant Life,* vol II (OUP 1943) 193.
13 *Acts of the Convocations of Canterbury and York*, ed. A. F. Smethurst and H. R. Wilson (SPCK 1961) 90–95.
14 Bursell, Rupert, *Liturgy, Order and the Law* (Clarendon Press 1996) 245.
15 *Church Acts and Measures* from *Halsbury's Statutes of England* (1969 Church Assembly Edition) 877.
16 *Kemp v Wickes* [1809] 3 Phill Ecc 265.
17 *Kemp* 273.
18 Norman Doe, *Christian Law* (CUP 2013) 269–70.
19 Ibid., 271.
20 Ibid., 305.
21 *Mastin v Escott* [1841] 2 Curt 748.
22 Constitutions & Canons Ecclesiastical, No. 68.
23 G. C. B. Davies, *Henry Phillpotts, Bishop of Exeter 1778–1869* (SPCK 1954) 172.
24 This is a theme recounted clearly in Julie, Rugg, *Churchyard and Cemetery: Tradition and Modernity in Rural North Yorkshire* (Manchester University Press 2013).
25 See Ronald Fletcher, *The Akenham Burial Case* (Wildwood House 1974).
26 *East Anglian Daily Times* 26 August 1878, cited in Fletcher, *Akenham*, 28.
27 From a sermon by Benson on 3 November 1889, reported in court by Swayne's solicitor (Arches Hh23).
28 Arches Hh23.

29 J. C. Chambers, "Decay of Discipline" in Orby Shipley (ed.) *Ecclesiastical Reform. Eight Essays by Various Writers* (Longmans, Green & Co 1873).
30 Neville Figgis, *Churches in the Modern State* (Longmans, Green & Co 1913) 60–70.
31 Chambers, *Decay*, 113.
32 Ibid., 118.
33 Ibid., 133.
34 Ibid., 134.
35 Ibid., 143.
36 Noted in the court papers, Arches H966/1–32.
37 Henderson, *The Devil's Law Cases* (2012) *15EccLJ* 28–58.
38 Ibid., 45.
39 Letter of Jenkins to Cook, cited at *Jenkins v Cook* [1875] LR 4 A&E 478.
40 Henderson, *Devil's Cases*, 46.
41 Letter of Cook to Jenkins, reported at *Jenkins* [1875] 480.
42 Letter of Jenkins to Bishop Ellicott, reported at *Jenkins* [1875] 484.
43 *Jenkins* [1875] 487–8. incl. letter of Ellicott to Cook reproduced at 488.
44 Henderson, *Devil's Cases*, 50–51.
45 *Jenkins* [1875] 468–475.
46 Ibid., 493.
47 Ibid., 493.
48 Ibid., 492.
49 Ibid., 492.
50 Henderson, *Devil's Cases* 52, adverting to *Jenkins* [1875] 495–8.
51 *Church Times*, 23 July 1875, 370.
52 Ibid.
53 *Crockford's Clerical Directory*, 8th Issue (Horace Cox 1876].
54 Henderson, *Devil's Cases*, 53.
55 *Jenkins v Cook* [1876] LR 1 PD 80, 9.
56 *Jenkins* [1876] 9.
57 *Jenkins* [1876] 10.
58 Letter of Jenkins to Bishop Ellicott, 06/09/1874, at *Jenkins* [1875] 485.
59 *Jenkins* [1876] 13.
60 Henderson, *Devil's Cases*, 55.
61 Flavel S. Cook, *Righteous Judgment. Six Lectures on Future Punishment* (Seeley, Jackson and Halliday 1878).
62 William Gibson and Joanna Begiato, *Sex and the Church in the Long Eighteenth Century. Religion, Enlightenment and the Sexual Revolution* (I. B. Tauris 2017) 115–18.
63 *Banister v Thompson*, Arches [1908] P372.
64 Bruce S. Bennett, "*Banister v Thompson* and Afterwards: The Church of England and the Deceased Wife's Sister's Marriage Act" *Journal of Ecclesiastical History* 49.4 (1998) 669.
65 *Banister* [1908] P363–4.
66 Bennett, *Banister*, 670.
67 *Banister* [1908] P370, footnote.
68 *Banister* [1908] P365–6, footnotes.
69 Bennett, *Banister*, 671.
70 *Banister* [1908] P381.
71 *Banister* [1908] P385.
72 *Banister* [1908] P385.
73 *Banister* [1908] P389.
74 *Banister* [1908] P393.
75 *Banister* [1908] P394.
76 Bennett, *Banister*, 673–4.
77 Brief summary of many *Church Times* reports, 1909–12.

78 *Church Times* editorial, 17 December 1909.
79 Bennett, *Banister*, 675.
80 Figgis, *Churches.*
81 Ibid., 4.
82 Ibid., 36.
83 Ibid., 45.
84 Ibid., 112.
85 Ibid., 115.
86 Ibid., 123.
87 Ibid., 124.
88 The Hon W. H. Fremantle, DD, Dean of Ripon, *Natural Christianity* (Harper & Brothers 1911).
89 Ibid., 104.
90 Ibid., 110.
91 Ibid., 124–5.
92 Ibid., 136.
93 Ibid., 136 footnote.
94 Henson, H. Hensley, *Retrospect of an Unimportant Life, Vol 1.* (OUP 1942) 301.
95 Augur Pearce, "Episcopacy and the Common Law" *7EccLJ* 204–5.

6. Reluctance to discipline

The beginnings of an important distinction

As noted towards the end of Chapter 4, historical periods tend in reality to overlap, and intermittent persecution for ritual offences continued beyond the 1890 Lincoln Judgment:

> the fact that visible forms of worship and architecture continued to provoke conflict well into the twentieth century reveals the profound weakness of both the Elizabethan Act of Uniformity and its 1662 successor in imposing uniformity on a church that was so often bent on reinterpreting the nature of its identity.[1]

However, the sense that Bishop King's trial stands at a turning point is perhaps reinforced by an important legal change that followed it in the form of the Clergy Discipline Act 1892. One of the standing complaints of both the alleged heretics like Head and Wilson, and the early Ritualists before 1874, had been that they were tried under the same legislation as drunks and adulterers, the Church Discipline Act 1840. It seemed, they felt, that the Church was procedurally unable to distinguish between matters of moral turpitude and spiritual controversies. The Public Worship Regulation Act of 1874 in a sense recognised this, by subjecting ritual controversy to a new and different procedure, but it was not successful.

According to Rodes, the presenting issue leading to the CDA 1892 was the problem of dealing with clergy whose behaviour was thought to be scandalous, but which was either not actually criminal, or not worth prosecuting by the secular courts. Inevitably, this was often about sex, for example: "It is one thing not to impose on an active homosexual the life imprisonment to which he was theoretically subject until 1967; it is quite another to leave him in charge of a parish."[2] The difficulty was that under a dictum of Sir Henry Hobart from the 1618 case of *Searle v Williams*, the absence of a secular conviction was a solid defence for the wicked clergyman, unless he could be found guilty of the ill-defined offence of 'scandal.'[3] This defence was swept away by the CDA 1892, which also made the helpful provision that clergy found guilty of serious crimes (those at the time including a sentence of hard labour) could be summarily deprived of their preferments.

The CDA 1892 also introduced a new and important provision. For centuries the Church of England had adhered to the tradition, embodied in Canon 76 of 1604, that Holy Orders could not be removed, and that clergy were by definition unable to relinquish the charge taken up. However, as noted above, the Clerical Disabilities Act 1870 (still in force) had made it possible to give up one's orders by a Deed of Relinquishment, freeing those who did so from the duties and obligations of the canons. What the 1892 Act did was to provide for bishops, if they felt the case merited it, to *depose* clergy from Holy Orders as an additional penalty (defining deposition as having the same force a voluntary Relinquishment).

There is a learned section in the first chapter of the 1954 Ecclesiastical Courts Report which attempts to expound the distinction between the medieval practice (lingering in attenuated form into the seventeenth century) of 'degradation' and the 'deposition' introduced by the 1892 Act.[4] In summary, degradation was a more complete reversal of ordination, including ritual unrobing, introduced in order to remove the benefit of clergy in order that guilty clergy could be handed over the secular authorities for punishment, notably including burning for heresy. Both are nonetheless frequently referred to loosely as 'defrocking.'[5] The draft Canon LII.2 of 1947 proposed reasserting the tradition that clergy could not relinquish their calling[6] but this of course conflicted with both the Clerical Disabilities Act 1870 and the Clergy Discipline Act 1892 (and the deposition provision was renewed in the Ecclesiastical Jurisdiction Measure 1963). I would conclude that this drove the compromise of Canon C1.2 promulged in the 1960s that a minister may relinquish or be deprived of the *exercise* of their orders, but that something undefined (though borrowed from the Catholic theology of ordination) called their *character* remains unalterable.[7] The only legal effect of this seems to be that in the rare cases (provided for by a 1934 Measure amending the 1870 Act) of a cleric wishing to resume their orders after relinquishment, they would not be re-ordained.

Criminal or not, defrocked or otherwise, the real significance of the 1892 Act for the purposes of this study is that it specifically excluded cases of doctrine or ritual, leaving them to the pre-existing uncertainties of the CDA 1840. This can only have been in the recognition, hard-won by the controversial and costly cases described in earlier chapters, that the Church needed a means of dealing with clergy guilty of crime or undisputed sin, but which did not look like a renewal of punitive jurisdiction over controversial categories of theological opinion or liturgical preference. Although Rodes notes a certain amount of difficulty in the courts in defining the 'immoral conduct' and 'immoral habit' referred to in the 1892 Act,[8] it still constitutes an important stage in the Church of England's wise recognising that the ecclesiastical courts were not the right place to settle ecclesiastical controversy. The exercise of this wisdom was to keep controversy out of the courts through most of the twentieth century.

An unlikely defence

The removal of doctrine and ritual was not wholly effective in preventing controversy in the most famous clerical trial since Dr Free, that of Harold Davidson,

Rector of Stiffkey, in 1932. Mr Davidson had devoted his life not to his quiet Norfolk cure, but to spending all his weekdays in London visiting and entertaining girls of low repute. Since the trial by Norwich Consistory Court was held in Church House, Westminster, the press were easily able to derive entertainment from the evidence of his uniquely foolish ministry. Unlike other clergy 'found out,' however, Davidson attempted a distinctive defence with at least a sliver of theological plausibility:

> For years I have been known as the Prostitutes' Padre – to me the proudest title that a true priest of Christ can hold. I believe with all my soul that if He were born again in London in the present day He would be found constantly walking in Piccadilly. He suffered the cruellest slander, but this did not deflect Him from solicitude for the fallen, and His attitude with the woman taken in adultery and still more his close friendship with the notorious harlot of Magdala ... has always been my inspiration and comfort in the difficult work I have humbly undertaken in His name.[9]

Even the implication of repeated adultery, and the shame of his longsuffering wife, was not enough to divert Davidson from invoking the image of Christ before his judges, just as had the Ritualist martyrs of a previous generation.

In this case, however, the court was not impressed, and Davidson was sentenced to deprivation on all charges, and to be deposed from Holy Orders. The sentence was solemnly executed in Norwich Cathedral, the custom being maintained that deposition, like medieval degradation, was carried out by the bishop in person, accompanied by his *familia* of dean and canons, and the deposition, read out over Davidson at the High Altar, referred to him being "removed, deposed and degraded."[10] A united conservative order of Norfolk church and squirearchy were determined to make an example, but it is also apparent that what was achieved was closer to pantomime, and did nothing for the credibility of ecclesiastical courts as a place where complex problems could be explored and resolved.

The Church crisis – controversy without courts

The fading away of theological controversy in the courts after the Lincoln Judgment 1890 did not reflect a diminishment of theological controversy *per se*, rather the increasingly fixed reluctance of bishops to see it resolved by law. As seen above with Wason and further below, bishops did attempt to use patronage and informal statements of discipline to keep order, and it could be argued that these are always properly the first recourse in such situations, with court action as in other areas of life the last resort. But it was knowledge that the last resort was in fact a futile one, for all the reasons explored, that rendered many preliminary steps of attempted discipline equally ineffective and allowed the life of the Church of England to continue to broaden according to the convictions and eccentricities of many.

Alan Wilson's study of the 'Church Crisis' of 1898–1904 offers an in-depth look at one episode of attempted non-legal maintenance of order, when Anglo-

Catholic worship in London was regularly disrupted by Protestant agitators led by John Kensit, and the whole controversy aired extensively in Parliament, where Sir John Harcourt supported the Protestant cause. This was a response to the frustration that they seemed to have no other means available given the episcopal veto of all attempts at prosecution under the PWRA. "By 1898, members of the Church Association were disillusioned, bitterly frustrated, and spoiling for a fight."[11] Kensit's response was to come up with ingenious ways of making publicity out of Anglo-Catholic practice – giving notice of intending to receive communion in a parish with a non-communicating High Mass, or at St Michael's, Shoreditch, getting his associate Daniel Hone to claim that he had suffered common assault by unwanted holy water at the Asperges.[12] The Anglo-Catholic clergy were equally controversialist, demanding the right to repel the Kensitites as depravers of the Prayer Book, and bolstered by E. G. Wood's argument that their ritual was simply the 'œcumenical custom' required by law.

Presiding over this undignified situation as Bishop of London was the gentle historian Mandell Creighton, who met patiently with controversialists from both sides who refused to acknowledge the real nature of his position. Wilson, writing long before he became a bishop himself, makes it sound very contemporary:

> Being a bishop in 1898 was far more a matter of reacting to pressure than taking initiatives. Both sides, however, found this hard to accept. The Catholic fantasy was that the bishops were princes of the church, able to resist the pressure of Harcourt and the mob if only they wanted to. The Protestant fantasy made them out to be officers of the law who could suppress any eccentricity at will, but were strangely reluctant to do so.[13]

In a series of letters to *The Times*, Harcourt appealed to the bishops to enforce the law as to public worship, but also showed signs of his belief that "Anglo-Catholic congregations were largely composed of queer aristocrats and cringing paupers, mostly women"[14] and challenged them to display an Anglo-Catholic grocer, who would presumably be an acceptable specimen of manly Englishness. In response, Creighton wrote thoughtful private letters to Harcourt, stressing the need to preserve the tender plant of liberalism from the competing passions of dogma and persecution.

An attempt to draw a line was made by the two Archbishops issuing formal rulings on their own undefined authority against the use of incense in 1899 and reservation in 1900 respectively, which produced some compromise but also continued defiance. Creighton unfortunately went down in Anglo-Catholic legend for his ill-judged attempt to lighten the mood when discussing incense with some of the defiant clergy, by asking them whether they thought that souls, like herring, needed to be cured with smoke. Back in the privacy of the SSC, the same clergy recorded their disgust that the bishop was known to dance.[15] But for all this bitterness, neither Creighton nor the other bishops took the relevant Anglo-Catholics to court. They had come to see that such discipline as could be obtained would come only by consent. After Creighton's death in 1901 his long-serving successor,

Winnington-Ingram, became notorious for his benevolent unwillingness to resist any ritual advance in his diocese.

Alternatives to the courts

One important outcome of the Church Crisis was the convening of the Royal Commission on Ecclesiastical Discipline, which heard at enormous length from across England of the reality of liturgical variety before reporting in 1906. The conclusions were simple and memorable. First, "the law of public worship in the Church of England is too narrow for the religious life of the present generation."[16] In other words, in the absence of much provision for variety in the Prayer Book, clergy and others had taken matters into their own hands and introduced great variations in both rite and ceremony, and in spite of the controversy, had supporters whose faith was sustained by them. Second, "the machinery for discipline has broken down,"[17] a conclusion readily supported by the accounts of the trials, and non-trials, the most important of which we have already described, even if such discipline had never really existed.

Although the Church continued to include many (including those who prosecuted Henly and Wason) who desired to restore discipline, in the world of liturgy there was a great diversion of effort from enforcement to liturgical revision. This has in more recent times come to be seen as the cautious beginning of the great explosion of official liturgical freedom which characterised the Church of England in the late twentieth century. At the time, however, it is important to recognise that for many "the *raison d'être* of the revision project was the re-establishment of order to parish services."[18] The argument was that once the liturgy had been revised and approved, divergences from it could be appropriately punished. In the event, the revision process took up over 20 years, so many bishops could postpone dealing with their undisciplined clergy with a clear conscience.

A side effect of the combination of anticipated revision and the known ineffectiveness of legal discipline was inadvertently to deepen the process of detachment of the most extreme Anglo-Catholics. Biographies and accounts of the movement, including Michael Yelton's several studies, make regular references to bishops placing their clergy 'under discipline,' the nature of such treatment being understood without being explained. Although it may have varied, this seems to have been an attempt to manifest episcopal displeasure (partly for the benefit of anti-Catholic critics writing cross letters) without resorting to costly or futile court cases. So, the 'discipline' was notified by formal letter, and took the form of the bishop refusing to visit the parish (including to confirm), sometimes refusing to license curates, not inviting the priest concerned to diocesan councils or synods and assuring them they would be refused future preferment.

Thus treated, the paradoxical consequence is that whilst some Anglo-Catholic clergy may have been worn down by isolation and confirmed in eccentricity (Yelton certainly offers many examples), they also turned even more for support to the various societies and fellowships which would fortify their views and endorse their suspicions about the legitimate authority of their bishops. In order to ensure that their parishioners were confirmed as they invariably believed vital, colonial bishops on furlough were often invited, with or without permission, again increasing the separation and culture of autonomy. This contributed to their vigorous opposition to Prayer Book revision in 1927–28, and delight in its eventual failure, with the apparent discrediting of the establishment, Erastian view of the Church of England.[19]

The revision of the Prayer Book leading to the Parliamentary votes of 1927 and 1928 can be seen as the first of three attempts to restore discipline and order in the Church of England, the latter two (distinct if somewhat interconnected) being the revision of Canon Law from 1947 onwards and the Ecclesiastical Jurisdiction Measure 1963, both to be discussed below. Prayer Book Revision has attracted far wider attention than the other two, each successive attempt involving the serious attention of a successively smaller and more specialist body of people. But in all three cases it is legitimate to ponder how seriously to take the expectation that discipline really would be restored. Maiden reports that there were various episcopal assurances in the 1920s that the new Prayer Book would be enforced, but "significantly, neither penalties for disobedience nor the procedures for enforcing discipline were prescribed within the revision proposals."[20] It seems quite possible that the new Book would have been no more enforceable than the old, a fact observed by the sharp mind of Dean Inge: "The rejection of the Book really saves them [the bishops] from a humiliating position; for they would not have been obeyed."[21]

Two other phenomena of the early twentieth-century Church of England may be noted as indirect responses to the discipline problem, or more positively, as signs of a change of temper from frustration at the disobedient to faint recognition that laying down and enforcing the law is an inherently problematic activity in the Christian Church. This is not to say that most churches, including the Church of England, do not apparently possess enforcement mechanisms: "The concept of an ecclesiastical offence is a common and fundamental feature of all the ecclesiastical disciplinary systems, as is the provision of sanctions."[22] But rather that the actual use of such mechanism in the Church of England, as this whole study reflects, has not functioned as the written law might suggest, and that here and there flickers of theological recognition of this problem can be spotted.

We have seen above how part of the response to the Church crisis at the turn of the twentieth century had been solemn declarations on Incense and Reservation by the two Archbishops. To such could be added, as it grew in maturity, some of the Acts of Convocation, in response to controversy, one of which was considered of "great moral force as the considered judgment of the highest and ancient synod of the province"[23] in the *Bland* case. These included the declarations of the bishops (constituted as the Upper Houses) after Parliamentary defeat in 1928 that they would attempt to hold the Church to the standards of the Deposited Book, and the acceptance (with reservations in Canterbury) of those declarations by the Lower Houses.[24] The response to the Matrimonial Causes Act 1937 has been noted earlier. However, it is also apparent that until the Convocation began to engage with the process of Canon Law revision in the 1950s, there are very few Acts which refer to issues of ongoing controversy such as ritual or doctrine.

The other non-disciplinary response to ongoing doctrinal controversy was the appointment in 1922 of the Doctrine Commission by the Archbishops. In his life of Davidson, George Bell recounts the "many appeals … that he should denounce particular writings or opinions as heretical"[25] and his patient reluctance to do so, and his general lack of interest in theological controversy. It represented a characteristic response therefore to accept the plea of the Bishop of Oxford and allies from 1920 that a Doctrine Commission should be set up, but no doubt with relief that it would take a long time to come to any conclusions – Bell wryly concluding his chapter on the subject with the footnote "The Commission is still sitting (1935)."[26] The resulting "pondered, rather dull document"[27] did something to reflect the growing acceptance of more Catholic doctrine, and offered a convoluted and ambiguous statement about the nature of Creeds and assent to them which reflects the difficulty of obtaining agreement and a deep reluctance to condemn particular views.[28] The implicit challenge to the Declaration of Assent from the Clerical Subscriptions Act 1865, with its requirement to assent to the 39 Articles, was not, however, taken up until the 1960s as seen below.

A clear and particular view

Further insight on the state of controversy over discipline in the first half of the twentieth century can be found in that reliably deep trove of opinions, the writings of Herbert Hensley Henson, candid and controversial as in so many other respects. Henson was an advocate of freedom of opinion, both for himself and others, but offers with particular clarity the dilemma of attempting as a long-serving bishop to maintain some sort of order with his deep suspicion of forms of coercive authority. As early as 1920 he could reflect that the bishops were "powerless now, save for the furtive oppression of latitudinarian curates"[29] and during the 1927–28 crisis over the Prayer Book, reflected on how the lack of obedience by clergy undermined the whole understanding of law by the Church: recalling being heckled in Barking in the 1890s that "It's all very fine for the Vicar to tell us to obey the law; but the Parsons break it soon enough when it suits them"[30] and finding himself for once stumped thereby.

In the event, the rejection of the revised Prayer Book drove Henson to favour disestablishment, believing that the Church could not live with being thus overridden. But towards the end of his ministry he was able, in a work of reflection on the Church he had served so long, to recognise the impracticality of doctrinal coercion and the wisdom of liberty. Although Henson was undoubtedly an individualist in many ways, I quote at length his summary of the wisdom of the Church of England of the time about compulsion (my italics):

> [W]e are confronted by a strange spectacle of doctrinal confusion which demonstrates the failure of Subscription to secure either of the two objects for which presumably it was designed. It does not provide any effective guarantee of the doctrinal soundness of the subscribing clergy, and it does not protect the people from heretical parsons. *The Church of England, at the present time,*

> *exhibits a doctrinal incoherence which has no parallel in any church claiming to be traditionally orthodox.* It is important that the character and extent of this phenomenon should be justly regarded, for it may well be the case that, when so regarded, it will be found less perplexing and indefensible that at first view it appears to be.
>
> The doctrinal incoherence of the Church of England, though it is unquestionably perplexing, practically embarrassing, and not infrequently scandalous, has its roots in something far more respectable than an indolent acquiescence in undiscipline or a reprehensible indifference to truth. *It reflects the reluctance of considering and responsible English churchmen to thrust the rough hand of authority into the sphere of religious opinion....* Christian history, as well ancient as modern, does not encourage the notion that error can most effectually be corrected by the action of official authority, nor does the Christian religion harmonize easily with methods of coercion, while its insistence on truth, and on the temper of sincerity, justifies, and even requires, a large acquiescence in the honest blundering of Christian scholars.
>
> "Doctor, doctor," said the large-hearted Tillotson to the learned but narrow-minded Beveridge, "charity is better than rubrics." It has been a happy thing, alike for the nation and for the Church, that the spirit of Tillotson rather than that of Beveridge has generally prevailed among the clergy of England.[31]

Episcopal indiscipline – three controversial bishops

Whilst the controversies referred to above largely concern the divergent opinions and practices of the clergy at large, or particular parties amongst them, it was inevitable that from time to time a bishop would arouse controversy. Sometimes a great controversy arises when a particular bishop is nominated, as with Hampden and Temple in the nineteenth century, and Henson himself in the early twentieth – the latter situation overcome by an impressively ambiguous Anglican manoeuvre whereby the controversial nominee issued a statement of belief: Henson claimed subsequently this was no recantation, many of his opponents suspected the same, but nonetheless peace was obtained. However, as noted in the Introduction and explored more fully below, the scrutiny of an individual's views at the point of admission to a particular office does not really constitute discipline in a proper sense. Whether at baptism and/or confirmation, ordination or consecration, the order of the Church has always involved some sort of public profession in order for the individual concerned to make the 'step up.' Whilst there may be controversy as to whether they have honestly made the profession, there is no real disagreement that some sort of profession is required, and if not made, precludes the relevant step.

Discipline, on the other hand, should mean the attempt to recall or reform individuals to a particular standard, and as this whole study explores, is a much more difficult and questionable enterprise. In three particular twentieth-century cases, spread out over more than 50 years, the response of successive Archbishops of Canterbury (even the supposedly disciplinarian Geoffrey Fisher) to bishops who had expressed opinions which might have demanded disciplinary action was to find a face-saving public solution avoiding any sort of trial of the facts or opinions of the bishop concerned.

The first bishop concerned, E.W. Barnes (Birmingham, 1924–53), managed two serious periods of controversy which involved the intervention of archbishops. Barnes was a modernist Protestant who was particularly unpopular with Anglo-Catholic clergy due to his open contempt for them as peddlers of quasi-medieval superstition, and matters came to a head when he refused to institute G. D. Simmonds to the parish of St Aidan, Small Heath, in 1930, on the grounds that he would not promise to end reservation of the sacrament there.[32] This appears to be the last case in which the patrons (including Bishop Walter Frere of Truro) sought the ancient writ of *quare impedit* from the High Court to compel the bishop to institute. Barnes stated that he would be willing to face imprisonment if defeated, and the press "gleefully pointed out that if the Bishop of Birmingham went to prison, it would be because the Bishop of Truro sent him there!"[33] The trustees accepted the need to avoid a court battle, and involved Archbishop Lang, who struggled to restrain Barnes's enthusiasm for letters to *The Times* and was eventually able to institute Simmonds himself after the lapse of patronage.[34]

Barnes's more serious episode of controversy, made so in part because of his existing reputation, followed his publication of *The Rise of Christianity* in 1947. This was his exploration of early Christianity from his characteristic scientific and rationalist viewpoint, without taking advantage of the best contemporary Biblical scholarship, and leaving the reader to doubt whether the bishop believed in either the Incarnation or the Resurrection in even the minimalist terms of the 1938 Doctrine Commission report. In his biography of Archbishop Fisher, Edward Carpenter follows the wave of controversy and pressure in response, that "something must be done."[35] Given the knowledge that any legal action (itself of doubtful basis given the lack of precedent for heresy trials of bishops) would be likely to lead Barnes to revel in an appeal to the Privy Council, and that extensive debate in Convocation would probably only display "much emotion and primitive witch-hunting"[36] Fisher took control by the non-legal approach of his own opening address to the Convocations on 15 October 1947. In a very carefully composed statement, he defended intellectual freedom and Barnes's personal integrity, but made clear his disapproval: "If his views were mine I should not feel that I could still hold episcopal office in the Church."[37] Although Barnes did not take the heavy hint and resign, this manoeuvre had the desired effect of calming the controversy, preventing an unedifying debate in Convocation, and appeasing many of the disgruntled of Birmingham.

Fisher's success is likely to have been in the mind of two of his successors faced with somewhat similar circumstances, and although the form of their responses differed, it is possible to see the process as kindred, and in particular as strategic evasion of anything resembling a trial. In 1963 Michael Ramsey was faced with the controversy surrounding *Honest to God*, a short book by J.A.T. Robinson, Bishop of Woolwich, repackaging fairly conventional mid-twentieth century philosophical theology and biblical criticism, but which achieved a wider impact through publicity in *The Observer* under the headline "Our Image of God Must Go."[38] Defying calls for stronger action, Ramsey instead turned to television interview and, like Fisher, his presidential address to Convocation, to defend open scholarship whilst deprecating some of Robinson's language and self-publicity.[39] *Honest to God* is recorded as one of the turning points in the change of attitude to Christianity in England in the period (the beginning of, for example, a sharp decline in both ordinations and confirmations)[40] but in the history of ecclesiastical discipline, only seemed to confirm that even bishops in the Church of England could consider themselves free to publish their variegated opinions at will.

The third bishop to complete the impression of episcopal indiscipline is David Jenkins (Durham 1984–94), who attracted controversy from his appointment onwards, being already known as a freethinking academic theologian, albeit one whose views were easily subject to misrepresentation. Impressive publicity was provided by a lightning strike on the south transept of York Minster on the night of his consecration, prompting both archbishops Habgood and Runcie to offer reassurance to the media that it was not a sign of divine wrath. The need to respond to the sense of controversy around Jenkins's published comments on the Virgin Birth and Resurrection was met more fully, however, by the stratagem of a deliberately convened General Synod debate on doctrine in February 1985.

Opening the debate, the Bishop of Winchester took care to assert that "in this debate no one is on trial"[41] and ruminated at length on the nature of faith and doubt. The long debate gave ample space for conservative opinion to be aired, critiquing "the House of Bishops in its cloistered towers"[42] but equally balancing it with those who did not want the Church narrowed in any way, and working over much of the ground in this study as a whole from both sides. This provided a suitable space for Archbishop Runcie to maintain a line not unlike his predecessors:

> a Church needs authority. It cannot do without authority. But if it became as tidy as the High Courts of Justice we should suspect it. The Church is not like a schoolteacher who must expel a boy from school lest he influence the others to wickedness. It is not like a king who must expel a troublesome subject. It is more like a parent with children, holding a lively family together. A Church cannot do without authority, but it ought to be gentle, calm, long suffering and, therefore, sometimes untidy.[43]

In relation to the Bishop of Durham and many others, the principle of keeping the family together (used regularly now by Archbishop Justin Welby) has outweighed the very vocal voices of those who are quite clear that a few need to be expelled to protect others from their wickedness. But those voices, whether Graham Leonard in the 1980s or Christian Concern today, continue to be heard, and their ability to be heard is a mark of the true liberalism prevailing in the Church.

The episcopal controversies referred to above are intended in part as a reminder of the state of heated and public doctrinal debate which characterised the Church of England through much of the twentieth century. What is remarkable is that whilst strident voices called from time to time for a disciplinary response, there was little connection made with the very real process of revision of Canon Law and the ecclesiastical courts, which took place largely amongst learned experts and effected fundamental changes in the possibilities of discipline within the Church of England. I will note three stages of change, of apparently diminishing significance for doctrinal order in the eyes of those who debated them at the time, but arguably increasing effect in the long term.

Canon Law reform

The first stage of reform was the long-drawn-out process of completely replacing the Canon Law of the Church of England from 1939–69. Although this work laid the foundation for the canonical framework which continues to govern the Church today, it has been given very little historical attention, except the habitual note that it was the favoured interest of Archbishop Fisher, and thus only showed his inattention to a changing world. I draw on the only prolonged study, by Canon Peter Boulton, who died in 1998 before he could submit it as an LLM thesis.[44] Although Boulton researched with great skill the many abortive stages before a proper Commission was appointed, it remains difficult to see why it was in 1947 rather than any other date that the Church found herself with a set of draft canons to work on under Fisher's headmasterly hand.

This process of revision occupied much of the working time of the Convocations during the 1950s, and Boulton credits Fisher with providing constant encouragement and reassurance to those who either feared their time was being wasted, or that new rules would mean new sanctions. Notable is his Presidential Address to the Church Assembly of January 1960, in which he praised those who had worked on the revision, and set out his assurances:

> I would emphasize again that while Canon Law along with the Statute Law and Common Law is part of the public law of England, it retains its own ethos which in the Church of England is not legalistic but domestic. Canon Law is a statement of the norm of family regulations to which Bishops, Priests and Deacons can willingly conform as members of the family and under its authority, and by which the laity can be secured in their domestic liberties and protected from disturbance of their rights.
>
> [T]he conception of Canon Law is not that of a rigid code of law, to be rigidly enforced. There must be an instrument of enforcement, and we can hope that before too long the Ecclesiastical Courts Measure will be before the Church Assembly. But the courts do not concern the ordinary law-abiding citizen at all and the administration of the Canons will be in the hands, amongst others, of Episcopal Pastors whose desire it will be always to avoid recourse to law as far as possible. And I know enough of the proposed Measure to be sure that it will not give any scope for the unreasonably litigious-minded. At this stage, anyhow, the Convocations are concerned only with

> producing what may be universally accepted as the norm, to be administered and obeyed by normal people, with, as its normal penalty, where a penalty is required, that of admonition.[45]

Among the remarkable features of the revision is the total absence of any provision for sanctions, unlike the fixed penalties (excommunication, suspension etc) provided in 1604. What is difficult to judge is the extent to which the revisers looked forward to the possibility of enforcement or were simply trusting in the existence of new and agreed canons to secure a new level of cooperation. Certainly, many of the controversies of the nineteenth century, for example over vestments or the material of altars, were laid to rest by canons allowing legitimate variation. The new canons followed those of 1604 in that some (particularly what became section A) are not concerned with any detail of church organisation, but to set out principles of the Church of England (such as the Royal Supremacy and episcopacy) as 'agreeable to the Word of God,' itself a magnificently opaque expression, but not as in 1604 to declare that those who impugn these principles are excommunicated *ipso facto*.

Another level of subtlety is given to the process by the recognition that under the Submission of the Clergy Act 1533, the new canons had to remain subject to the statute law, including of course all the Measures passed by the Church Assembly since its inauguration in 1920. This had the effect of constraining the new canons from dealing with many matters, particularly with relation to property and pastoral organisation. Combined with the desire to lay to rest controversy, this had a curious effect on the process, and Boulton suggests a further reason:

> all through the Canon Law Report and the revision process, it seems that the tactical aim of 'tailoring' the final product so as to make rejection by Parliament virtually impossible had almost overtaken the stated aim, that is, to provide the church with an up-to-date set of workable canons. There is no doubt that the rejection of the 1928 Prayer Book had left traumas in the minds of the church's senior administrators and lawyers which they were unwilling to risk re-opening.[46]

Within a 2003 article,[47] Augur Pearce identifies Sir Thomas Barnes as the government solicitor who came to be in effect an in-house adviser to the Canon Law revision process, gaining the full confidence of Archbishop Fisher and resisting all claims to renewed ecclesiastical authority.

Boulton goes on to identify four areas which remained problematic late in the process, precisely because of their relevance to what might be considered questions of discipline. Fisher's advice in 1960 that 'if … the degree of substantial agreement necessary for action cannot be achieved, that Canon should be left alone for the time being'[48] was to be closely followed. The first, admission to communion, will be considered separately as our third item below. On the seal of the confessional the device, still in force, was adopted that the relevant proviso of the 1603 Canons should be left unrepealed, supported by resolutions of the

Convocations, in recognition that Parliament was unlikely to agree to the resulting change in the laws of evidence.

Most interesting is the interaction between the canons and the law of marriage, where the draft Canons XXXVI and XXXVII had wanted to allow the Church of England to declare annulments after civil divorce, and to forbid the unbaptised to marry in church, in both cases responding to widespread opinion within the Church desiring to control marriage in these ways. Both would have represented a renewal of ecclesiastical discipline. To implement the first a procedure to declare annulments would have to be invented (for which reason three of the Commission, including the chair, Archbishop Garbett, dissented from Canon XXXVI) with the consequence that some divorcees would have been *denied* such an annulment and forbidden to marry in church. Whilst the vast majority of clergy in the 1950s would have exercised their freedom under the Matrimonial Causes Act 1937 to refuse to marry divorcees, this would still have restricted the couple's undoubted legal freedom to marry, and the draft was replaced by a canon simply asserting the Church's teaching. The Home Office regarded XXXVII as unacceptable in restricting the common law right of all to marry in their parish church, and it was passed to the 1966 Chadwick Commission on Church and State.[49] This in turn, whilst musing on the various possibilities, inconclusively suggested that it was better not to restrict the clergy's pastoral discretion.[50]

In relation to discipline as a whole, the draft canons had attempted to respond to this by the catch-all Canon IX, responding to "infraction of, or neglect to observe … Canon Law"[51] with reference to the extensive penalties for the clergy (all in force under existing law) and in the case of the laity "by removal from such office or membership as aforesaid, refusal of the benefit claimed, of exclusion for an appropriate period from the Holy Communion."[52] It is striking that a century after the Church had lost her real power to excommunicate, the spirit to do so remained, even if the penalty of refusing communion was supposedly a punishment for failing to receive communion, that being one of the few definable duties of the ordinary laity. Boulton records that the whole canon was dropped on the advice of the Home Office, who still regarded *Middleton v Crofts* (1736) as sacrosanct.[53] The canons also did not attempt to set out the expectations of the laity, enforceable or otherwise, but the Act of Convocation of 1954 on 'The Duties of Church Membership' was passed as a sort of substitute.[54]

Underlying this is the wider issue of the discipline of the laity, and its interaction with the almost impossible problem in the Church of England of defining membership (requested by the Convocations in 1948, but never obtained)[55] and therefore to whom any such discipline could apply. In the 1950s, this difficulty was complicated further in relation to the canons because those were passed by the entirely clerical Convocations, albeit with constant reference to the House of Laity. Boulton suggests rather easily that the coming of General Synod in 1970, including the laity in all canon-making, eliminated this difficulty,[56] but ongoing disquiet about whether the modern House of Laity is truly representative suggests that this may have been overoptimistic.

Reform of the courts

The process of reconstituting the ecclesiastical courts ran slightly behind, but in some ways in parallel with, the revision of Canon Law, and built upon rather more numerous previous reports reflecting on the excessive number of courts and in particular of overlapping Acts for different contexts, each with different procedure. The resulting Ecclesiastical Jurisdiction Measure 1963 built on the last report of 1954[57] with a comprehensive overhaul, providing the simple structure of one Consistory Court for each diocese, with appeals to a Provincial Court (called the Court of Arches or Chancery Court of York as required) for the majority of cases, which it was recognised would be faculty business which is not the subject of this study. Rodes notes that the EJM, like some of the revision of the canons, seemed strangely concerned to lay to rest controversies of the nineteenth century which might already have been thought ancient history:

> I cannot leave the Ecclesiastical Jurisdiction Measure, 1963, without noting a certain oddity about it. It is full of antiquarian allusions. Reading it, one keeps noting which nineteenth century problems are dealt with by which sections. Here in Section 10 (1) (b) is the provision for the *Gorham* case. Here is Section 40 to take care of the accusation against Bishop King. Here is Section 45 (3) to cut loose from the old and hated decisions of the Judicial Committee, and claim for the Church of England the same liberty that the South African church was read out of its endowments for claiming. These problems were so long dormant in 1963 that one is surprised that anyone was still interested in solving them. It is the kind of surprise one feels at finding that a figure out of a dim period of history is still alive.[58]

The main interest of the 1954 Report and 1963 Measure for this study is that they built on the distinction, made by the Clergy Discipline Act 1892 but now fully examined and explained, between moral offences or serious neglect of duty, and "doctrinal, ritual, ceremonial, and simoniacal offences; and in addition a number of heterogenous offences, difficult to classify, such as disobedience to the Canons," the 1954 Commission defining cases arising from the latter as 'reserved' cases. They recognised that these were likely to be cases of great difficulty and controversy, and so lifted them up from diocesan level to a new national court, the Court of Ecclesiastical Causes Reserved, to consist of present or former bishops and senior judges, to provide the best chance of a sound and widely accepted judgment.[59] Eric Kemp attributes this idea to Bishop Chase (Ripon 1946–59), who had sat on the Canon Law Commission and offered it as a compromise to Fisher, Ramsey and others wrestling with the problem.[60]

In terms of this study, the Court of Ecclesiastical Causes Reserved has been the dog that didn't bark for over 50 years. It has only sat twice, in the 1980s, in both cases to consider questions which had arisen in faculty cases (that of St Stephen's Walbrook has been referred to above, and in the other the response was that it should never have come to them anyway). Never has the power to try clergy guilty of heresy, ritual, simony or disobedience of the canons been exercised,[61] and so it is impossible to say whether or not the high and learned tribunal would be more respected than the Judicial Committee of the Privy Council which many were so anxious for it to replace.

More frustratingly, it is difficult to know whether or not many of those in 1954–63 involved in inventing it *expected* it to be used or not. There are a few hints in the papers of the Church Assembly Revision Committee on the 1963 Measure. In October 1961 the Committee received a letter from the Archdeacon of Lindisfarne, who was concerned that "this Measure seems to be widely regarded as a device by which the laity may obtain their legal rights from the clergy" and that "there is all the difference in the world between a legal system which is frankly in desuetude and a legal system which is being purposefully dusted down and burnished ready for use."[62] The Committee however rejected his concerns and those of a Major Monckton, who seemed to regard church courts *per se* as insufficiently spiritual,[63] and continued burnishing. A rather better informed and serious alternative proposal from Chancellor Garth Moore will be discussed below.

Some measure of the public ignorance of the whole business is provided by a cutting from the *Guardian* of 23 February 1962 (NB at this date this is the modern secular newspaper, ex-*Manchester Guardian*, not the Tractarian periodical) archived with the Revision Committee papers, claiming anachronistically of the church courts that "on lay members they can enforce, on pain of imprisonment, public penance." The article acknowledges the decent work of reform, but reflects "Church courts, which enjoy the same status [as Crown courts] have glided down the back passages of time, sheltered from the winds of change and heavy with the must of the Star Chamber"[64] before recommending wholesale disestablishment of the Church of England.

There are a number of reasons why no cases of controversy have ever reached the Court of Ecclesiastical Causes Reserved, not all of which may prove the *Guardian* unjustified. Unease with assent to the 39 Articles, led by Ian Ramsey, Bishop of Durham, led to a Doctrine Commission Report debated by the Church Assembly in 1969[65] and thence to Amending Canon 4[66] which substituted the present looser Declaration of Assent. Issues of liturgical dispute were channelled into the proposals for new rites which led eventually to the Alternative Service Book 1980; we have already seen the disinclination of the Church to persecute supposed heretics over a long period; any case brought would be likely to summon up the spirit of the controversies of 1850–90.

Yet it seems likely that the sheer heaviness of the CECR, including the provision for a preliminary hearing by a committee of Convocation,[67] with its concomitant costs (especially for the High Court judges)[68] acted as a discouragement to its use in the first instance. Ironically given that any case would be likely to be one of great preceding controversy, the only sentence the CECR can impose for a first offence is monition,[69] which if treated with Mackonochie-like defiance, would resolve nothing. And after 50 years' quietude, the total lack of any developed jurisprudence within the Court means that it would be difficult to predict the outcome of any decision. Although the bishops appointed have been those with as far as possible some knowledge of relevant law, the obvious failure of Eric Kemp in *re. St Stephen's Walbrook* to refer to the Holy Table Measure 1964, as noted in Chapter 3 above, gives some indication of the level of doubt involved.

Excommunication and intercommunion

Between 1947 and 1970 the Church of England achieved a subtle revolution in discipline of the laity, little remarked upon at the time, in spite of the depth of breach effected with ancient tradition. As noted, in the 1947 draft Canon IX, provision was suggested, but later abandoned, to use exclusion from communion as a penalty for breaches of the canons. What remained was the draft Canon XXI, providing a replacement for the ambiguous provisions of the old Canons 26 and 27, and the rubrics of the Prayer Book about 'notorious and open evil livers' so thoroughly debated in *Jenkins v Cook, Banister v Thompson* and *Rex v Dibdin*. This stated that a minister could refuse to communicate any "who be openly known to live in sin notorious without repentance, or any who have maliciously or openly contended with their neighbours"[70] provided he told the bishop within 14 days and then followed his instructions. In revision to become Canon B16, the order was reversed to "malicious and open contention with his neighbours, or other grave and open sin without repentance,"[71] echoing Dibdin's views in 1908 that the main purpose of repulsion was the peace of the community rather than the punishment of sin, and removing the rather obviously sexual implications of 'live in sin' of the draft. The clergy were also forbidden to repel until they had consulted the bishop, except for "grave and immediate scandal."[72] It is notable that in Doe's *Legal Framework* the only judgments cited to support the application of Canon B16 are those discussed in the previous chapter,[73] and there would seem little certainty of the courts today adopting the precedents in very different circumstances.

This provision was also, unusually, incorporated into the text of the Prayer Book itself by Section 3 of the Prayer Book (Miscellaneous Provisions) Measure 1965.[74] The relationship between this and the Sacrament Act 1547 has never to my knowledge been tested in court. Recalling however that the original function of the Prayer Book rubric had been to refer cases to the ecclesiastical courts whose original business much involved determining and revoking excommunications, the nearly contemporary Ecclesiastical Jurisdiction Measure 1963 removed all possibility of a church court imposing general excommunication. All repulsion from communion can only now be a response to a pastoral situation, and it is notable that in the widespread controversy over sexuality in recent decades, for example, the House of Bishops has consistently advised that there can be no bar on communion for individuals.[75]

The final stage of abandonment of any version of the ancient doctrine of excommunication occurred in 1969–70, not it would seem by design, but as the incidental outcome of generous ecumenism. The question of intercommunion between churches had been passed from the Canon Law process to a separate Commission which reported in 1968. However, a long debate in Church

Assembly led to the adoption of the proposal of Geoffrey Lampe.[76] This resulted in a draft Canon B15A, which was debated by the new General Synod, most decisively in July 1971, providing for members of other churches in good standing to be freely admitted to communion. The debate recognised that in practical reality, many people had thus communicated as unchallenged guests for many years, the Chairman of the House of Laity for example responding to the rigorists:

> How many parsons in this country ever challenge anyone who presents himself at the communion rail? In fact, it is only those who are sufficiently conscientious to see the parson and ask if they would be welcome, who are virtually ever turned away. To legislate on these lines seems to me unreal and, though I know it is not intended in this way, hypocritical.[77]

Although there were fears that the result would be "merest Congregationalism … far removed from any Catholic conception of Church and sacrament, to say nothing of any regard for the balance of good order in the Church"[78] the proposal was passed by a large majority.

More striking is that although there were fears raised about confirmation and the rather general sense of catholic sacramental order, there was no reference to the historic relationship between communion and moral discipline. This is more surprising when one considers that a large number of churches were then still refusing communion to remarried divorcees, and certainly refusing to marry them. But as soon as B15A was passed this becomes nonsense – one may refuse to marry Mr Jones to the second Mrs Jones, and repel them from communion. They go down the road and are welcomed with open arms at the United Reformed Church, both to marry and worship. A few months later, they begin to return occasionally as visiting members of the URC, and canon dictates they must be welcomed at communion after all.

An alternative vision?

The evolution of the Church of England's legal system in the postwar period, although it offered a forum for the ongoing tension over liturgical issues in particular, was not seriously contested by those involved. However, in the writings and more particularly the actions of one significant commentator, E. Garth Moore (d. 1990), it is possible to make out an alternative perspective, strongly echoing the canonical tradition. Moore's significance as a commentator and teacher is now complicated by the fact that (whilst this work was in progress) he was identified as the perpetrator of serious sexual abuse over many years, and the inadequate response of the Church of England to his victims remains the subject of publicity at the time of writing. Although there has been public controversy over other cases of posthumous identification of alleged abusers, notably Bishop George Bell, in Moore's case both the agreed payment of compensation by the Church of England and the apparently uncontested report of his deathbed repentance leave the matter beyond doubt.[79]

Moore's obituaries recognised him as an eccentric[80] and that some found him "a difficult, prejudiced pedant."[81] Any reckoning of character in this assessment has been set aside but the implicit theology of church law emerging in this study stands distinctly against his. As well as being one of very few academics in the field of Canon Law, Moore was by 1957 Chancellor of the dioceses of Southwark, Durham and Gloucester, and had built a reputation by bold judgments in faculty cases which saw "the Church of England freed from the shackles of many nineteenth century judgments concerned with ritual and ceremonial."[82] In a context where the canons were also being revised to remove such shackles, he captured the spirit of the period and the sympathy of more catholic-minded Anglicans, notably Eric Kemp, whose collaborator he was in promoting the study of law in the Church of England and eventually contributing to the founding of the Ecclesiastical Law Society.

During the revision of what became the Ecclesiastical Jurisdiction Measure 1963, Moore contributed to the Revision Committee a memorandum[83] proposing a noticeably different structure for dealing with doctrinal cases, whereby they would be heard by the Chancellor of the diocese at first instance, with a first appeal as in faculty and conduct cases to the provincial court, and the Court of Ecclesiastical Causes Reserved deployed only as a court of final appeal. The proposal was rejected by the Committee at their first meeting, but it is possible to see in Moore's proposal an aspiration that chancellors such as himself might return to something like their medieval status, settling many difficult questions decisively as the bishop's judicial *alter ego* and restoring some of the lost orderliness of the Church of England. Moore subsequently (and perversely, given his complicated proposals?) attacked the Measure as unnecessarily complex in the debates in the Church Assembly.[84]

Moore's 1967 textbook on Canon Law famously begins with the text of Genesis 1.1, presenting his theology that the law of the Church is but the local and subsidiary application of the law of God in creation.[85] His commentary upon the courts, however, is largely a clear description of the structures and their functioning, lamenting only that the new structure introduced by the EJM 1963 is still as "complicated and cumbersome"[86] as the old and not admitting to his disappointment that his preferred proposals were not adopted. A clearer perspective on his particular views is offered by the most important disciplinary case to be brought under the 1963 Measure, in which neither the accused nor the judge were the 'normal people' Archbishop Fisher had spoken of, and which for many decisively confirmed the ineffectiveness of the Church of England's judicial systems.

The case of Mr Bland

The case of Michael Bland, Rector of Buckland with Laverton and Stanton with Snowshill, in the diocese of Gloucester, was heard before Chancellor Garth Moore and assessors at Gloucester Consistory Court in 1969 and before the Court of Arches in 1970, and an analysis by Stephen Pix including unpublished papers was published in 2001,[87] and is referred to extensively below. Mr Bland seems to have been an aggressive, difficult man, ill at ease with his genteel Cotswolds parishioners. Moore's judgment was of deprivation, but most of the charges were successfully appealed, resulting in only a rebuke. The whole case can be seen as a desperate and ultimately disastrous attempt to remedy a pastoral disaster, not least because Mr Bland remained in post until 1987, shortly before his death.[88] The charges against him were four of neglect of duty and four of conduct unbecoming, but Pix's account makes it clear that all in fact involved somewhat similar clashes in which the Rector's defensive personality was manifest. The charges will be explained before looking at the case under two interrelated themes: as an exercise of judgment by Garth Moore as Chancellor, and manifesting some of his distinctive concerns as noted above; and as in the end an expensive failure which led many to regard the disciplinary provisions in the 1963 Measure as worse than useless.

Although taken in the opposite order in the courts, the more straightforward part of the case concerned the conduct unbecoming, which although gathered under four headings all concerned Bland's rude and aggressive behaviour, whether in writing or in person. The excerpts from letters and incidents described by Pix are interesting for showing not only Bland's personality, but as in other noted cases above like Mr Davidson or Dr Free, a determined self-defence based upon his own dearly-held principles, in this case his rights as incumbent and belief that all his parishioners should adhere loyally to the churches in his idiosyncratic charge. Particularly remarkable is his letter to a Lancashire clergyman who was to officiate at the marriage of his god-daughter, a parishioner of Bland's who had outraged him by preferring to worship and marry at neighbouring Broadway. He lectures the unfortunate on the "gross perversion of your duties"[89] for allowing her to do so and including the grandiose claim:

> it would be more seemly if future ceremonies of this kind were to be by licence obtained from the surrogate, rather than by banns. It is extremely distasteful to me to be forced by law to proclaim at divine service the unprofessional and ungentlemanly conduct of a fellow-clergyman. As it is, you can be assured that the worship of a small country parish, despicable though it may be, has been entirely upset for the past six weeks by this unnecessary formality.[90]

The charges of neglect of duty were more complex, because each of the three serious charges (Bland was acquitted of the first charge, leaving church early) potentially involved a doctrinal element, which he used in his defence. The second charge was of refusal to baptise, specifically the third child of a Mr and Mrs Haynes, on the alleged grounds that the request came from Mr Haynes, who never attended church, although the conversation reported was not conclusive. Significantly, Bland offered the defence that his real reason was a doctrinal objection to indiscriminate infant baptism, and that if tried at all, this should be by the Court of Ecclesiastical Causes Reserved and not the Consistory Court. This is the charge which provides the most interesting display of Moore's viewpoint.

The third charge was that Bland had prevented a Mr Bryant from entering church in order to hear and object to his son's banns of marriage, and the transcript cited by Pix gives a lively account of his inexplicable behaviour. Finally, the fourth charge was that he had repelled from Communion a reporter, Paul Raymer, on no other grounds than that he was a reporter, although Bland made the defence that he had received no notice of intention to communicate. Unfortunately, the published report of the appeal judgment omits the reasoning for the Court of Arches allowing the appeal on these charges, and so it is difficult to provide closer analysis.

In Moore's judgment of the charge of failure to baptise, it was necessary to show with clarity that the law of the Church offered Bland no freedom for his 'conscientious objection' to indiscriminate baptism to be entertained as a serious doctrinal question, and that he had simply failed in his pastoral duty to baptise as required of all parish clergy as defined by Canons 68 and 69 of 1604. In responding to this difficulty, Moore took the opportunity to restate his disapproval of the distinction between conduct and reserved cases, arguing that since the allegation was not about Bland's doctrinal opinions, but about his actions, it was a conduct matter only. The interpretation here is that it suited Moore's own conception of his role to call Bland to account as Chancellor and not pass jurisdiction to the CECR. This view was accepted by the Court of Arches, perhaps without the same justification, but nonetheless willing to avoid further complicating an already difficult case.

Moore was faced with the difficulty that although the canons on baptism (B21–25) had been the subject of recent debate, the controverted encounter with Mr Haynes had happened in October 1966, before the new-minted canon had been promulged, and so the relevant provision remained the old Canon 68 of 1604, which carried an anachronistic fixed penalty of three months suspension. Leaning on the surprising claim that he had been unable to obtain a copy of the new canons (even given the technology of the time, this seems remarkable for a leading scholar of Canon Law who had also been a member of the Church Assembly), Moore chose to base his instruction to the assessors on an altogether different ground (my emphasis, italics original):

> the offence, if offence there be, springs from the jus commune, the Common law of the Church, part of the law of this land, and I am not proposing to give an exhaustive exposition of the law as it relates to baptism, because it is not necessary for the purposes of this case. Let it suffice to simply say this: that there is in law – **and I so rule** – there is in law a *prima facie* duty on an incumbent to baptise the children of his parishioners.[91]

The Court of Arches found a number of reasons to reject Moore's reasoning and conclude that he had misdirected the assessors, particularly his introduction of an irrelevant analogy about the nature of negligence. However, in responding to the section above, they made careful reference to the drafting of the canons[92] and the existence (unmentioned by Moore) of the 1957 Act of Convocation setting out in different but related terms the duty of clergy to prepare parents before a baptism,[93] giving succour to the many clergy like Bland who were hesitant about indiscriminate baptism.

In the light of that critique, it is possible to see quite how presumptuous Moore's ruling actually was. He had recently in his own writings condemned the 1604 Canons by quoting with endorsement the disparaging words of Hensley Henson that they could only be read "with a feeling of dismay, so remote are they from the circumstances of … life, so harsh their tone, so frankly impractical … their practical requirements."[94] Yet rather than heed the recent wisdom of the Convocations in both their Act and painstaking drafting, he turned to the idea that *he* could authoritatively declare the true law of the Church, based on the medieval concept of a natural unity of Canon Law. It is likely that Moore had read Edmund Wood's *Regal Power of the Church*, republished in 1948 by his friend Eric Kemp, and his argument carries more than a little of Wood's appeal to 'œcumenical custom' that overrode the disappointingly provincial rules of the Church of England.

The Court of Arches found many other areas to criticise Moore's reasoning, but the most significant was the censure of deprivation, where he was to be most roundly criticised, 'much to his grief and chagrin.'[95] His sentencing suggests again a magnification of the role of the chancellor:

> When it comes to selecting the sentence or censure which I should impose in this case, I remind myself that it has long been the practice of the courts spiritual to pass sentence pro salute animae – for the good of the soul – and I give that a wider interpretation, and say that I think it is my duty to pass sentence pro salute animarum – for the good of souls, which includes both the accused, the convicted clerk himself, and the souls of those who were committed to his care.
>
> I am quite convinced that I should be failing in my duty if I did not do all that lies in my power to ensure that the convicted clerk and the cures where he was now working part company now for ever. I know of no way in which I can ensure this except by the censure or sentence of deprivation.[96]

The Court of Arches was blunt: "In our judgment this was a wholly wrong approach."[97] They went on to in effect accuse Moore of beginning with the assumption that Bland had to be removed from his parish, and judging all the offences worthy of deprivation, without discrimination, to achieve that aim. Having allowed the appeal on all charges except the offensive letters, they found this far too severe, and reduced the censure to a rebuke, with the result that, as noted, Mr Bland and the people of Buckland had to rub along together for another 16 years.

The subtleties of the theology of ecclesiastical law were of course not closely followed by most; the conclusion given by Pix is simple "the case lay in ruins, and along with it any expectation that the Ecclesiastical Jurisdiction Measure 1963 would solve all the problems associated with enforcing discipline among the clergy, where previous legislative efforts had failed."[98] One may speculate whether if the first such case had been heard before a less particular Chancellor than Garth Moore the whole system might in fact have been inaugurated in a less hopeless way. Combined with the expense, the effect of the Bland case was to reinforce the longstanding mindset of the bishops to avoid court at all costs in cases of difficult clergy. The legislative response, in the form of the Incumbents (Vacation of Benefice) Measure 1977, which prescribed a non-condemnatory process to identify pastoral breakdown, has been little used, and a generation passed before a new spirit of discipline hovered over the Church of England.

Notes

1 Mark Chapman, *Anglican Theology* (Bloomsbury T&T Clark 2011) 76.
2 Robert E. Rodes Jr., *Law and Modernisation in the Church of England* (Notre Dame 1991) 217.
3 Ibid., 216–18.
4 *The Ecclesiastical Courts. Principles of Reconstruction* (SPCK 1954) 16–20.
5 For reasons of its own, the *Church Times* always uses 'unfrocking,' or so I was told when I wished to use 'defrocking' in an article on the subject a few years ago.
6 *The Canon Law of the Church of England* (SPCK 1947) 141.
7 *The Canons of the Church of England* (SPCK 1969) 31.
8 Rodes, *Modernisation,* 218–19.
9 Letter of Davidson to the Bishop of Norwich, quoted in *The Times*, 28 May 1932.
10 *The Times*, 22 October 1932.
11 Alan Wilson, *The authority of church and party among London Anglo-Catholics, 1880–1914, with special reference to the Church Crisis, 1898–1904* (unpublished Oxford DPhil thesis, 1988) 43.
12 Ibid., 60.
13 Ibid., 49.
14 Ibid., 68.
15 Ibid., 111.
16 *Royal Commission on Ecclesiastical Discipline* (HMSO 1906) conclusion.
17 Ibid., conclusion.
18 John G. Maiden, "Discipline and Comprehensiveness: The Church of England and Prayer Book Revision in the 1920s" in *Studies in Church History 43. Doctrine and Discipline* (Boydell 2007).
19 Michael Yelton, *Anglican Papalism* (Canterbury Press 2005) Ch. 4.
20 Maiden, *Discipline*, 385.
21 A. Fox, *Dean Inge* (1960) 216, cited in Yelton, *Papalism,* 78–9.
22 Norman Doe, *Christian Law. Contemporary Principles* (CUP 2013) 154.
23 Mark Hill, *Ecclesiastical Law* (2nd ed. OUP 2001) §1.33, 17.
24 *Acts of the Convocations of Canterbury and York*, ed. A. F. Smethurst and H. R. Wilson (SPCK 1961) 62–4.
25 G. K. A. Bell, *Randall Davidson* (OUP 1935) 1134.
26 Ibid., 1150, note 3.
27 Adrian Hastings, *A History of English Christianity 1920–1990* 3rd Ed. (SCM Press 1991) 261.
28 *Doctrine in the Church of England* (SPCK 1938) 37–9.
29 H. Hensley Henson, *Retrospect of an Unimportant Life, Vol II* (OUP 1943) 28.
30 Ibid., 235.
31 H. Hensley Henson, *The Church of England* (CUP 1939) 108–10.

32 Robert Beaken, *Cosmo Lang, Archbishop in War and Crisis* (I. B. Tauris & Co, 2012) 175.
33 John Gunstone, *Lift High the Cross. Anglo-Catholics and the Congress Movement* (Canterbury Press 2010) 212.
34 Beaken, *Lang*, 176–8.
35 Carpenter, Edward, *Archbishop FISHER – His Life and Times* (Canterbury Press 1991) 295–305.
36 Ibid., 304.
37 Ibid., 300.
38 Hastings, *English Christianity*, 536.
39 Owen Chadwick, *Michael Ramsey, A Life* (OUP 1991) 371–2.
40 Hastings, *English Christianity*, 551–2.
41 *GSP* 13 February 1985, 128.
42 P. A. Lovegrove, at *GSP* 13 February 1985, 135.
43 See *GSP* 13 February 1985, 143.
44 Edited and published as Peter Boulton "Twentieth Century Revision of Canon Law in the Church of England" *5EccLJ* 353–68 (2000).
45 *Chronicle of Convocation*, 19 January 1960, 9.
46 Boulton, *Revision*, 357.
47 Augur Pearce, "Episcopacy and the Common Law" *7EccLJ* 203–6.
48 *Chronicle of Convocation*, 19 January 1960, 8.
49 Boulton, *Revision*, 364.
50 *Church and State. Report of the Archbishops' Commission* (General Board of Finance of the Church of England 1970) 61–3.
51 *The Canon Law of the Church of England* (SPCK 1947) 109.
52 Ibid., 109.
53 Boulton, *Revision*, 366–7.
54 *Acts of the Convocations*, 172–3.
55 Boulton, *Revision*, 367.
56 Ibid., 366.
57 *The Ecclesiastical Courts.*
58 Rodes, *Modernisation*, 362.
59 *Ecclesiastical Courts*, 53–6.
60 E. W. Kemp, *Shy But Not Retiring. The memoirs of the Right Reverend Eric Waldram Kemp. Edited and prepared for publication by Jeremy Matthew Haselock* (Continuum 2006) 125–6.
61 See Sir Mark Hedley "Practical Aspects of the Clergy Discipline Measure" Lecture to the Ecclesiastical Law Society, 11/10/17, 1.
62 Letter to the Revision Committee 12 October 1961, at EJ17, Church of England Records Office.
63 Letter of Major R.P.F. Monckton, EJ14.
64 Cutting from *The Guardian*, 23 February 1962, filed with 'EJ' papers, without number.
65 Church Assembly Report of Proceedings, vol. 49 (1969) 165–193.
66 Substantially debated in 1972, cf. *General Synod Proceedings* 3.4, pp. 789–804, but not promulged until 1975 since it could not issue until the passage of the Worship and Doctrine Measure 1974.
67 *EJM* 1963 §42.
68 I am grateful to Mr Sion Hughes Carew, present Secretary to the Clergy Discipline Commission, for this point.
69 Mark Hill, *Ecclesiastical Law* 2nd ed. (OUP 2001) 160.
70 *Canon Law*, 118–19.
71 *Canons*, 14.
72 *Canons*, 1.

73 Norman Doe, *The Legal Framework of the Church of England: A critical study in a comparative context.* (Clarendon Press 1996) 344–5.
74 *Church Acts & Measures*, 3rd ed., 964–5.
75 e.g. House of Bishop Statement on Civil Partnerships, §23, www.churchofengland.org/sites/default/files/2017-11/House%20of%20Bishops%20Statement%20on%20Civil%20Partnerships%202005.pdf (accessed 15 December 2017); House of Bishops Pastoral Guidance on Same Sex Marriage, §18, www.churchofengland.org/sites/default/files/2017-11/House%20of%20Bishops%20Pastoral%20Guidance%20on%20Same%20Sex%20Marriage.pdf (accessed 15 December 2017).
76 Boulton, *Revision,* 363.
77 *GSP,* 13 July 1971, 292.
78 Ibid., 286.
79 *Church Times*, 4 December 2015, 5.
80 Obituary, *2EccLJ* 63.
81 *Church Times*, 15 June 1990, 4.
82 Obituary, *2EccLJ* 63. The most significant example of Moore's judgement in faculty cases (allowing provision for reservation) is *Rector and Churchwardens of Bishopwearmouth v Adey* [1958].
83 At EJ1, Church of England Records Office.
84 Stephe Pix "Archdeacon of Cheltenham v. Bland: a sledgehammer to crack a nut" *6EccLJ* 135.
85 E. Garth Moore, *An Introduction to English Canon Law* 1st ed. (OUP 1967) 1–5.
86 Moore, *Canon Law*, 138.
87 Pix, *Bland,* 135–49.
88 *Crockford's Clerical Directory,*www.crockford.org.uk/people/23696/the-revd-michael-bland (accessed 19 April 2016).
89 Pix, *Bland*, 145, citing the transcript *Pleadings*, 32.
90 Ibid., 144–5, from the same source.
91 Ibid., p. 63, at *6EccLJ* 138.
92 [1971] 3 W.L.R. 711–13.
93 *Acts of Convocation*, 155.
94 Moore, *Canon Law*, 6, quoting Henson, *Retrospect*, vol. I, 299.
95 Pix, *Bland,* 147.
96 [1971] 3 W.L.R. 716.
97 [1971] 3 W.L.R. 716.
98 Pix, *Bland,* 148.

7. The lingering temptation

I have set out a thesis that from the experiences of having her deepest divisions fought through the ecclesiastical courts in the nineteenth century, the Church of England lived through the twentieth largely in the wisdom that a broad and even sometimes chaotic liberty was the better path. This wisdom, only explicitly recognised by a few such as Hensley Henson, continued to be challenged by those who continued to favour judicial vengeance upon their opponents, but was embodied in the revision of the Church's law in the post-war period at least as much by pragmatic accident as inspired design. After noting an interesting case of non-judicial interaction between liberal breadth and the canonical tradition, this chapter will look at the revision of the disciplinary structures of the Church since 1990, noting how narrowly the return of an active jurisdiction over doctrine and liturgy was avoided, before considering the effect of the law on the current controversies over sexuality.

The Freeman case

With each generation comes a new subject for Christians to disagree about, and in the later twentieth century this was the very doctrine of God himself. Building on sources going back as far as Feuerbach in the nineteenth century, but also in traceable relationship to Bultmann, Tillich and Jenkins, a school of theology which had branded itself the Sea of Faith Network evolved in the 1980s around Cambridge academic Don Cupitt. Cupitt's movement towards a Christianity in which God was increasingly spoken of as a projection of human aspiration aroused great controversy, not least because the direct alternative – describing God as a knowable object – is clearly also an inadequate theology. Cupitt himself was comparatively invulnerable to ecclesiastical attack in his academic position as Dean of Emmanuel College, Cambridge, and so the significant fire fell upon one of his associates.

Anthony Freeman, having known Eric Kemp as his chaplain at Exeter College, Oxford, had then as a young priest followed Kemp from Worcester to serve as his chaplain in Chichester, followed by a parish and then a small parish combined with the diocesan role of Continuing Ministerial Education Advisor from 1989. However, as Kemp wrote with a hint of betrayal and scandal, "*without any of us knowing*, he had become involved with a group led by the radical Cambridge theologian, Don Cupitt, calling itself 'The Sea of Faith'" (italics original).[1] The particular manifestation of Freeman's involvement was that he had written up his thoughts as *God with Us: The Case for Christian Humanism*, and Kemp as bishop felt that this represented an extreme of theological modernism which he could not tolerate, particularly in a staff member responsible for clergy education. It is possible that any other bishop at the time might have felt similarly, but we can note that, as with Phillpotts or Ryle, it takes an authoritarian bishop *and* a controversial cleric to generate a serious clash.

In fairness to Kemp, his response was staged, and sought alternative ways out. He arranged for Freeman to meet 'retired professors (chums of his)'[2] in an attempt to move his theological position to a place he could tolerate. Kemp rather brusquely concludes "Anthony therefore left the diocese. He has not been in touch with me since."[3] This glosses over what in fact occurred. As can be traced readily in the *Church Times*, he used his absolute discretion over the continuance of Freeman's licence as Continuing Ministerial Education officer to withdraw it, leaving him in an unsustainable position as priest of a tiny parish.[4] Freeman comments "I thought I was treated very fairly, being allowed to continue on full pay and living in my vicarage for a full year with only the lightest of duties."[5] When the year was up, however, Kemp wrote with his unambiguous opinion that he must leave in a letter, like others below, which Anthony has kindly shared with me:

> It is clear … that your position has not changed and that you are still asserting that God is nothing more than the sum of human aspirations and has no objective existence. This is so far removed from the assertions of the Christian creeds and the foundation documents of the Church of England that none of us [i.e., himself and his suffragan bishops] could receive the Declaration of Assent from you with a good conscience knowing the interpretation that you would be putting on it.[6]

In response, Freeman acknowledged his bishop's power to remove him (because the parish post was tied to the CME one) and that he would have to go, but registered his protest:

> This does not mean that I accept your opinion that my theology prevents my holding office in the Church of England. The Declaration of Assent does not require ministers to interpret the concept of God in any particular way. To insist that all clergy must affirm the 'objective existence' of God would be to beg questions which have long been debated among Christian theologians.[7]

Freeman duly left his parish in August 1994, prompting his supporters in the Sea of Faith to write to the Archbishop of Canterbury that their conference:

> deeply regrets that for the first time this century a Church of England parish priest has been removed from his living for publishing views unacceptable to his bishop. The conference fully and unreservedly supports the Revd Anthony

> Freeman in his efforts to preserve a liberal and tolerant spirit within the Church of England.[8]

From the viewpoint of the interaction of law and discipline, the significance of the Freeman case is not only that it was a rarity, but that it was only possible to proceed as it did because Freeman did not in fact hold the living (as the Sea of Faith casually referred to it) but was a licensed priest-in-charge, with no security of tenure. He was therefore removed from post without any due process beyond Kemp's consultation with his suffragans and was not placed on the official black list afterwards. Had he published his book as an incumbent in the diocese of Chichester, it would have been necessary for Kemp to promote a case against him before the Court of Ecclesiastical Causes Reserved, and it seems unlikely that even as an enthusiast for that court with whose invention he had been so involved and of which he was an episcopal judge, Kemp would have considered it worth the expense and uncertainty. The Freeman case was, however, almost certainly among the situations in the mind of those who came to revise the structures of both clergy discipline and terms of service in the 2000s, with the result that a different situation would prevail today.

A coda to the Freeman story is provided by the fact that although he has not in any way significantly altered his theological opinions, he has been gradually rehabilitated into the Church of England's ministry. At the time of his departure from Chichester, he found that the bishops of the Church of England (and Rowan Williams, then at Monmouth) closed ranks in refusing to consider him for any position, and that although Richard Holloway of Edinburgh and Jack Spong of Newark were sympathetic, they did not have any practical opportunities available.[9] Having subsequently moved to Devon, Freeman some years later sought, with the support of the local PCC, for permission to officiate. Not being on the black list, there was no formal procedure, but after interviewing Freeman, the bishop of Exeter, Hewlett Thompson, wrote a careful letter giving the rector of Crediton permission for 'AF' to take services in Crediton only, with strong caveats, including the statement:

> it would be inappropriate for anyone to imply that the modest development you can foster amounts to a "rehabilitation" of AF by the Church of England. He was not formally tried in the courts and so the Church has not given a verdict on his theological teaching. The Bishop of Chichester, as entitled, withdrew his licence to minister in a particular parish because in his judgment AF's teaching in certain respects contravened accepted understandings. It is not inconsistent with that discipline if I give my goodwill to a limited development. The Anglican way does not stifle public theological exploration; but it must be clearly understood that such exploration belongs to the seminar, lecture room and published material, but not to the pulpit; and as I have written above, published material should not imply that AF is in some formal way a priest of this diocese.[10]

Two years' later, upon the appointment of a new bishop, Michael Langrish (and incidentally when Eric Kemp had retired) Freeman sought a wider Permission to Officiate. This was refused in favour of formalising his position with an official PTO for Crediton only, Langrish being unwilling to authorise an itinerant preaching ministry, stating

> I continue to be concerned about your theological position and it does seem to me that you have not fully grappled with, for instance, John McQuarrie's [sic] assertion that the dangers of denying the reality of God are greater than those of affirming it.

He also noted that Freeman's theology was still developing and seeing 'preaching as a pastoral activity rooted in a particular context' guided him to develop his ministry in the community where he was known as the most 'fertile soil for future growth.'[11]

In 2009, however, when in response to the need to renew all Permissions to Officiate throughout the diocese as part of safeguarding proceedings, Freeman was issued with a new PTO, he noticed that it was no longer limited to Crediton, and he attributes this to an oversight by diocesan staff.[12] Alternatively, it may have been considered that theological debate in the Church had moved on in such a way that adherence to the Sea of Faith was no longer considered dangerously heretical. The final and perverse result, however, was that when Freeman moved in 2013 to live in Chichester, he was issued with an unrestricted PTO by the Bishop of Chichester, Martin Warner, valid until 2018[13] and no doubt renewable thereafter. Whilst it is arguable that Eric Kemp upheld the discipline of the Church by removing Freeman from post, he in the end failed to terminate his ministry as a priest, and almost certainly gave much incidental publicity to the theology and personalities of the Sea of Faith.

I have not found any real parallel to the Freeman story in the Church of England, but there is an indirect comparison from Ireland in Andrew Furlong, Dean of Clonmacnoise, who held a distinctly non-real account of the Christian faith. In his own words:

> The story of the Son who is sent by his Father to leave heaven, who lives out a human life and then who dies for the salvation of the world is not, I consider, a true story in a literal sense. Nor is the story about his being raised from death and his returning to his heavenly Father an account to be taken literally. In my view, nothing like that ever really happened.[14]

As told in his verbose memoir, the response of his bishop to online parish magazine articles in 2002 expressing views of this sort was to suspend him and announce the convening of a provincial court to try him for publishing "beliefs contrary to the doctrine of the Church of Ireland."[15] In the event Furlong resigned his deanery before the trial could proceed, and so it is impossible to say whether the Church of Ireland would have had any greater success running a heresy trial than the Church of England.

Women priests – controversy, division and a new sort of court case

The second great subject of dispute in the Church of England towards the end of the twentieth century was whether or not women should (or, for some, could) be ordained priest, and then after some delay, bishop. It is not relevant here to recount the full progress of debate through Synod, from votes of principle in the 1970s, unsuccessful legislation on priests in the 80s and successful in the 90s, but three elements of the debate add to the picture of indiscipline in the Church built up here.

The first was a consequence of the staged progress of approval of women's ordination around the Anglican communion, which meant that by the 1980s there were women priests in Hong Kong, the USA and Canada among others, when the Church of England was still debating the subject, and in 1986 General Synod failed to approve a Measure which would have allowed such overseas priests to minister in England. However, a pattern of private celebrations by women ordained abroad, either visiting or now resident in England, grew and became a matter of controversy between those promoting such services and those decrying them as 'illegal.'[16]

Particular flashpoints included: a celebration in 1982 by Elizabeth Canham in the Deanery at St Pauls, which prompted the then Bishop of London, the conservative Graham Leonard, to a public repudiation;[17] a celebration by Joyce Bennett at a private meeting of the Movement for the Ordination of Women which happened to use a room at Church House, Westminster, leading to repudiation from the Archbishop of Canterbury and apologies by the conservative Chair of the House of Laity, Oswald Clark and the Home Secretary to the Queen in the (incorrect) belief that the room was within her jurisdiction (presumably as part of the curtilage of Westminster Abbey);[18] and the expulsion of the St Benet's Community from the use of the chapel of Queen Mary College in East London by Leonard.[19] Although Leonard was able to achieve the last by threatening action for trespass (the chapel, though ecumenical, was diocesan property) there was in fact a standoff between the legal opinions that the failure of the Women Ordained Abroad Measure forbade such celebrations, and a 1977 judgment of the Dean of Arches that it was not illegal in an unconsecrated space.[20] Whilst celebrations by women in church do not seem to have been attempted, there was little that the authorities could effectively do to inhibit private celebrations.

The second area which might be called indiscipline, in one of the many ironies which occur in the political history of the Church of England, also involved Graham Leonard, not in his role as enforcer but rather rebel against authority. This was the so-called Tulsa Affair, when Leonard accepted the invitation of a dissenting congregation of the Episcopal Church in the United States at Tulsa, Oklahoma, to visit and confirm in defiance of the jurisdiction of the ECUSA episcopate and the characteristically over-subtle discouragement of Archbishop Robert Runcie.[21] Conspicuous was Leonard's expressed frustration at what he perceived as the liberal defiance of authority combined with a certain presumption about his own role as a bishop being freely transferable outside his own jurisdiction.

In the long run, however, it could be argued that although disastrous for ecclesiological coherence, the Tulsa Affair revived the visiting-colonial-bishop tradition among Anglo-Catholics and so prepared for the provisions of the 1993 Act of Synod, providing alternative episcopal oversight for those unable to receive the ministry of women priests. Arguably, this thereby diverted into a sort of internalised schism a good deal of dissent which might otherwise have been engaged in breaches of discipline. This principled living-with-difference was formalised during the later stages of the agonised women bishops debates into the *Five Guiding Principles* (to which as a Diocesan Director of Ordinands supervising candidates I am now required to secure the assent of all ordinands) representing a success in accommodating deep difference in a way that is truly liberal in the older sense.

The final area of interest from a disciplinary viewpoint arose after the passage of the Measure to ordain women, in attempted judicial reviews of the decision of General Synod, firstly by the Church Society against the Ecclesiastical Committee of Parliament for the Measure, and then by Revd Paul Williamson, Rector of Hanworth, against the Archbishops, for the Canons made under the Measure. The first was heard by the Divisional Court in October 1993 and the latter by the Court of Appeal in March 1994, and both were dismissed on the solid grounds that the 1919 Enabling Act gave to the General Synod power to make Measures with the effect of statute, and which were therefore beyond any judicial review.[22]

Whilst these cases are perhaps marginal as far as discipline is concerned, being ultimately fruitless attempts to enlist the secular courts in support of religious conservatism, they represent the first attempt to enlist the courts in critique of the Church of England's higher authorities, which has been picked up in a different way under the Human Rights Act 1998, as seen below. Although expressing great reluctance to intervene, the High Court also upheld the episcopal order against conservative rebellion in *Gill v Davies* [1997], granting an injunction to prevent an ordination by an external bishop of a prospective curate unable to accept his incoming diocesan bishop's liberal views on sexuality.[23]

Renewed reform of clergy discipline for the twenty-first century – the first attempt

Particularly scandalous cases of indisciplined clergy tend to give rise to a legislative response. As the Church Discipline Act 1840 was the last bastard child of Dr Free, and the Incumbents (Vacation of Benefices) Measure 1977 that of Mr Bland, so it is possible to see the Clergy Discipline Measure 2003 as the offspring of Mr Tyler, who was tried under the 1963 Measure for adultery in 1991 and 1992. As a pure scandal case, it is not strictly relevant to this study, but the difficulties, notably a mistrial (one of the original assessors compromised his independence) overall cost and prurient media interest, were a major contribution to the belief that a new disciplinary system was needed. The lengthy disputes amongst the Chapter at Lincoln Cathedral in the late 1980s also contributed. A General Synod Working Party was therefore set to work, reaching its conclusions in the 1996 report *Under Authority*.

The report begins with caution, noting that 'All forms of authority are treated with suspicion and the exercise of discipline is unpopular.'[24] After a short survey of difficult cases since 1963 (Bland, Tyler, the Dean of Lincoln and the Freeman case) there is a degree of insider wisdom, noting "much anecdotal evidence that bishops are unwilling to utilise the 1963 Measure because of the cost, both in human and financial terms."[25] Yet after these nods to what we have noted as the Church's established wisdom, a concise theological section is followed by proposals for a radical revision of the system of clergy discipline. The theology is disappointing in feeling able to draw a theory of discipline undigested from the New Testament and early Church sources without any thorough consideration of the sorts of issues raised in this study about the realities of exercising discipline in a Church of flawed sinners. In particular, the report proposed abolishing the distinction between reserved and conduct cases, bringing all cases before the same new tribunals, although their examination of the disadvantages and advantages of the 1963 Measure (Chapter 2 of *Under Authority*) had not discussed the reasons behind the distinction, embodied in ecclesiastical law since 1892.

In proposing categories of offence under new legislation, *Under Authority* proposed five categories of offence, starting from scratch and abandoning the clear distinction between conduct and reserved cases made in the EJM 1963 and implicit since the Clergy Discipline Act 1892. Three covered the more conventional conduct or scandal subject matter: "neglect, culpable carelessness or gross inefficiency," "conduct inappropriate or unbecoming," and secular conviction.[26] The former reserved cases were proposed to be caught up under two headings. Ritual and ceremonial offences would be treated as "wilful disobedience to or breach of the laws ecclesiastical." This seems to show a certain naivety, since even if diversity in vesture and liturgy has broadened yet more since 1996, it is known that Eric Kemp as Bishop of Chichester certainly presided at Benediction, for example, a rite almost certainly in breach of the published laws ecclesiastical.

Most importantly, the report proposed identifying a new offence, as follows (my italics):

> TEACHING, PREACHING, PUBLISHING OR PROFESSING DOCTRINE OR BELIEF INCOMPATIBLE WITH THAT OF THE CHURCH OF ENGLAND AS EXPRESSED WITHIN ITS CREEDS AND FORMULARIES
>
> 6.18 Belief in central in a Christian Church and the Church of England is founded upon the teachings of the Scriptures, the ancient Creeds and its historic formularies. Our clergy are called upon to make a clear and consistent reiteration of the essentials of the faith. The Church of England represents a breadth of theological approach. It has been described as having a *hard central core (represented by the Scriptures and Creeds), and a less clear-cut, more fuzzy circumference*. If this is so, and if the Declaration of Assent taken by all in Holy Orders is to have any meaning, then there must be a limit to the breadth of doctrinal expression. Denial of the central core *must be excluded* if the community of faith is to retain any distinctiveness. This is not to suggest a

> denial of free speech, simply to insist that some doctrinal positions are inconsistent with being an authorised guardian or teacher of the church.[27]

This paragraph would appear to beg a number of questions, some of which will be explored in the conclusion of this study, particularly the idea that exclusion is necessary to secure identity. The central emphasis highlights an image which is not a direct quotation, but which echoes many of the speeches in the 1985 Synod debate on doctrine, notably that of Archbishop John Habgood, although I have also heard it attributed to Bishop John Robinson.[28] I have highlighted 'professing' as although it was probably intended to mean public statement, it sounds close to identifying 'thought-crime' which would take us right back to Elizabeth I. In the event, Synod was to respond decisively to the suggestion.

The Synod working party had received many submissions from interested parties, the one with almost certainly the most relevant expertise coming from of a parallel working party convened by the Ecclesiastical Law Society.[29] The ELS submission has many points in common with *Under Authority*, including the important view that reserved matters, i.e. concerning doctrine, could and should be considered by the same tribunals as conduct matters. This point carries, however, the following footnote recording a clear difference of opinion, prophetic for how General Synod was to respond (my emphasis, italics original):

> When the final draft of this paper was considered by the General Committee of the Ecclesiastical Law Society **a significant majority** of those present considered that the composition of any clergy disciplinary tribunal which had to consider a matter of *doctrine* should be differently constituted as is the case at present. The working party remains of the opinion that its recommendation at 5.6.17 is appropriate and adequate.[30]

Under Authority received its first hearing at General Synod in November 1996. In his introduction, Canon Hawker responded to the concerns including:

> the fear of witch hunts or heresy trials. Either could happen now even under the EJM. Our proposals introduce new safeguards, for the doctrine of the Church of England should not, and cannot, be determined by a disciplinary tribunal or court. To do so would be an abuse of process.[31]

As at several points in this period, it is very difficult to see whether those advocating a renewed disciplinary jurisdiction expected them to be actually used, or had thought out the likely long-term effects if they were. Synod accepted the report, but in debating how to take it forward, shaped the process decisively by accepting amendments.

The significant amendment for this study was that of the Archdeacon of Surrey, Robert Reiss, who proposed to omit the recommendation to bring reserved matters under the new tribunals. He cited the effects of historical perspective, the disastrous effect had such procedures been applied to Bishop Robinson or Bishop Jenkins, and finally:

> I am sure that it will lead to an endless series of complaints in some parishes where those who believe that they have a firm hold on the doctrine of the Church of England will think that their incumbent has not, and any expression that their incumbent might make that is considered too liberal or too Catholic or too Protestant will be the source of complaint.[32]

After two speeches from lay members which broadly stated the 'something must be done' position (the second referring extensively to Anthony Freeman), the Bishop of Guildford responded, attacking 'any suggestion that bishops and clergy are not engaged in a living relationship of communion'[33] and urging caution about bringing in judicial discipline. After such a very brief debate Synod, short of time as often, voted. The vote was given by hands in favour of the amendment 185–168, and being close was repeated by division, 222–208. By only 13 or 14 votes after a debate of four speeches the Church of England decided not to revive her legal jurisdiction for heresy.

Having removed reserved cases from the jurisdiction of the new tribunals, Synod spent many hours over many years until what became the Clergy Discipline Measure 2003 was finally passed. Since then the system shows many signs of having settled down to a low murmur, in part precisely because the cases considered normally involve incontestable crime or scandal (the distinction made in the Preface of 'I didn't do it' instead of 'it's no crime, you know') and because bishops have exercised their freedom to dismiss complaints which they think not appropriate (including one notable case below). The main content of the low murmur is that the unavoidable result of a complaint which gives the bishop a determining role is to distance the accused cleric from episcopal pastoral care; dioceses vary in the success with which they make alternative provision for this.

Periodic reportage of the progress of the CDM[34] does however draw attention to the fact that whilst many CDM cases are summary decisions following a criminal conviction, and a large number involve what might simply be termed unprofessional behaviour, typically involving drunkenness or financial irregularity, the one area of possible controversy where the Church does appear to be able to enforce a standard of discipline slightly above that of any other walk of life remains that of sex, in that a small number of cases have involved particularly scandalous adultery. Yet even this may not be wholly accepted, as Bursell muses:

> More worrying, however, is the anecdotal evidence of surprise in some clerical quarters that matters relating to the "private lives" of the clergy should be the subject of any complaint under the Clergy Discipline Measure. If this anecdote is accurate, it raises questions as to the training given to ordinands about Christian morality but also in relation to the standards of behaviour expected of the clergy, and the law applicable to them once ordained.[35]

Reform of clergy discipline for the twenty-first century – the second attempt

The Synod debate of November 1996 may have manifested the reluctance of the Church to restore a heresy jurisdiction, but it was not enough to permanently put off the House of Bishops. Recognising the difficulties in getting any version of the Clergy Discipline Measure into law at all, they allowed it to continue its slow progress whilst commissioning a new working party to look again at the problem of reserved cases under the leadership of the Bishop of Birmingham from 2000–02, succeeded by the Bishop of Chester who presented it for debate at Synod in July 2004. The paper (GS1554) sets out with some care the history of doctrinal controversy in the Church of England, and we shall return to consider its somewhat contradictory theology in the Conclusion. In practical terms, it proposed creating a doctrinal offence in the following terms (italics original):

> *professing, advocating or promoting beliefs which are incompatible with the doctrine of the Church of England by preaching or teaching or publicly communicating such beliefs.* [36]

Having reached a definition, rather than attempting any precise definition of 'the doctrine of the Church of England' the working party recommended a panel of theological experts to advise, appointed by the House of Bishops. A new tribunal, with both preliminary process and procedure closely following that of the CDM, was proposed, although leaving the CECR at a final court of appeal.

Bringing the new report before Synod in July 2004, amongst his commendations the Bishop of Chester uttered the following paragraph:

> Many in the Synod will ask themselves whether establishing a new tribunal system along these lines would increase the likelihood that a tribunal would consider actual cases. The group considered that very carefully, and ultimately found itself unable to answer such a hypothetical question. We have attempted to set the initial requirements for disciplinary proceedings to be instituted at least as high as under the EJM, and in certain respects significantly higher. We certainly saw it as no part of our purpose to increase the likelihood that new procedures would be invoked.[37]

Given that the 'increase' to which he referred was over a baseline of zero cases in 40 years, it is baffling that the learned working party was unable to say whether or not the fine system they were proposing would ever actually be used.

The debate gave space for a variety of viewpoints, including the Bishop of Rochester's assertion, rejected by his brother of Chester in his summing up, that the Church of England considered discipline a mark of a true church. Judge John Bullimore presented the view that any doctrinal courts would not work, both because of the difficulty of taking evidence for someone's views out of context, and because the standard against which to judge them was deeply problematic:

> We have a wide definition of doctrine: it is grounded in the Holy Scriptures, and in such teachings of the ancient Fathers and Councils of the Church as are agreeable to the said Scriptures. Then there is reference to the Thirty-nine Articles, and so on. This is a very elastic standard by which to judge someone's teaching. Is it not a fact that, over 2,000 years, almost any view on a particular doctrine has been held by someone over the centuries, who might otherwise be revered for other things that they have been taught, and anyone who is facing a tribunal could appeal to them?
>
> No one proclaims themselves as being unorthodox or a heretic: they believe that they have some extra insight or understanding.
>
> Nothing like this will do anything to change minds or correct error. Let us face it, no proceeding which does not involve copious amounts of firewood has ever produced even an apparent recantation. Some, at least, think that those days are over! The only thing that overcomes bad theology is good theology, not dismissals or inhibitions or whatever.[38]

To Bullimore's legal wisdom was added the more direct fear of liberals like John Drury, Dean of Christ Church that 'the drawbridge is creaking up, to cut the Church off from the world.'[39] Others weighed in for the defence of doctrine, including Richard Reiss who had changed his mind since 1996. Stephen Trott, though professing his own conservatism, echoed the wisdom of the Church:

> We are a broad Church, and I thank God for it. I belong to a very conservative doctrinal tradition myself, but I welcome the breadth and the splendour of the Church of England. It seems to me, to quote Bishop Gibson who is quoted in this report, [from his appendix to the 1906 Report on Ecclesiastical Discipline] "Every attempt to enforce the strict letter of the law by coercive measures has proved disastrous".
>
> We are a broad Church not by design but by accident, because the warring parties have fought themselves to a standstill.[40]

The vote was in the event dramatically close, with two-thirds of the bishops and three-quarters of the laity endorsing the recommendation to prepare legislation. But the House of Clergy voted 103–99 to reject it. This time by only four votes, in one house, was the Church of England spared 'an unsatisfactory situation in which case law was once again defining the Church's doctrine.'[41] Trott's 'standstill' is standing still, but it had not been so close to overturn for over a century.

Controversies anew – sex again

As noted above, the debate over women's ordination has reached a broad conclusion with only limited reference to the courts, but things have not been so simple in the world of sexuality, the overlapping subject of bitter controversy for some decades at the time of writing. Even so, there has been comparatively little in the sexuality debate for students of ecclesiastical discipline to investigate. There are several reasons for this. The first is that as a result of the history of criminalisation, the culture of homosexuality has been until recently in Britain shaped by a need for secrecy resulting in both concealment by gay people themselves, and the unwillingness of others to discuss openly. The response within the Church of England, encouraged by the advice not to pry in the 1989 document *Issues in Human Sexuality* has given rise to a 'don't ask, don't tell' culture where the official teaching that clergy may not be in same-sex relationships is belied by the reality of at least several hundred, including this author, who are. The second is that in this area, a degree of exclusion is effectively exercised by the selection process for ordination, because openly gay candidates will often be either directly discouraged or come to realise that they are not really wanted. This applies also to the ability of bishops or others to refuse appointments, including selection as bishops. Finally, as the teaching of the House of Bishops is based on forbidding actual sex and not relationships *per se*, there has naturally been a lack of direct evidence of disobedience available to give life to disciplinary action.

There is a further and rather complex reason, which is most relevant to this study. It is easy to identify an apparently clear set of authoritative texts which contain the Church of England's teaching on homosexuality: the motion passed overwhelmingly by General Synod in 1987 condemning 'homosexual genital acts,'[42] the document *Issues in Human Sexuality* produced by the House of Bishops and defined by them as setting the expectation of ordinands, and the resolution 1.10 of the 1998 Lambeth Conference (albeit the last has never been formally received in the Church of England). All these might be considered within the area of 'ecclesiastical quasi-legislation' identified by Norman Doe,[43] of uncertain legal standing until tested in court. However, the reality is that it has been clear for at least the last 20 years that there are strong and divergent views within the Church of England on the subject.

The result has been a textbook case of conflict avoidance, with major voices on either side reluctant to press matters to a crisis, and direct debate on the principle of same-sex relationships kept judiciously off the agenda of General Synod. The indirect result of this has been that the present position relies heavily on principles, such as Canon B30 on marriage (written when sex between men was still illegal in England) and the 1987 motion (adopted long before civil partnerships, let alone same-sex marriage, had been thought of) which have become outdated by changing society, but which the Church has been unable to either reaffirm or reform. In this context for the most part the strategy of the House of Bishops has been, at least until recently, very much in the spirit of wisdom identified above, to see that no good can come of court battles on the subject.

A new legal angle – the Case of John Reaney

Into this context appears a case, the cause of considerable tension and bitterness within the relevant diocese in the memory of the author, but whose interest for this study lies not so much in either the positions of the protagonists or the decision, but the nature of the case. The Reaney case is significant as the first case I have encountered where an aggrieved member of the Church (Reaney) sought remedy against the authorities of the Church (the Bishop and Diocese of Hereford) at a secular employment tribunal on a question of ethics or doctrine (as opposed to employment, raised by *Coker* [1997] and *Barthope* [1979][44]), building in that sense on the attempted judicial review of the ordination of women by Paul Williamson in the 1990s. This response has only really been possible since the Human Rights Act 1998, incorporating key elements of the European Convention on Human Rights into UK law, including the construction of all relevant law, including Church of England measures and canons, of whatever date. As perspicacious scholars of ecclesiastical law noted immediately,[45] the potential for impact within the Church of England was considerable. *Reaney* can be seen therefore as a partially successful attempt to impose a secular liberal discipline upon the Church and is of significant interest for that reason. It should also be noted, according to a recent study[46] that the Archbishops' Council deliberately and successfully lobbied for a broad religious exception clause to be included in the Employment Equality (Sexual Orientation) Regulations 2003 which were introduced pursuant to the HRA 1998, and maintaining the exception in the subsequent Equality Act 2010.

As noted above, a 'fence' against gay people in positions of responsibility has been only intermittently maintained in the modern Church of England, but it can be achieved by refusing appointments. What happened in Hereford in 2006 seems to have been the result of a failure of internal communications, and the subsequent result across the Church has been a tendency to much clearer advance statement for all posts of the relevant expectations. The situation arose out of the appointments process for a Diocesan Youth Worker, and is set out in great detail in the judgment of the subsequent tribunal.[47] Fortunately, most of the significant facts of the case are not in dispute, although both sides maintained their position after the judgment,[48] and the then Diocesan Secretary of Hereford, John Clark, maintains[49] that the diocese was let down by their legal team, who introduced the defence of religious exemption to indirect discrimination too late in the hearing.

In the shortlisting of candidates for the vacant post, a meeting on 30 May 2006 chaired by the Chair of the Board of Education, John Chapman, at which the Bishop was neither present nor directly represented, drew up a shortlist which included John Reaney, who had declared in his application that he was gay but presently single, the meeting believing that this would therefore not be a problem.[50] Subsequently at a meeting of the Bishop's Staff, the bishop, Anthony Priddis, voiced his concerns, confirming at the Tribunal that he had felt "great care was needed and there was a need to ask more about the Claimant's lifestyle."[51] 'Lifestyle' is in this context the accepted if peculiar code for sex life. It was agreed that in the course of the interviews, the Director of Education, Ian Terry, would discuss *Issues in Human Sexuality* with all four candidates in order to be assured of their agreement to abide by it. It was noted by the Tribunal that no such requirement was made of candidates interviewed at the same time for the parallel post of Schools Officer.

During the interview process, Terry was content that Reaney, being single and willing to remain so, complied with *Issues* and therefore when he was strongly endorsed by the interview panel as the strongest candidate, Terry informed him that he was appointed subject to meeting the Bishop. The tribunal records them discussing start dates and housing, confirming John Clark's view that Terry 'over-offered,'[52] giving Reaney the false impression that the job was his, but raising suspicions that the Bishop would wish to ask more about his 'lifestyle,' as was indeed the case. At the meeting between Reaney and Priddis (John Chapman also being present) on 19 July 2006, Reaney's relationship history (specifically, a gay relationship which had recently ended) and his present and future intentions were discussed at length. This forms the crux of the case, since Priddis's subsequent judgment was that Reaney was insufficiently stable in his emotional life to make the commitment to singleness which he believed the post required as the only acceptable alternative to heterosexual marriage.

In all fairness to the bishop, there is a certain amount of evidence in the case to suggest that he may have been right. In response to being asked about what he would do if he met a potential partner, Reaney had apparently answered that he would 'discuss it with the Bishop.'[53] Given the dialogue between them, the only likely expectation of such a discussion (strengthened by Reaney's previous experience in the Diocese of Chester) would be that such a discussion would lead to a demand for his resignation if a relationship had commenced. Reaney's emotional protestation in subsequent conversation with Priddis that he was being denied the support of a loving relationship[54] might also confirm the judgment of emotional rawness, although the tribunal preferred that it was a response to the circumstances of his non-appointment. More significantly, it suggests that Reaney may have hoped that *Issues* would be interpreted for him as for clergy in many dioceses, i.e. as the turning of a blind eye, and he was chiefly disappointed that this was not the case with Priddis. But the conclusion of the tribunal was that the Bishop did not have the right to make such a judgment, correct or otherwise, and should have relied upon the references given which evidenced his general trustworthiness:

> We do not consider it to be reasonable to rely upon some vague idea that a person whose relationship had recently come to an end cannot be relied upon to state a future intention because of the fragility of that person's mind, as for example a person who has suffered recent bereavement. Indeed, the contrary appears to be the case in that, despite having positive endorsements of the Claimant.... Bishop Priddis either ignored such views or gave them very little weight. It may well be that there was some unconscious discrimination on the part of Bishop Priddis in the refusal to accept the assurances of the Claimant because he was a gay man.[55]

The decision of the tribunal was, however, only a partial success for Reaney. His claim that the meeting with the Bishop amounted to harassment was not successful, and the tribunal did accept that although a layman, the post of Diocesan Youth Officer was one to which the legitimate exemption of the Church of England from the Discrimination Act could be applied (although also possibly contradicting themselves by saying "It may be that ... [Priddis] was confusing the stricter standards which would be expected of Clergy to that of a lay person such as a Diocesan Youth Officer."[56]) The main claim for direct discrimination was found on the basis that had Reaney not stated he was gay, the particular enquiries (both the questioning of all candidates about *Issues* and the Bishop's interrogation of his lifestyle) would not have happened. Efforts are now made (e.g. the requirement of *all* ordinands, even married heterosexuals, to declare their conformity to *Issues*) to avoid singling out gay candidates in this way.

The tribunal also found that the diocese was indirectly discriminating, by requiring singleness of all gay candidates as against the possibility of heterosexuals to marry – a significant finding, as this would apply equally to all clergy and lay officials. It was in relation to this claim that the legal team brought the defence under the Discrimination Act too late,[57] worsening the case for Hereford, but meaning that in future this defence is available. The diocese was ordered to pay £45,000 compensation and the costs were a further c.£40,000, which were met from an anonymous donation,[58] causing a mixture of relief and disquiet in the diocese. More serious was the sense that the Church of England was trying to uphold its teaching in an inconsistent manner, and Bishop Priddis was declared 'Bigot of the Year' by the campaigning charity Stonewall (which had financed Reaney's case).

In the study of discipline, the Reaney case fits the pattern that law progressively achieves clarity as well as liberty. Priddis had attempted to rely on his pastoral judgment; the tribunal refused him that freedom in favour of the need for transparency about whom he would appoint and why. In the deeply confused world of the Church of England's teaching and practice around homosexuality, it would be difficult to claim that the Reaney tribunal let in much daylight, but it did help to clarify that the terms of an appointment need to be clear in advance, and that it is unjust to allow any individual discretion to decide whether to accept another's word or not.

Same-sex marriage – the game changes

As noted, a particular aspect of the present undisciplined situation of the Church of England with relation to sexuality has been the ongoing change in society and the law of the land, to which the Church has responded (in the only partially representative form of the House of Bishops) whilst being unable to find the internal consensus to either reaffirm or reform its overall position. In response to the introduction of civil partnerships in 2005, the bishops issued a Pastoral Statement[59] which carefully preserved the existing ambiguities. Significantly in relation to the laity, the bishops resisted any idea that civil partnerships might provide an opportunity for conservative churches to impose discipline on their laity:

> The House considers that lay people who have registered civil partnerships ought not to be asked to give assurances about the nature of their relationship before being admitted to baptism, confirmation and communion.... we believe an unconditional welcome should be given to children in our

> churches.... In relation to infant baptism, Canon B 22.4 makes it clear that, while baptism can be delayed for the purposes of instruction (including on marriage and the family), it cannot be refused.[60]

In relation to the clergy, the statement adopted the ingenious position that civil partnerships (which were, of course, an entirely new invention) were not marriages, and did not *necessarily* constitute the legal formalisation of same-sex sexual relationships (note particularly the line, "The Church should not collude with the present assumptions of society that all close relationships necessarily include sexual activity").[61] Whilst continuing to maintain the need for clergy to conform to *Issues* (i.e. not at all in many cases) this meant that clergy were able to, and did, participate in the freedom to enter civil partnerships with limited hindrance. Following debate on a Private Member's Motion in February 2010, General Synod also agreed to treat surviving civil partners equally to widows and widowers for the purposes of clergy pensions, displaying a pragmatic readiness to recognise their importance to those involved.[62]

The introduction of civil partnerships is likely to be seen in retrospect as only a stage in the changing understanding of sexuality in Britain which led, surprising some, to a Conservative-led government introducing same-sex civil marriage by legislation in 2013. In response to the opposition of religious groups, the Church of England's official spokespersons prominent among them, the Same-Sex Marriage Act included clear protection for all faiths to be able to undertake same-sex marriages only when they had agreed through their own governing processes. Great care was taken, with the assistance of the Church of England Legal Office,[63] to ensure that Church of England weddings, defined by canon as between a man and woman, should remain only that unless and until the Church decided otherwise through Synod.

Once the Act had passed through Parliament and it was clear that same-sex marriage would become law, the House of Bishops again resorted to a pastoral letter to set out their position.[64] For the laity, this followed that of 2005 in resisting any possibility of exclusion:

> We recognise the many reasons why couples wish their relationships to have a formal status. These include the joys of exclusive commitment and also extend to the importance of legal recognition of the relationship. To that end, civil partnership continues to be available for same sex couples. Those same sex couples who choose to marry should be welcomed into the life of the worshipping community and not be subjected to questioning about their lifestyle. Neither they nor any children they care for should be denied access to the sacraments.[65]

In relation to the laity at any rate, the bishops of the Church of England appear to have accepted the effects of the history above, that the Church can have no meaningful discipline over them. The bishops also reiterated their view of 2005 that they could not authorise any order of service following a same-sex marriage.

In spite of this, it is anecdotally known that many clergy across the country have officiated in such services, and in the vast majority of cases been subjected to no more severe ecclesiastical discipline than the officiants at such other canonically disallowed rites as solemn Benediction, or a main Sunday service consisting only of praise music and extemporary prayer with no attempt to conform to the rubrics of a *Common Worship* Service of the Word.

In relation to the clergy themselves, however, the statement expounds the relevant sources of the Church's teaching on marriage, before declaring that the House "considers that it would not be appropriate *conduct* for someone in holy orders to enter into a same sex marriage, given the need for clergy to model the Church's *teaching* in their lives"[66](my emphases). Anecdotally, the effect of this has been that a significant proportion of clergy in civil partnerships who might have wished to marry have not done so, and clergy forming new partnerships have continued to register civil partnerships rather than marry. However, given that it was assumed that at least some clergy would marry, speculation arose as to whether or not it would be possible to bring charges against them under the Clergy Discipline Measure, with many conservative voices opining that it would, and that this would be a good thing.

Only about a dozen clergy have definitely entered same-sex marriages,[67] giving rise to cases which indicate that clergy discipline in the 2010s is as complex and unclear a subject as it has ever been. One was Andrew Cain (Foreshew-Cain after marrying), Vicar of St James, West Hampstead with St Mary with All Souls, Kilburn. In his and similar cases the bishops were faced with a dilemma, knowing that any attempt to bring clergy discipline proceedings would be subject to two possible objections. First, it could be alleged that in spite of the bishops' declaration that such a marriage would be bad *conduct*, the extensive reference to it contravening the Church's *teaching*, assuming that word to be synonymous with doctrine, would imply such cases could only be heard by the Court of Ecclesiastical Causes Reserved. There does not seem to be any clarity as to who, in the last resort, determines a disciplinary case as doctrinal, but my reading would be that in the absence of any provision in the CDM this remains as defined in the EJM, a matter for the relevant chancellor (as it was for Moore in *Bland*), a curious result since the chancellor now has no involvement with clergy discipline. Alternatively, it may be the duty of the President of the Tribunals to resolve this when a case comes first before a tribunal.[68] In the unlikely event that such a case arose, a further disincentive to the use of the CECR is the provision that for a first offence the only available penalty is monition: clergy who have made lifelong commitments in (same-sex) marriage should be only too happy to be told they should not do so again.

The second is that statements of the House of Bishops do not constitute law in the Church of England. Mark Hill classifies them with Acts of Convocation as 'quasi-legislation,' citing the Court of Arches in *Bland*, "Such pronouncements are not law *per se*, nor do they have the force of a statute, but they have 'great moral force as the highest judgment of the highest and ancient synod of the province.'"[69] I would be amongst those who would question Hill as to whether a statement of the House of Bishops which has neither sought nor obtained the voted agreement of the other Houses can be considered to have the same authority as an Act of Convocation or Synod. In relation to an entirely different disciplinary matter, membership of racist political parties, the House of Bishops was, after much debate, given power by the Clergy Discipline (Amendment) Measure 2013 to designate particular parties as unacceptable.[70] Not only is the power quite specifically defined, the House of Bishops is required to record a two-thirds approval of the designation, and Synod retains a power to question such designation on the request of 25 members. Any attempt to use the February 2014 pastoral statement as a tool of discipline in the same way could be open to judicial challenge as lacking in similar authorisation. This is not to say that a determined disciplinary attempt might not pass such hurdles, but the uncertainties seem to have dictated caution.

However, a different approach seems to have been agreed upon. After a guarded meeting with his area bishop at which he confirmed his intention to enter a same-sex marriage, and then actually doing so, Andrew Foreshew-Cain received a letter from the Bishop of Edmonton, which like others below he has kindly shared with me. After reviewing their meeting, the letter declares:

> you have chosen to marry, knowing that for an ordained priest to enter into a same-sex marriage is contrary to the teachings of the Church of England and the clear content of the House of Bishops' Pastoral Statement. You have acted in a way which is inconsistent with your ordination vows and your canonical duty to live in accordance with the teachings of the Church of England. I therefore have no alternative but to rebuke you for your conscious and public decision to act in a way which does not model these teachings.
>
> I am issuing this rebuke in my role as your Area Bishop under the authority delegated to me under the London Area Scheme. A copy of this rebuke will remain on your file. Whilst it will not be entered on the Archbishop's List maintained under the Clergy Discipline Measure, I am nonetheless copying it to the Archbishops of Canterbury and York, as we have been requested to do in such cases.[71]

This text is interesting mainly because of what it is not. Because Foreshew-Cain contested the claim that same-sex marriage was necessarily contrary to the teachings of the Church of England (because of the complete silence of authorised canon and liturgy on the subject) and because (I suggest) for the reasons noted above, the bishop did not wish to bring a case before a disciplinary tribunal where all the relevant law could have been contested openly, instead a 'quasi-rebuke' was issued, having no more legal authority than the fact that the bishop had issued it. It would seem at least possible that in the absence of the due and agreed process under the CDM for a rebuke, this was a miscarriage of justice.

However, since Foreshew-Cain remained in secure possession of his benefice, it is also possible to concur with those who felt that the Church's only response to his marriage was a letter telling him he had been a very naughty boy and not to do it again. Amongst those unhappy with the outcome was another clergyman in the Diocese of London, who made a complaint under the CDM that Foreshew-Cain's marriage constituted conduct unbecoming. The complaint was however dismissed by the Bishop of London on the basis that no further action was required than the Bishop of Edmonton's letter, and that he did not have a proper interest under the CDM as a complainant.[72] In the accompanying legal advice from the Registrar, the question of proper interest is dealt with fairly easily, as the complainant was in no way directly connected with Foreshew-Cain's parish, and knew of the marriage only through media reporting.[73]

The section of the advice on whether or not the marriage was actually conduct unbecoming is less clear-cut, and after noting that the marriage was undoubtedly a legal civil marriage and not in church, is worth quoting at length [*my emphases*]:

> The issues of same sex relationships and same sex marriage are sensitive and controversial ones within the Church at the moment. The House of Bishops' report referred to above concludes with the following paragraph:-
>
> > "The Church of England has a long tradition of tolerating conscientious dissent and is seeking to avoid drawing lines too firmly, not least when an issue is one where the people of God are seeking to discern the mind of Christ in a fast changing context. Nevertheless, at ordination clergy undertake to "accept and minister the discipline of this Church, and respect *authority duly exercised* within it".
>
> It has been suggested by some that this is an issue which pertains to doctrine, and the accordingly it cannot be dealt with appropriately under this Measure. Alleged offences involving ritual, ceremonial or doctrine are, of course, subject to the provisions of the [EJM], not the [CDM].
>
> "Doctrine" on a literal interpretation encompasses all the teachings of the Church. Those teachings include the premise that marriage is between one man and one woman (Canon B30).
>
> But the teachings include much that would undoubtedly be regarded as misconduct – theft, adultery, etc. cannot sensibly be regarded as doctrinal matters in this context whereas, say, an unorthodox interpretation of the Resurrection probably would be.
>
> In the Church of England it is *presumably for the House of Bishops to give a lead as to what should and should not be regarded as doctrine.* The Bishops have said in clear terms (see below) that their view is that it would be inappropriate conduct for a member of the Clergy to enter into same sex marriage.
>
> What the Complainant is alleging is essentially unbecoming or inappropriate conduct. That is a specific category provided for under the 2003 Measure.
>
> In my view there is therefore a strong case for saying that a member of the Clergy who enters into a same sex civil marriage at the present time is acting "inappropriately" contrary to Section 8(1)(d) of the Measure.[74]

He then quotes the House of Bishops' statement that entering a same-sex marriage is not appropriate conduct, before offering a little more freedom to manoeuvre:

> Having said that, not all forms of misconduct are appropriately dealt with by way of penalty or process under the Measure.
>
> Discipline is essentially a matter for the Bishop. Although the Measure provides a formal process by means of which complaints may be brought, discipline in its wider sense extends beyond the Measure.[75]

In the advice it is possible to observe the tension between the idea that the House of Bishops is empowered to act as a sort of corporate *magisterium* to declare and enforce the teaching of the Church, and the difficulty that this authority is not clearly grounded in law. Some of the theology of this will be discussed in the conclusion, but the suggestion of this study is that in practical reality, this case is yet another example where it was in fact most helpful to find a loophole that avoided an open legal clash and anything that could be construed as persecution.

This is confirmed by the response of the President of the Tribunals to an appeal by the complainant, in which he had made the argument that his experience of the marriage and public reaction to it gave him a proper interest after all. In his response, Sir Andrew was able to rely upon the clause in the CDM which limited his power to overturn the bishop's dismissal to cases where the bishop was 'plainly wrong.' This gave him space to acknowledge the complainant's concerns and arguable case, whilst concluding that 'the Bishop had a margin of discretion'[76] and had acted on sound legal advice, and so although the case was arguable, he was not "plainly wrong." In a coda to the affair which also says something about opinion in the Church of England, in the elections for General Synod in 2015, the clergy electors (only a few of whom are likely to have known the details above) elected Andrew Foreshew-Cain as a proctor for the Diocese of London. Only since then, and for other personal reasons, Foreshew-Cain has left his parish, and so his exclusion from active ministry in the Church of England.

My suggestion that a common quasi-disciplinary response has been devised for same-sex marriages is strengthened by two other cases. Geoffrey Thompson, priest-in-charge of St Stephen's, Norbury in the diocese of Southwark, was already in a civil partnership at the beginning of 2015. Thompson relates[77] that in early 2015 he approached the diocese, eventually meeting with the bishop of Croydon, to explain that he and his partner intended to convert their partnership into a civil marriage that October. The bishop was personally supportive but officially neutral. In a semi-comic element to the story, when Thompson and his partner visited the register office in April 2015 to make arrangements for their forthcoming marriage, the registrar had erroneously believed that they wished to convert there and then, and they were presented with a marriage certificate (made out, as all are, from the date of their original civil partnership).

At first the only 'disciplinary' response by the diocese was to refuse to place a stipendiary curate in the parish, and in November 2015 Thompson was instituted as Vicar. In January 2016, however, he received a letter from the bishop of Croydon. Thompson read me the text – it is extremely close to that sent to Andrew Foreshew-Cain, verbatim in the central legal section, but with warmer pastoral words from a supportive bishop, who has apparently also told Thompson that his marriage would not preclude another appointment in Southwark diocese. But in an addition obviously provided by the Hobbs complaint case above, there is a warning that the 'rebuke' does not preclude a complaint under the CDM, but only from a properly interested party.

The battle goes on – the Pemberton Case

The final case of same-sex marriage is complicated both because it involves a new appointment and two dioceses, and because at the time of writing it was the subject of ongoing legal proceedings. It manages to combine elements of the Freeman, Reaney and Foreshew-Cain cases, and has been the subject of widespread publicity and competitive interpretation. Jeremy Pemberton was a chaplain at Lincoln hospital, but lives in Southwell in the diocese of Southwell and Nottingham with Laurence Cunnington, whom he married in April 2014.[78] This was in fact the first clergy same-sex marriage, but the complexity of the case makes it easier to explain in the light of all the cases above. At the time of his marriage, he held a licence from the Bishop of Lincoln but also Permission to Officiate (PTO) in the diocese of Southwell and Nottingham. The responses from the two dioceses at first appear to be inconsistent: from the bishop of Lincoln he received an informal rebuke similar to those already described above,[79] whereas the diocese of Southwell and Nottingham withdrew his PTO.[80]

Social media and press commentary on the situation, and the airing of issues in the employment tribunal, has made much of this inconsistency, suggesting *inter alia* that it represented a difference of approach between different bishops, or even different archbishops (the decisions of the diocese of Southwell and Nottingham having been made by an acting bishop, Richard Inwood, who may or may not have consulted with the archbishop of York). Even if this is true, however, it overlooks the differences of law which in my view dictated the options open to the relevant bishops. The bishop of Lincoln could only have removed Pemberton's licence after due process under the CDM, which as explained seems to have been viewed as an impractical and undesirable response. However, there is no legal requirement for due process in the withdrawal of PTO, which is simply an expression of episcopal approval and generally intended for retired clergy with no pecuniary need to exercise their ministry, and so the acting bishop had complete freedom to withdraw it. In respect of the diocese of Southwell and Nottingham, Pemberton found himself in the same position as Anthony Freeman, who was deprived of his licence without legal process, albeit that the CDM had extended the protection of due process to licensed clergy between the two cases.

More serious complexity arose when in June 2014, Pemberton was offered by Sherwood Forest Hospitals NHS Trust the post of Head of Chaplaincy, a promotion within his career of hospital chaplaincy[81] and incidentally closer to his home. However, in accordance with normal practice, the NHS expected him to be able to verify his good standing in the Church of England by obtaining a licence from the relevant diocese, in this case Southwell and Nottingham, and this was not forthcoming. Pemberton had previously had a difficult meeting[82] with Bishop

Inwood, although he had been allowed to carry on with his job application without any proper warning that a licence would definitely be refused. The issue of a licence has never, unlike institution to a benefice, been subject to the historic legal restraints of *duplex querela* and *quare impedit*, with the understanding that bishops may grant a licence or not as they judge right, generally in connection after all with an appointment simultaneously in their gift. And in justice to Bishop Inwood, the refusal to grant a licence in Southwell and Nottingham did not impede Pemberton's continued employment (and therefore livelihood) as a hospital chaplain in Lincoln. The contrast between Pemberton's apparent unproblematic continuance as a chaplain in Lincoln with his apparent total unsuitability as a chaplain in Nottinghamshire, however, led him to seek redress at an employment tribunal.

All the claims made by Pemberton were dismissed by the employment tribunal,[83] and his subsequent appeal was also dismissed. The published record of the appeal tribunal[84] enters in some depth into the questions of whether or not the Diocese of Southwell and Nottingham was, for the purposes of the case, a qualifications body under Section 53 of the Equality Act 2010 (concluding with the initial tribunal and against a cross-appeal from Bishop Inwood that it was) and Pemberton's claim of harassment (dismissed). Most important to the disciplinary case, however, is that the Appeal Tribunal accepted without significant demur that:

> the Respondent had been entitled to rely on the House of Bishops Guidance (of particular significance as anything on doctrinal matters had to be approved by the House of Bishops before being passed (or not) by the General Synod) as evidencing the beliefs of the Church.'[85]

On that basis, Bishop Inwood was able to rely on the exemption in the Equality Act as sufficient defence for his decisions, even if Judge Eady remarked that she found in the original tribunal 'the reasoning is hard to follow in places.'[86] Pemberton appealed further but the Court of Appeal upheld the Employment Appeal Tribunal judgment in all essentials and he has announced that he will not pursue the case further.[87]

Tribunals aside, what is uncontested is that Jeremy Pemberton remained a full-time minister in his position at Lincoln hospital until 2016, and held a licence in the diocese, and so once again it is doubtful whether anything that could really be called discipline was effectively enforced. It is also interesting to note that in addition to dividing opinion within the Church of England (the July 2015 General Synod was notable for 'Justice for Jeremy' badges distributed amongst sympathisers) the legal teams themselves indicate the division, with Justin Gau, Chancellor of Bristol, and Alan Wilson, Bishop of Buckingham, appearing in support of Pemberton.[88] This supports my contention that this, like all the other situations in which discipline has proven impossible, is really a division within the Church and not an attempt by authority to bring erring members into line. In parallel, a Private Members Motion placed before General Synod in 2015–16, calling for more active steps to be taken against clergy in same-sex marriages, failed to attract the 100 signatures within three sessions required for debate and so lapsed, confirming that even among the disapproving there is little appetite for persecution.

Undisciplined consecrations

Defiance of authority as a consequence of divisions over sexuality has not been confined to gay clergy marrying but can be found in a different form on the conservative side. Convinced of the need to form alternative structures against a perception of current or imminent heterodoxy by the whole Church of England, two different conservative Evangelical groups obtained episcopal consecration for clergy associated with them in 2017. Unlike the Provincial Episcopal Visitors under the 1993 Act of Synod or the Bishop of Maidstone, those consecrated have no official recognition as bishops in the Church of England. These were Jonathan Pryke, curate of Clayton Memorial Church, Jesmond (commonly known as Jesmond Parish Church) in South Africa on 2 May[89] and Andy Lines, General Secretary of the mission agency Crosslinks in Wheaton, Illinois, on 30 June.[90]

In both cases the consecrations attracted critical comment and calls for responses from on high, but the actual disciplinary actions undertaken by bishops of the Church of England fell into the same pattern already noted. The Bishop of Newcastle has confirmed that she has written to Pryke asking him to refrain from exercising episcopal ministry,[91] but he remains licensed as curate at Jesmond (although I note that his consecration is not recognised by Crockford,[92] which may amount to some sort of non-recognition by the Church of England). The vicar at Jesmond, David Holloway, demonstrated his clear understanding of the situation by arguing that any disciplinary action against Pryke would require the invocation of the inactive Court of Ecclesiastical Causes Reserved, and threaten 'reciprocal heresy trials.'[93] The only relevant canon seems to be B43.5, forbidding clergy to participate in the laying on of hands in churches not in communion with the Church of England, but there is no history of enforcement.

By contrast, Lines held no licenced post but only PTO in the dioceses of Southwark and Canterbury. It has been reported that his PTO in Southwark was not renewed by the Bishop of Southwark[94] and as he is no longer listed with a personal entry in Crockford's,[95] it seems probable that his Canterbury PTO has also terminated, and so he is now not only not a bishop, but not a minister of the Church of England at all. The status and future activities of these independently-styled bishops remains uncertain, but, regardless, the means available to the Church of England to constrain their activities are much the same as those available to constrain their direct opponents. It seems likely that the sexuality debate will continue to generate examples of calls for discipline, but given the well-established legal limits on episcopal power, the actual actions will mostly be comparatively disappointing for those calling for them.

Notes

1 E. W. Kemp, *Shy But Not Retiring. The memoirs of the Right Reverend Eric Waldram Kemp. Edited and prepared for publication by Jeremy Matthew Haselock* (Continuum 2006) 191.
2 *Freeman Correspondence*, email of Anthony Freeman to the author, 22 July 2015.
3 Kemp, *Shy*, 191.
4 *Church Times*, 27 August 1993, 4.
5 *Freeman Correspondence*, email of Anthony Freeman to the author, 22 July 2015.
6 *Freeman Correspondence*, letter of Kemp to Freeman, 9 March 1994, quoted by permission of Canon Clay Knowles and Dr Andrew Foster, Literary Executors to Bishop Eric Kemp. They have asked for the full text to be provided, which runs as follows:

Following our discussion on Monday afternoon I promised to write to you, and I do now with sadness to tell you that it will be necessary for you to leave Staplefield by the end of July this year. You will remember that last July I wrote to you, after the meeting you had with Bishops John and Ian and myself, and I said that we would allow you to remain at Staplefield for 12 months. We did so in the hope that a period of reflection and consultation with Professor MacQuarrie and others would help you to move sufficiently from the position that you had stated in your book to make it possible that I could licence you to another post. It is clear, however, from what you said to us and from the text of the lecture you gave to us that your position has not changed and that you are still asserting that God is nothing more than the sum of human aspirations and has no objective existence. This is so far removed from the assertions of the Christian creeds and the foundation documents of the Church of England that none of us could receive the Declaration of Assent from you with a good conscience knowing the interpretation that you would be putting on it.

I am very sorry that things have worked out in this way and for all the distress and difficulty that it will cause you. We shall always be grateful for the work that you have done in the diocese for the education of the clergy and as a parish priest and I hope that you and Jacqueline will be able to find satisfactory employment. As I said I am willing to do everything that I can to help you in this matter.

7 *Freeman Correspondence*, letter of Freeman to Kemp, 11 March 1994.
8 *Church Times*, 5 August 1994, 3.
9 *Freeman Correspondence*, email of Anthony Freeman to the author, 4 August 2015.
10 *Freeman Correspondence*, letter of Hewlett Thompson to Revd Anthony Geering, 17 July 1999, quoted with permission.
11 *Freeman Correspondence*, letter of Michael Langrish to Freeman, 4 October 2001, quoted with permission.
12 *Freeman Correspondence*, email of Anthony Freeman to the author, 4 October 2015.
13 *Freeman Correspondence*, copy of Permission to Officiate in the Diocese of Chichester, 2 February 2013.
14 Andrew Furlong, *Tried for Heresy. A 21st-Century Journal of Faith* (O Books 2003) 11.
15 Petition in the Court of the General Synod, cited at Furlong, *Tried for Heresy*, 69.
16 *Church Times*, 27 January 1984, 1, 20.
17 Peart-Binns, John S. *Graham Leonard, Bishop of London* (Darton, Longman & Todd, 1988) 224.
18 *Church Times*, 10 October 1986, 1; Furlong, Monica, *C of E, The State It's In* (Hodder & Stoughton 2000) 135. Furlong dates the Church House event to 1989, but even though she was probably present, I assume that it only happened once, and that the *Church Times* date is correct.
19 Furlong, *C of E*, 135 – again, she states '1987' though it appears in *Church Times* reports of July and October 1988.
20 *Church Times*, 10 October 1986, 24.
21 Peart-Binns, *Leonard*, 184–215.
22 As reported in Hill, Mark, *Ecclesiastical Law* 2nd ed. (OUP 2001) 665–81.

23 Hill, *Ecclesiastical Law*, 707–12.
24 *Under Authority. The Report of the General Synod Working Party reviewing Clergy Discipline and the Working of the Ecclesiastical Courts* (Church House Publishing 1996) Foreword.
25 Ibid., 4.
26 Ibid., 52–3.
27 Ibid., 53.
28 By the present Bishop of Hereford, in conversation 26 February 2018.
29 Published at *4EccLJ* 510–19.
30 Ibid., footnote.
31 GSP 26/11/1996, 868.
32 Ibid., 891.
33 Ibid., 894.
34 See Rupert Bursell "Turbulent Priests" *9EccLJ* 250–63 (2007) and "More Turbulence?" *11EccLJ* 154–168 (2009) and Adrian Iles "The CDM 2003; A Progress Report" *16EccLJ* 3–17 (2014).
35 Bursell, *More Turbulence*, 168.
36 *GS1554*, 30.
37 *GSP* 10 July 2004, 82.
38 Ibid., 87–8.
39 Ibid., 90.
40 Ibid., 99.
41 *Church Times*, 16 July 2004, 6.
42 *GSP* 11 November 1987, 955–956.
43 See Norman Doe, "Ecclesiastical Quasi-Legislation" in Doe, Hill and Ombres, *English Canon Law. Essays in Honour of Bishop Eric Kemp* (University of Wales Press, 1998).
44 Hill, *Ecclesiastical Law*, 700ff.
45 For example, Mark Hill, at *5EccLJ* 431–39.
46 Johnson, P and Vanderbeck, R, "Sexual Orientation Equality and Religious Exceptionalism in the Law of the United Kingdom: the Role of the Church of England" *Oxford Journal of Law and Religion* 29 August 2017.
47 *Reaney v Hereford DBF*, Cardiff Employment Tribunal, case no 1602844/2006, 17 July 2007.
48 *Church Times*, 27 July 2007, 7.
49 In conversation with the author, 11 April 2016.
50 *Reaney v Hereford DBF*, 6–7.
51 Ibid., minutes of the Bishop's Staff Meeting cited at 8.
52 In conversation, 11 April 2016.
53 *Reaney v Hereford DBF*, 13.
54 Ibid., 16.
55 Ibid., 39.
56 Ibid., 39.
57 *Church Times*, 27 July 2007, 8.
58 In conversation, 11 April 2016.
59 *Civil Partnerships – A pastoral Statement of the House of Bishops of the Church of England*, 25 July 2005, At www.churchofengland.org/media-centre/news/2005/07/pr5605.aspx (accessed 22 April 2016).
60 *Civil Partnerships*, §23–25.
61 *Civil Partnerships*, §20.
62 *Church Times* 19 February 2010, 31–2.
63 From conversations of the author with members of the Legal Office, date unrecorded.
64 *House of Bishops Pastoral Guidance on Same-Sex Marriage*, 15 February 2015, at www.churchofengland.org/media-centre/news/2014/02/house-of-bishops-pastoral-guidance-on-same-sex-marriage.aspx (accessed 22/04/2016).

65 *Same-Sex Marriage*, §18.
66 *Same-Sex Marriage*, §27.
67 I am grateful to Alan Wilson, Bishop of Buckingham, for this estimate.
68 Clergy Discipline Measure 2003 as amended by the Clergy Discipline (Amendment) Measure 2013§4 (2).
69 Hill, *Ecclesiastical Law*, 1.33, 17.
70 CDM 2003 as amended, §8 (4)-(10).
71 *Foreshew-Cain Correspondence*, Letter of Bishop Peter Wheatley to Andrew Foreshew-Cain, 27 June 2014, quoted with permission
72 *F-C Correspondence*, letter of the Registrar to Foreshew-Cain, 4 September 2014.
73 *F-C Correspondence*, Registrar's advice of 4 August 2014, §4(a).
74 Ibid., §4(b).
75 Ibid., §4(b).
76 *F-C Correspondence*, letter of Sir Andrew McFarlane to the complainant, copied to Andrew Foreshew-Cain, 10 October 2014, quoted with permission
77 In conversation with the author, 25 April 2016, the source for all this section.
78 *Church Times*, 17 April 2014.
79 As described in conversation with the author in 2015.
80 *Church Times*, 27 June 2014.
81 *Church Times*, 11 July 2014.
82 Conversation with the author.
83 *Church Times*, 6 November 2015.
84 UKEAT/0072/16/BA.
85 UKEAT/0072/16/BA, §64, 23–4.
86 Ibid., §113, p43.
87 *Church Times*, 29 March 2018, 6.
88 *Church Times*, 19 June 2015.
89 *Church Times*, 12 May 2017, 2–3.
90 www.thinkinganglicans.org.uk/archives/2017_06.html and links (accessed 27 September 2017).
91 *Church Times*, 30 June 2017, 8.
92 www.crockford.org.uk/people/25911/the-revd-jonathan-justin-speaight-pryke (accessed 27 September 2017).
93 *Church Times*, 12 May 2017, 2.
94 Conversation of the author with Southwark General Synod members, July 2017.
95 www.crockford.org.uk/yearbook-organisation-detail/1499/crosslinks (accessed 27 September 2017).

Conclusion

The journey to indiscipline

The Church of England has reached its present state with respect to discipline, I would argue, in a series of phases which can be traced in the history in preceding chapters. First, from the Glorious Revolution until the mid-nineteenth century, the remnants of legal ecclesiastical discipline over the faith and morality of the laity declined until abolition, leaving an assumption that it was no longer the place of the Church to regulate the lives of its members in a decisive manner. This was understood and feared in the period immediately after 1688 but came to be accepted reality. This assumption was sufficiently deep-seated to resist the aspirations of a few, mostly Anglo-Catholics such as R. Wilberforce and Chambers, to revive it alongside the revivals of liturgy and Patristic scholarship that did endure. It also contributed to the failure of the few attempts at the use of repulsion from Holy Communion as a tool of discipline to reach the courts.

By contrast, in the mid-nineteenth century it might have been thought that the courts would afford a forum to resolve doctrinal and liturgical disputes in the maintenance of good order. However, the difficulty of defining and condemning heterodoxy, and the civil disobedience of liturgical innovators, ensured that by the end of the century it was recognised that in matters of controversy the ecclesiastical courts were no more effective at regulating doctrine and liturgy than they had been at controlling fornication or defamation. This resulted in a quiescence in the early twentieth century in which consistent efforts were made to resolve conflicts without use of legal mechanisms. Only in the past 30 years has the possibility of legal discipline been seriously revived, but without practical effect as yet. At the time of writing, with Church politics dominated by the sexuality debate, it remains the case that for those attempting to maintain a particular standard in public worship or the conduct of the clergy, the only tools are patronage (or denial thereof) and public statement. It is to be hoped that in time the wisdom of mutual acceptance which eventually dispelled the bitterness of the doctrinal and ritual disputes of the nineteenth century will come to prevail in those of the early twenty-first.

A new angle on an old problem

Looking at the issues more generally, it is clear that since the so-called Council of Jerusalem (Acts 15) the Christian church has wrestled with the problems of defining its membership and rules. This was for many centuries encompassed chiefly within the debates about canon law in many churches, but can now be considered the field of ecclesiology, the study of the nature of the Church, of which law is the practical outworking. What I claim as modest originality is that as far as I have been able to ascertain, there is no previous work that begins from the problematical outworking of law as discipline and attempts to draw ecclesiological conclusions from its history in the Church of England. It is possible to trace, in the history summarised again above, three interweaving causes of the notoriously undisciplined state of the Church of England. These will then lead on to the question of what impact this knowledge ought to have on our ecclesiology.

The first is sheer accident in the formation of the ecclesiastical settlement in England, arising from, among other things, the lifetimes of particular monarchs, and other subsequent causes. It is known that Archbishop Cranmer began to draft a new Canon Law for the Church of England but was not able to bring it into effect; had Edward VI lived to reign long, the Church might well have been founded upon a solid and enforceable basis from the start, with utterly different consequences. The same could be said had either Charles II or Queen Anne left legitimate issue. Less accidental, but equally unintentional, has been the continued establishment of the Church of England for all sorts of reasons independent of discipline, but which has continued to ensure the ambiguity of ecclesiological boundaries.

Second, is the fascinating interaction observable in so many of the cases above between difficult theological problems and the legal system of the established Church, which has almost always resulted in greater freedom and the failure of discipline. Two factors have conspired together: the complexity and obscurity of process preventing effective prosecution; and the requirements of the law for clarity and proof typically not available in questions of religious conscience. The former was predominant in the eighteenth century and the latter in the nineteenth, although both can be observed throughout. A tradition which began as the protection of property rights, either of laity to receive the Church's ministry or clergy to enjoy their livings, can be seen as giving rise to the idea of legal protection for religious freedom itself, even within the Church.

Third, arising particularly from the controversies of the mid-nineteenth century but with deeper roots (not least 1 Corinthians 6.1–8), has been the idea that there is something particularly iniquitous about using legal process to resolve spiritual conflict. In the minds of those wrestling as to whether to exercise their theoretical authority, notably bishops, this has sometimes looked like little more than dispirited cynicism that resort to the courts is self-defeating. Yet here and there, as with Creighton,[1] Henson and Habgood, deeper wisdom shows up that even if law is needed, it becomes 'unlaw' (to use Pusey's word)[2] when it is deployed by one set of Christians against another. Donald McKinnon in 1969 linked this back to the kenotic Christology of Charles Gore, quoting with approval Gore's statement that the self-emptying of God in Christ was 'so that He could verily live through all the stages of a perfectly human experience and restore our nature from within by a contact so gentle that it gave life to every faculty without paralysing or destroying any.'[3]

This history has given a peculiar character to the question of discipline in the Church of England, even if this is still not well understood. The statement of Principles of Christian Law mentioned in the Introduction, derived from the several Anglican-Roman Catholic colloquia on Canon Law and the comparative work of Norman Doe, identifies that all churches generally always have some understanding of and mechanism to achieve discipline, intended 'to glorify God, to protect the integrity and mission of the church, to safeguard the vulnerable from harm, and to promote the spiritual benefit of its members.'[4]

Yet, as even one of the relevant colloquia recognised, "The Church of England, being established, is in a different situation."[5] My contention is that the particular nature of discipline in the Church of England is that although it functions in a fairly conventional way as regards safeguarding the vulnerable, it has come to recognise that such ideas as 'the mission and integrity of the church' (or indeed Church), 'spiritual benefit' and most difficult of all, the glory of God, are both difficult to define, and positively damaged by the use of legal coercion of one set of Christians by another.

I have not, however, found any Anglican source which summarises the idea that the Christian faith in its very essence rejects the idea of compulsion with the same effectiveness as *Dignitatis Humanæ*, the 1965 document by which the Second Vatican Council famously endorsed the religious freedom of the later twentieth century, even if then or since this has not been systematically worked into the practice of the Roman Catholic Church. The central section on *Religious Freedom in the Light of Revelation* sets out first the abstract reasoning that faith must be free before defending it with concise observations from the gospel story:

> The act of faith is of its very nature a free act. Man, redeemed by Christ the Saviour and called through Jesus Christ to be an adopted son of God, cannot give his adherence to God when he reveals himself unless, drawn by the Father, he submits to God with a faith that is reasonable and free. It is therefore fully in accordance with the nature of faith that in religious matters every form of coercion by men should be excluded.
>
> This fact received its fullest manifestation in Christ Jesus … who … acted patiently in attracting and inviting his disciples … supported and confirmed his preaching by miracles to arouse the faith of his hearers and to give them assurance, but not to coerce them … left vengeance to God until the day of judgment … did not wish to be a political Messiah who would dominate by force but preferred to call himself the Son of Man who came to serve and "to give his life as a ransom for many" … he bore witness to the truth but refused to use force to impose it on those who spoke out against it.[6]

To this Christological understanding of freedom arising from the very manner of Christ's work and redemption it is logical also to add a pneumatology. The work of the Holy Spirit in human lives can likewise be seen as inviting voluntary cooperation with the divine prompting, and to be something that is invalidated by external compulsion. A systematic theology exploring this in depth would be likely to lead to a deepening understanding that the heart of Christian discipleship must be informed by the patristic theology of the Two Wills, divine and human, in the incarnate Christ, which co-exist in harmony without the divine overcoming the human, lest the real humanity itself be extinguished. Back to ecclesiology, though ...

Must law be enforceable?

As already noted, the last 30 years or so have seen a distinct renewal of interest in church discipline, focussed on but not limited to the need to reform the process of dealing with errant clergy. The relevant reports offer good summaries of much of the history but are prone to a question-begging thinness at the critical theological point. So, to repeat an earlier quotation from the 1996 Hawker Report, the definition of the proposed offence of teaching or preaching incompatible doctrine states (my italics):

> Belief is central in a Christian church ... clergy are called upon to make a clear and consistent reiteration of the essentials of the faith. The Church of England represents a breadth of theological approach ... having a hard central core ... and a less clear-cut, more fuzzy circumference. *If this is so, and if the Declaration of Assent is to have any meaning, then there must be a limit to the breadth of doctrinal expression. Denial of the central core must be excluded if the community of faith is to retain any distinctiveness.* [7]

This passage reveals yet again the difficulty of doing anything at all when working in the realm of the 'more fuzzy,' or more particularly, where there is no consensus as to what is fuzzy and what is hard.

The deeper question, though, is whether or not there is any reason to accept the assumption that distinctiveness of belief requires exclusion of some sort. Whilst it is true that the particulars of the Christian faith held by the Church of England can be defined (but recalling Geoffrey Fisher's dictum that the Church of England holds no tenets of faith not common to Christians in general) and that this *definition* can exclude other possibilities, that does not necessitate taking positive action to *exclude individuals* who are unable to subscribe to the official definition, as long as it can be maintained by a sustainable structure of authority.

The corporate life of the Church of England affords more than adequate safeguard against the seemingly feared collapse of meaning which the Hawker report and others appear to display. In part, this is because of what we may call 'subscription.' Although the elastic boundaries of membership of the Church of England are precisely one of the causes of anxiety to some, the practical reality is that most ordinary worshippers will find themselves reaffirming the basic tenets of the

Christian faith regularly, in the liturgical use of the Creeds in particular, perhaps at annual renewals of baptismal promises, and will have done so as individuals at their baptisms and/or confirmations, and potentially the baptisms of their children. Of course, it is possible to worship regularly in the Church of England and do all these things insincerely or stay strategically silent like Mr Evanson. Certainly, the average congregation reciting 'We believe …' masks a good deal of honest doubt. But the words continue to make the call to belief with integrity.

For the clergy this is rightly amplified, both in the formal Declaration of Assent and throughout the process of selection and training. Again, it is possible (if extremely unwise) to seek to minister from an insecure or insincere faith, and some clergy carry on as belief fades. But, again, the manifest existence of a visible standard acts to uphold Christian doctrine amongst those charged with teaching it. The reality is that those who find themselves professing the faith, either as worshippers or particularly as clergy, with complete insincerity, are far more likely to have the integrity to leave of their own accord than to need expelling by legal processes of dubious merit. This does mean, though, that the processes of selection and training need to be rigorous enough to save prospective ordinands, not least for their own sake, from the hypocrisy of ministering a faith which they themselves lack.

The wisdom of elusive authority

The second, more substantial reason why it is not necessary to assume that a lack of definitive line-drawing will result in a collapse of meaning is that the Church of England does still possess a definite structure of authority, even if that is more diffused and less willing to make authoritative declarations than many would like. The original source of the diffusion is inherent in being a Protestant church, in the sense of accepting (at least in the 39 Articles and the Declaration of Assent) the principle that all decisions and determinations are only valid inasmuch as they conform to Scripture. This basic fact, set out in Article XX (*it is not lawful for the Church to ordain anything that is contradictory to God's word written*) is treated very strangely in the 2004 House of Bishops report on doctrinal discipline. There it is presented after the question-begging assertion 'authority is properly a quality of persons, not of documents. Documents have authority only in a secondary sense, derived from the authority of those persons who have written or approved them.'[8] This claim appears to then be wholly contradicted by the full citation of Article XX which follows, setting out the inability of the Church (persons) to act beyond what Scripture (document) permits. The same document also cites Article XXI, which declares among other things that General Councils "may err, and sometimes have erred," and can only be accepted if in conformity with Scripture, followed by the non-sequitur "thus the authority of councils such as Nicaea and Chalcedon is assured."[9]

The difficulty for any Church accepting the primacy of Scripture as a written authority prior to all ecclesiastical institutions (which is surely the position of the Church of England, the logic of the 2004 General Synod paper on doctrinal discipline (GS1554) considered above notwithstanding) is that controversies will typically be manifest as arguments between differing interpretations of Scripture, with neither side willing to accept the determinations of courts or bishops when they conscientiously believe their own interpretation to be Scriptural. This is why in practice the settlement of differences within the Church has come down to law and, owing to the subtleties of the governance of the Church of England, it is very difficult to put into law anything which diminishes the inherited breadth and liberty. Articles 6 and 7 of the Constitution of General Synod, originating in the Enabling Act 1919 as provisions for the Church Assembly and renewed as a Schedule to the Synodical Government Measure 1969, set out the additional conditions for any Measure of General Synod considered to involve doctrinal change: special majorities in all three Houses; the privilege of the House of Bishops to prepare the final text; the veto of each of the four Houses of the Convocations; consultation with dioceses; all this on top of the usual scrutiny by the Ecclesiastical Committee of Parliament. Nonetheless, where there is real agreement, measures can clamber over the necessary hurdles: women priests and bishops, and as mentioned above, the agreement to debar from ministry all those who are members of explicitly racist political parties such as the BNP.

As noted when discussing the sexuality controversy in particular, there remains some uncertainty about the place of decisions or declarations by the House of Bishops. Whilst the Synodical Government Measure 1969 gives the bishops a sort of negative privilege, that all doctrinal or liturgical Measures must be finally drafted by them, this is not the same as conferring on the House a sort of corporate *magisterium* to declare the doctrine of the Church of England, and their actions in relation to the sexuality debate have done much to question the credibility of this approach. A happier example can be found in the 'Five Guiding Principles' document which, although produced by the bishops, was offered for and received the warm commendation of Synod as a whole, and now appears to be enshrined as a sort of dogmatic text as noted above. The significance of the Five Guiding Principles is that they represent an extremely subtle reconciliation of the positions in the debate about women's ministry, enabling both sides to claim a degree of victory and for practical working together by those who are theologically far from reconciled. This most Anglican of results was prophesied by T. S. Eliot in a commentary on another controversy, that of reunion in South India in the 1940s, when Anglicans were fiercely divided by whether to recognise the ministry in a united church where not all ministers would have been episcopally ordained (an issue which may be about to be sprung from the history books by the nature of the proposed mutual recognition of Anglican and Methodist ministries at the time of writing):

> The essential point about these extraordinary differences … is that we do not agree to differ. We do not say that these things do not matter.
>
> The Church of England maintains its unity in spite of the differences, and *because* we do not agree to disagree. Each party in this Church can defend its

> own doctrine, in the conviction that its doctrine is the true doctrine of the Church of England.[10]

This living with disagreement is a direct if unintended result, and a happy one, of the failure of discipline in the Church of England over the last three centuries. In the ongoing controversy over sexuality, this living with disagreement was recognised more explicitly than ever before in the process of Facilitated Conversations in 2015–16. I can do no better than Rodes (writing in 1991 before women priests) with a final comment on how the Church of England collectively copes with division (my italics):

> the Anglican synthesis continues to survive internal shocks that would tear any other organisation apart. In one crisis after another, people have ringingly predicted that failure to decide the question of the moment their way will wreck the establishment, drive great numbers of Anglicans into schism, or both. *They have always been wrong*. In each case, there have been a few scattered withdrawals – often of prominent churchmen to be sure – and a few scattered rumblings about disestablishment, and all has gone on as before.[11]

A vision of a free Church

Although in 2017 the Church of England continues to wrestle with controversy, most clearly over sexuality, and the spirit of persecution remains alive in some quarters (including those vehement liberals who wish to denounce what they perceive as subordinationism in the Trinitarian theology of 'headship' conservative Evangelicals), the greatest fears of most are not about internal strife but declining numbers and public irrelevance. As the proportion of the English population calling themselves Christians of any sort falls below those who identify as of no religion, it becomes steadily harder to endorse the optimistic vocation of the Church of England identified by Rodes's conclusion, inspired by other thoughts from Vatican II:

> [the Church of England] can give a deeper significance to the historical and cultural identification that so many people feel who are not active worshippers. If we take the claim of *Gaudium et Spes* seriously, peripheral identification with the church is not a mere accident of history; it is the human condition. It is not a consequence of indiscriminate infant baptism; it is a consequence of being born into a world whose redemption the church proclaims.
>
> On this understanding, the gathered church is a sign to the wider society.... The state, by maintaining a residual establishment, and the people, by claiming nominal membership in the church and approaching it for their rites of passage, are recognising and accepting the presence of that sign among them. In the long history of England, that presence, that recognition, that acceptance, have had a profound and salutary effect.

Please God, they will continue to do so.[12]

Hard as the truth is to face, it seems likely that whatever exertions are made in renewal and evangelisation, the hopelessly skewed age profile of the Church of England means that steady decline in active membership in the next quarter-century is unavoidable and irreversible. Under these circumstances widespread nominal allegiance will become a thing of the past, and as one critical account of establishment puts it tactfully, "the departure of the present much-respected and long-reigning monarch will expose the underlying assumptions of the British monarchy and its relations with the established churches."[13] That said, the same study also notes the persistent attachment of the Anglican hierarchy to the advantages of establishment, and the British constitution has been astonishingly resistant to the open exposure of its multiple and subtly complex assumptions for many centuries.

If the Church of England does manage at some point in the next couple of decades to achieve a stability in numbers and finances which means that there is some freedom from the unenviable duty of ongoing reorganisation and the disposal of thousands of redundant buildings, and the painful little cuts of diminishing establishment, the potent question will be what sort of a Church she wishes to be. For three centuries we have seen the amazing persistence of an Erastian model of inclusion and public service in spite of the theological dominance of the competing exclusive models presented by the Anglo-Catholic and Evangelical movements, which can be seen as joint heirs to the High Church movement after 1688. My hope is that, unable to resolve her differences neatly and above all recognising that enforcement of discipline is unchristian as well as impractical, the Church of England can remain the model to every other church, that in a world where we have no choice but to live in the uncertainties between Pentecost and *paligenessia*, the true calling of the Christian Church is to include all who will come, and as far as possible leave the judgment to God.

Notes

1 As at Mandell Creighton, *Persecution and Tolerance* (Longmans, Green & Co 1895) 42–3.
2 E. B. Pusey, *Unlaw in the Judgments of the Judicial Committee and its Remedies* (Parker & Sons and Rivingtons 1881).
3 Donald McKinnon, *The Stripping of the Altars* (Collins 1969) 13, quoting Gore, Charles *Dissertations on Subjects Connected with the Incarnation* (John Murray 1895).
4 *Principles of Christian Law V.1.5, 19EccLJ* 146 (2017).
5 Hill (ed.) *Faithful Discipleship. Clergy Discipline in Anglican and Roman Catholic Canon Law* (Centre for Law and Religion, Cardiff University 2001) 2, footnote 4.
6 *Dignitatis Humanæ*, §10–11, in *Vatican Council II*, ed. Austin Flannery, O.P. rev. ed. (Dominican Publications 1992) 807–8.
7 *Under Authority. The Report of the General Synod Working Party reviewing Clergy Discipline and the Working of the Ecclesiastical Courts* GS1217, *§6.18*, 53.
8 GS 1554 §26.
9 GS 1554 §27.

10 T. S. Eliot, *Reunion by Destruction* (Council for the Defence of Church Principles Pamphlet 7, undated) quoted at Robert E. Rodes Jr., *Law and Modernisation in the Church of England* (Notre Dame 1991) 364.
11 Ibid., 366.
12 Ibid., 374–5.
13 R. M. Morris (ed), *Church and State in 21st Century Britain: The Future of Church Establishment* (Palgrave Macmillan 2009) 3.

Bibliography

Primary sources (in chronological order)

The Church Times, many dates, as given in text, consulted at www.ukpressonline.co.uk

The Times for 1932, consulted at www.thetimes.co.uk/tto/archive

Chronicle of Convocation and *General Synod Proceedings*, dates as referred, consulted in the bound volumes at Church House and the Church of England Records Centre.

Constitutions & Canons Ecclesiastical (1604) – my (undated) copy bound up in *The Book of Common Prayer* (*OUP* 1859).

Bury & Norwich Post, and Suffolk Herald, 11 September 1850.

Crockford's Clerical Directory, 8th Issue (Horace Cox 1876).

and *Crockford Online*, www.crockford.org.uk

Court papers for *Swayne v Benson*, 1889, filed at Arches Hh23, Lambeth Palace Library.

Royal Commission on Ecclesiastical Discipline (HMSO 1906).

Doctrine in the Church of England (SPCK 1938).

Certain sermons or Homilies appointed to be read in churches in the time of Queen Elizabeth of famous memory (SPCK 1938).

The Canon Law of the Church of England (SPCK 1947).

The Ecclesiastical Courts. Principles of Reconstruction (SPCK 1954).

Acts of the Convocations of Canterbury and York, A. F. Smethurst & H. R. Wilson (eds) (SPCK 1961).

Papers of the Revision Committee for the 1963 Ecclesiastical Jurisdiction Measure, Church of England Records Centre, filed under "EJ."

Church Acts and Measures from Halsbury's Statutes of England, 1969 Church Assembly Edition.

Church and State. Report of the Archbishops' Commission (General Board of Finance of the Church of England 1970).

Under Authority. The Report of the General Synod Working Party reviewing Clergy Discipline and the Working of the Ecclesiastical Courts GS1217 (CHP 1996).

Freeman Correspondence refers to papers (dates and authors noted in text) kindly supplied to the author by Revd Anthony Freeman.

Vatican Council II. The Conciliar and Post Conciliar Documents, Austin Flannery, O.P. (ed.) new rev. ed. (Dominican Publications 1992).

Clergy Discipline Measure 2003 as amended by the Clergy Discipline (Amendment) Measure 2013.

GS1554. Clergy Discipline (Doctrine): Report of a Working Party of the House of Bishops 2004.

Civil Partnerships – A pastoral Statement of the House of Bishops of the Church of England, 25 July 2005, at www.churchofengland.org/media-centre/news/2005/07/pr5605.aspx (accessed 22 April 2016).

House of Bishops Pastoral Guidance on Same-Sex Marriage, 15 February 2015, at www.churchofengland.org/media-centre/news/2014/02/house-of-bishops-pastoral-guidance-on-same-sex-marriage.aspx (accessed 22 April 2016).

Foreshew-Cain Correspondence refers to papers kindly supplied to the author by the Revd Andrew Foreshew-Cain.

Cases cited (in chronological order)

Pelling v Whiston (1712) 1 COMYNE 199

Middleton v Crofts (1736) RIDG t.H 109

King's Proctor v Stone (1808) 1 HAG. CON. 424

Kemp v Wickes (1809) 2 PHILL. ECC. 264

Free v Burgoyne (1826) 5 B & C 400

Burgoyne v Free (1829) 1 HAGG. ECC. 456

Breeks v Woolfrey (1838) 1 CURT. 880

Mastin v Escott (1841) 2 CURT. 692

Sanders v Head (1843) 3 CURT. 565

Hodgson v Oakeley (1845) 1 ROB. ECC. 322

Gorham v Bishop of Exeter (1849) 2 ROB. ECC. 1

Gorham v Bishop of Exeter. The Judgment of the Judicial Committee of Privy Council (as published by Seeleys, London 1850)

Heath v Burder [1862] UKPC 10

Williams v Bishop of Salisbury (1863) I MOORE N.S. 375

Martin v Mackonochie (1868) V MOORE N.S. 500

Noble v Voysey (1871) VII MOORE N.S. 167

Hebbert & Elphinstone v Purchas (1871) L.R. 3 P.C.605

Sheppard v Bennett (2) (1871) IX MOORE N.S. 149

Jenkins v Cook (1875) L. R. 4 A. & E. 463

Jenkins v Cook (1876) L.R. 1 P.D. 80

Julius v Bishop of Oxford (1880) H.L.(E.) 214

Bishop of Oxford v Henly [1907] P. 88

Banister v Thompson [1908] P. 362

Bishop of Oxford v Henly [1909] P. 319

Rex v Dibdin [1909] P. 57

Bland v Archdeacon of Cheltenham [1971] 3 W.L.R. 706

In re St Stephen's, Walbrook [1987] 3 W.L.R. 726

Reaney v Hereford DBF (2007) Cardiff Employment Tribunal, 1602844/2006

Secondary literature

Adam, Will *Legal Flexibility and the Mission of the Church* (Ashgate 2011)

Ashcraft, Richard "Latitudinarianism and toleration; historical myth versus political history" in Kroll, Ashcraft and Zagovin (eds.) *Philosophy, Science and Religion in England 1640–1700* (CUP 1992)

Baker, J. H. *Monuments of Endlesse Labours. English Canonists and their work, 1300–1900* (Hambledon Press 1998)

Beaken, Robert *Cosmo Lang, Archbishop in War and Crisis* (I. B. Tauris & Co 2012)

Bell, G. K. A. *Randall Davidson* (OUP 1935)

Bennett, Bruce S. "Banister v Thompson and Afterwards: The Church of England and the Deceased Wife's Sister's Marriage Act" *Journal of Ecclesiastical History* 49.4 (1998) 668–682

Bennett, G. v *The Tory Crisis in Church and State 1688–1730. The Career of Francis Atterbury, Bishop of Rochester* (Clarendon Press 1975)

Bennett, G. v "Conflict in the Church" in Holmes, Geoffrey (ed.) *Britain after the Glorious Revolution 1689–1714* (Macmillan, St Martin's Press 1969)

Bentley, James *Ritualism and Politics in Victorian Britain: The Attempt to Legislate for Belief* (OUP 1978)

Bisse, Thomas *The Ordinance and Office of the Magistrate*, sermon preached to the Mayor of Hereford 4 October 1725 (Innys, London 1726)

Bohun, William *A Brief View of Ecclesiastical Jurisdiction, as it is at this day practised in England* (London 1733, reprinted Boston, New England, 1765)

Boulton, Peter "Twentieth Century Revision of Canon Law in the Church of England" (2000) *5EccLJ* 353–368

Briden, Timothy and Mason, Nigel "Recent Court Cases" (1995) *3EccLJ* 424–30

Brown, H. Miles *A Century for Cornwall* (Oscar Blackford Ltd 1976)

Burns, Arthur *The Diocesan Revival in the Church of England c.1800–1870* (OUP 1999)

Bursell, Rupert *Liturgy, Order and the Law* (Clarendon Press, 1996)

Bursell, Rupert "Turbulent Priests" (2007) *9EccLJ* 250–63

Bursell, Rupert "More Turbulence?" (2009) *11EccLJ* 154–168

Carpenter, Edward *Archbishop FISHER – His Life and Times* (Canterbury Press 1991)

Chadwick, Owen *The Victorian Church. Part 1 1829–1859* 3rd ed. (SCM Press 1971)

Chadwick, Owen *The Victorian Church. Part II 1860–1901* 3rd ed. (SCM Press 1972)

Chadwick, Owen *Michael Ramsey, A Life* (OUP 1991)

Chambers, J. C. "Decay of Discipline" in Shipley, Orby (ed.) *Ecclesiastical Reform. Eight Essays by Various Writers* (Longmans, Green & Co 1873)

Chapman, Mark *Anglican Theology* (Bloomsbury T&T Clark 2012)

Clamp, Peter "Bishop Wilson's Discipline: Language, Schooling and Confrontation in the Isle of Man, 1698–1755" *Journal of Religious History* 15.2 (1988)

Clements, Keith W. *Lovers of Discord. Twentieth Century Theological Controversies in the Church of England* (SPCK 1988)

Coffey, John *Persecution and Toleration in Protestant England 1558–1689* (Longman 2000)

Coffey, John "The Toleration Controversy during the English Revolution" in Durston, C. and Maltby, J. *Religion in Revolutionary England* (Manchester University Press 2006)

Cook, Flavel S. *Righteous Judgment. Six Lectures on Future Punishment* (Seeley, Jackson & Halliday 1878)

Creighton, Mandell *Persecution and Tolerance* (Longmans, Green & Co 1895)

Culver, Thomas *Excommunication in the Church of England* (unpublished Cardiff LLM thesis 1996)

Davies, G. C. B. *Henry Phillpotts, Bishop of Exeter 1778–1869* (SPCK 1954)

Dewhurst, Russell *The High Church Reactions to the Reforms of the English Ecclesiastical Courts 1830–1861* (unpublished Cardiff LLM thesis 2010)

Ditcher, Joseph *A Statement of the Proceedings in the Case of Ditcher v Denison* (Hatchard, 1858)

Ditchfield, P. H. *The Old-Time Parson* (Methuen & Co 1908)
Doe, Norman *The Legal Framework of the Church of England: A Critical Study in a Comparative Context* (Clarendon Press 1996)
Doe, Norman "Ecclesiastical Quasi-Legislation" (1998) in Doe, Hill and Ombres, *English Canon Law. Essays in Honour of Bishop Eric Kemp* (University of Wales Press, 1998)
Doe, Norman *Christian Law. Contemporary Principles* (CUP 2013)
Every, George *The High Church Party 1688–1718* (SPCK 1956)
Farrant, P. W. S. *The History and Development of Ecclesiastical Law and the Bishop's Courts in the Diocese of Sodor and Man* (unpublished Cardiff LLM thesis 1998)
Figgis, Neville *Churches in the Modern State* (Longmans, Green & Co 1913)
Fletcher, Ronald *The Akenham Burial Case* (Wildwood House 1974)
Foster, Michael *An Examination of the Scheme of Church-Power, laid down in the Codex Juris Ecclesiastici Anglicani, &c* (published anonymously, London 1735)
Fremantle, W. H. *Natural Christianity* (Harper & Brothers 1911)
Furlong, Andrew *Tried for Heresy. A 21st-Century Journal of Faith* (O Books 2003)
Furlong, Monica *C of E, The State It's In* (Hodder & Stoughton 2000)
Gibson, Edmund *Codex Juris Ecclesiastici Anglicani* 2nd ed. (London, 1761)
Gibson, William (ed.) *Religion and Society in England & Wales 1689–1800* (Leicester University Press 1998)
Gibson, William *Enlightenment Prelate: Benjamin Hoadly, 1676–1761* (James Clarke & Co 2004)
Gibson, William and Begiato, Joanna *Sex and the Church in the Long Eighteenth Century. Religion, Enlightenment and the Sexual Revolution* (I. B. Tauris 2017)
Gunstone, John *Lift High the Cross. Anglo-Catholics and the Congress Movement* (Canterbury Press 2010)
Harris, Troy L. "The Work of the English Ecclesiastical Courts 1725–1745" in Harris T. L. (ed.) *Studies in Canon Law and Common Law in Honor of R. H. Helmholz* (Robbins Collection 2015)
Hastings, Adrian *A History of English Christianity 1920–1990* 3rd ed. (SCM Press 1991)
Hastings, Adrian *Robert Runcie* (Mowbray 1991)
Havard, Neast *A Word at Parting: being a few observations on a mutilated sermon and an Epistle Dedicatory to the Worthy Inhabitants of Tewkesbury, &c* (London 1778)
Hedley, Sir Mark "Practical Aspects of the Clergy Discipline Measure" Lecture to the Ecclesiastical Law Society, 11 October 2017
Helmholz, Richard "Notable Ecclesiastical Lawyers: IX. Sir George Lee (c.1700–1758)" *17EccLJ* 348–54
Henderson, Duncan "The Devil's Law Cases" (2012) *15EccLJ* 28–58
Henson, H. Hensley *The Church of England* (CUP 1939)
Henson, H. Hensley *Retrospect of an Unimportant Life, Vol I* (OUP 1942)
Henson, H. Hensley *Retrospect of an Unimportant Life, Vol II* (OUP 1943)
Hill, Mark *Ecclesiastical Law* 2nd ed. (OUP 2001)
Hill, Mark (ed.) *Faithful Discipleship. Clergy Discipline in Anglican and Roman Catholic Canon Law* (Centre for Law & Religion, Cardiff University 2001)
Iles, Adrian "The CMD 2003: A Progress Report" (2014) *16EccLJ* 3–17
Ingram, Robert "'The Clergy who affect to call themselves Orthodox': Thomas Secker and the defence of Anglican orthodoxy, 1758–68" in *Studies in Church History 43. Doctrine and Discipline* (Boydell 2007)
Jacob, W. M. *Lay People and Religion in the Early Eighteenth Century* (CUP 1996)
Jacob, W. M. *The Clerical Profession in the Long Eighteenth Century 1680–1840* (OUP 2007)

Janes, Dominic *The Victorian Persecution: Anglo-Catholics & Martyrdom* (Anglo-Catholic History Society 2010)

Johnson, John *The Clergyman's Vade Mecum* (London 1731)

Johnson, Malcolm *Victorian Worthies* (Darton, Longman & Todd 2014)

Kemp, E. W. *Counsel and Consent. Aspects of the Government of the Church as exemplified in the history of the English Provincial Synods* (SPCK 1961)

Kemp, E. W. *Shy But Not Retiring. The memoirs of the Right Reverend Eric Waldram Kemp.* Edited and prepared for publication by Jeremy Matthew Haselock (Continuum 2006)

Knight, Frances "Ministering to the Ministers: The Discipline of Recalcitrant Clergy in the Diocese of Lincoln 1830–1845" in *Studies in Church History 26. The Ministry: Clerical and Lay* (Blackwell 1989)

McCart, Thomas K. *The Matter and Manner of Praise. The Controversial Evolution of Hymnody in the Church of England 1760–1820. Drew Studies in Liturgy Series, No.* 5. (The Scarecrow Press 1998)

MacCulloch, Diarmaid *A History of Christianity* (Allen Lane 2009)

MacKinnon, Donald *The Stripping of the Altars* (Collins 1969)

Maiden, John G. "Discipline and Comprehensiveness: The Church of England and Prayer Book Revision in the 1920s" in *Studies in Church History 43. Doctrine and Discipline* (Boydell 2007)

Marshall, Nathaniel *The Penitential Discipine of the Primitive Church* (Oxford 1844, original ed. London 1714)

Marshall, William *Church Life in Hereford and Oxford, 1660–1760. A Study of Two Sees* (Carnegie Publishing 2009)

Moore, E. Garth *An Introduction to English Canon Law* 1st ed. (Clarendon 1967)

Morris, R. M. (ed.) *Church and State in 21st Century Britain: The Future of Church Establishment* (Palgrave Macmillan 2009)

Outhwaite, R. B. *Scandal in the Church. Dr Edward Drax Free 1764–1843* (Hambledon 1997)

Outhwaite, R. B. *The Rise and Fall of the English Ecclesiastical Courts, 1500-1860* (CUP 2006)

Palmer, Bernard *Gadfly for God* (Hodder & Stoughton 1991)

Palmer, Bernard *Reverend Rebels. Five Victorian Clerics and their Fight Against Authority* (Darton, Longman & Todd 1993)

Pattison, Stephen *A Critique of Pastoral Care* 3rd ed. (SCM 2000)

Pearce, Augur "Episcopacy and the Common Law" (2003) *7EccLJ* 195–209

Pearce, Edward *The Great Man. Sir Robert Walpole: Scoundrel, Genius and Britain's First Prime Minister* (Pimlico 2008)

Peart-Binns, John S. *Graham Leonard, Bishop of London* (Darton, Longman & Todd, 1988)

Peart-Binns, John S. *Herbert Hensley Henson. A Biography* (Lutterworth Press, 2013)

Pix, Stephen "Archdeacon of Cheltenham v Bland: a sledgehammer to crack a nut" (2001) *6EccLJ* 135–49

Potter, Harry *Hanging in Judgment. Religion and the Death Penalty in England* (Continuum 1993)

Proctor, Francis and Frere, W. H. *A New History of the Book of Common Prayer* (Macmillan & Co. 1929)

Pusey, E. B. *Unlaw in the Judgments of the Judicial Committee and its Remedies* (Parker & Sons and Rivingtons 1881)

Reed, John Shelton *Glorious Battle. The Cultural Politics of Victorian Anglo-Catholicism* (Tufton Books 1998)
Rodes Jr, Robert E. *Ecclesiastical Administration in Medieval England* (Notre Dame 1977)
Rodes Jr, Robert E. *Lay Authority and Reformation in the English Church. Edward I to the Civil War* (Notre Dame 1982)
Rodes Jr, Robert E. *Law and Modernisation in the Church of England* (Notre Dame 1991)
Rowell, Geoffrey (ed.) *Gareth Bennett: to the Church of England* (Churchman Publishing 1988)
Rugg, Julie *Churchyard and Cemetery: Tradition and Modernity in Rural North Yorkshire* (Manchester University Press 2013)
Smith, Charlotte "Martin v Mackonochie/Mackonochie v Penzance: A Crisis of Character and Identity in the Court of Arches?" *The Journal of Legal History*, 24.3 (2003) 36–58
Smith, Charlotte "Ridsdale v Clifton: Representations of the Judicial Committee of the Privy Council in Ecclesiastical Appeals" *King's Law Journal*, 19.3 (2008) 551–574
Smith, Charlotte "The Quest for an Authoritative Court of Final Appeal in Ecclesiastical Causes: A Study of the Difficulties, c.1830–76" *The Journal of Legal History*, 32.2 (2011) 189–213
Smith, M.G. *Pastoral Discipline and the Church Courts: the Hexham Court 1680–1730* (University of York, 1982)
Sowerby, Scott *Making Toleration. The Repealers and the Glorious Revolution* (Harvard University Press 2013)
Sykes, Norman *Church and State in England in the XVIIIth Century* (CUP 1934)
Sykes, *Norman Edmund Gibson, Bishop of London 1669–1748. A study in Politics and Religion in the Eighteenth Century* (OUP 1926)
Thornton, W.H. *Reminiscences of an Old West Country Clergyman*, Duff Hart-Davis (ed.) (Excellent Press 2010)
Trollope, Anthony *The Warden* (J. M. Dent & Sons 1907)
Ussher, R. *Notes on White Sheet Confessions in Churches and Market Places* (privately published, 1934)
Waddams, S. M. *Sexual Slander in Nineteenth-Century England. Defamation in the Ecclesiastical Courts 1815–1855* (University of Toronto Press 2000)
Whyte, William *Unlocking the Church* (OUP 2017)
Wilberforce, R. I. *Church Court and Church Discipline* (John Murray 1843)
Wilson, Alan *The Authority of Church and Party among London Anglo-Catholics, 1880–1914, with Special Reference to the Church Crisis, 1898–1904* (unpublished Oxford DPhil thesis, 1988)
Wood, E. G. T*he Regal Power of the Church. The Fundamentals of Canon Law by the late Canon E. G. Wood.* Preface by the Rev E. W, Kemp, Fellow of Exeter College Oxford (Dacre Press 1948)
Woodforde, James *The Diary of a Country Parson 1758–1802.* Passages selected and edited by John Beresford (OUP 1949)
Yates, Nigel *Anglican Ritualism in Victorian Britain 1830–1910* (OUP 1999)
Yelton, Michael *Anglican Papalism* (Canterbury Press 2005)

Index

For Product Safety Concerns and Information please contact our EU
representative GPSR@taylorandfrancis.com
Taylor & Francis Verlag GmbH, Kaufingerstraße 24, 80331 München, Germany

www.ingramcontent.com/pod-product-compliance
Lightning Source LLC
Chambersburg PA
CBHW070827150926
51501CB00043B/1003
9780367586256